BECOMING A CITIZEN OF THE KINGDOM

Patrick Whitworth

Terra Nova Publications

Cover design by Roger Judd

Cover image: The Return of the Prodigal Son, Murillo
Photograph courtesy of the National Gallery of Ireland

ISBN 1901949451

Printed in Great Britain
by Bookmarque Ltd, Croydon

Contents

FOREWORD

Reading this book in preparation for writing a Foreword has been a strange experience. For a variety of reasons I have had to read it on my laptop —which is not my normal way of reading books. One consequence of this is that I have not quite known what was coming next! So as I read the first part, which focusses on Jesus' parables, I kept saying to myself, "I hope he writes later about *this*, or *that*." This is because of the whirlwind of events which are going on at the present time, and which provide, for me at any rate, four underlying contexts for any contemporary understanding of the kingdom of God.

The first context is the latest set of devastating, interlocking clashes in the Middle East, affecting members of the three monotheistic world religions. There are many (from a variety of religious backgrounds) who are being woefully selective about history, and my sadness about what is happening is compounded by the way in which such conflicts are reported – very selectively – so that many ordinary people are unaware of what is really going on.

The second context, which worryingly links into the first, is the failure amongst many Christians to balance the "now" with the "not yet" in Jesus' teaching about the kingdom of God. Admittedly, Jesus says, "My kingdom is not of this world..." (John 18:36) —but he also instructs his disciples to pray, "Your kingdom come, your will be done on earth, as it is in heaven…" (Matthew 6:10). The distorted thinking which leads some Christians to be so exclusively other-world-focussed that they have no care either for this earth or the wellbeing of its inhabitants is a mockery of Jesus' down-to-earth, practical kingdom teaching about how we are to live in this world.

The third context, which Anglican Christians and many others are caught up in at the present time, has to do with how we interpret the Scriptures. The presenting issues may well concern sexuality, the ministry of women or other matters; but the underlying question is about the extent to which we believe that the teaching of the Scriptures, and especially the teaching of Jesus, give us the framework for living – as individuals and in community – that offers some future for the world. It is as we study the Scriptures, and as we let the Holy Spirit speak to us through the teaching of the Bible – rather than reading into it what we want – that we get to the core of compassionate holiness which marked out Jesus' life and message.

Jesus came to inaugurate a kingdom which will transform the world —and living in this kingdom involves our seeking to live out the same powerful mix of prayer and action, of contemplation and service, as did Jesus in his earthly life. Many Christians of my generation have had to learn how to bring these aspects together, as we were brought up to believe that one was more "spiritual" than the other. We need to learn from the naturally holistic understanding of many young Christians today. This is exemplified – the fourth "context" in which I write – by the "Soul in the City" concept of mission, involving teaching, community service and street witness. The idea comes from "Soul Survivor", starting some years ago in Manchester and London, and now spreading (to my knowledge) to Nairobi in the summer of 2006 (organised by Kenyan Youth Pastors with over 5,000 Kenyan young people taking part), Kampala in 2007 and Durban in 2009.

As I began to read the later sections of this book, I was delighted to find that, one after the other, Patrick addresses these four contexts (along with much other relevant teaching), in a fresh and very readable style which can sometimes mask the depth of the insights he offers.

In order to get a proper perspective in our thinking and kingdom action, we need balanced, accessible exposition of what Jesus teaches in his parables. Patrick provides just this, and I trust that my few words will encourage the reader to take the teaching to heart.

Don Brewin
National Director, Sharing of Minstries Abroad UK
24th July 2006

PREFACE

This is the third of a trilogy in which the common thread is the word "becoming". In each of these three books I have taken a vital aspect of human life and tried to explore its meaning. In *Becoming Fully Human* and *Becoming a Spiritual Leader* and now *Becoming a Citizen of the Kingdom*, I have tried to show that, although a start must be made in each of these areas, they all involve a process. To become fully human is to become more like Jesus who is the model for all humanity; to become a spiritual leader often involves pain, struggle and joy not unlike those of the apostle Peter, around whom *Becoming a Spiritual Leader* was written; and to become a citizen of the kingdom involves discipleship which is enduring. It also requires keeping our eye on the main goal: the King himself and his kingdom. His kingdom is an all-encompassing reality of both the present and the future. We can only become fully human as members of this kingdom and we need spiritual leaders to point us to the King and his kingdom so that we become his fulfilled humanity. We cannot do it alone, nor were we ever meant to. In these and other ways this trilogy, I hope, hangs together. Although each stands alone they complement each other.

I am glad to offer this book because I have not found much written on the subject in recent years, and, although Jesus spoke constantly of the kingdom, many Christians are uncertain about what it means.

My hope is that this will help the reader to gain a vision of what the kingdom is, and some awareness of what it is not. We need to have a true idea of what we are called into. One of the reasons why I, and possibly many others, have a weak understanding of what the kingdom is all about is because much of our Christian upbringing has firmly rested on the teaching of Paul. No one explains more fully the "mechanics" of salvation and its implications, especially to a readership many of whom had been or were influenced by Judaism, but there is little mention *per se* of the kingdom in his writing. How different to Jesus who spoke continuously of the kingdom. The kingdom which was rumoured in the Old Testament was his world-view and the meta-narrative of all his teaching.

Though this book is about the kingdom, no book can ever adequately explain its meaning. All the shortcomings are mine. But I am grateful to those who have helped me. I recall particularly a series of excellent talks given by Canon David Cook at a Stewards Trust Teaching Week at Uppingham in 2003; to a number of authors whose works are listed; and to John Wimber who, building on the theology of Eldon Ladd, taught on the kingdom in a vivid and practical way.

I would like to thank my publisher, Terra Nova Publications, for their encouragement, for their patience and hard work in preparing this book for publication; Don Brewin, for kindly writing the Foreword just before leaving for Soul Nairobi 2006, and hearing the news, richly deserved, that he has been awarded the Medal of St Augustine for his service to the Anglican Communion by the Archbishop of Canterbury; my family for their support; and for the church I serve, All Saints, Weston, Bath, who have given me the opportunity to think, write, teach and consider what the kingdom might mean. I hope that we might be a signpost to the kingdom where we are, and to them I dedicate this book.

Patrick Whitworth
August 5th 2006
—Incidentally the Feast of King Oswald of Northumberland,
who himself received the kingdom and was later martyred.

PART I

SETTING THE SCENE

Chapter One

SEEING THE KINGDOM

It was the first night of a four-day vigil in our parish church, called Advent Prayer. It was the second such time of prayer in 2004. There had been an earlier one that year, from Ascension Day to Pentecost, which had continued for ten days. Members of the church led these ten days of uninterrupted prayer, day and night. These prayer vigils raised the temperature of the spiritual life of the church towards what Bishop Michael Marshall once called apostolic boiling point.

Each night during our Advent prayer unchurched kids roamed the churchyard, up to their usual mischief. And every night of the four days of prayer they came into the church and drifted round the various stations for prayer, entitled turning, yearning, listening and lamenting. At times they were so disruptive they had to be asked to leave. The lamenting station was a tent erected in a side-chapel. It was naturally a favoured spot for some kids, not because they had a lot of lamenting to do necessarily but because being further out of sight inside the tent, within the chapel, inside the church they felt free to do whatever they liked! Like figures in the innermost part of a Russian doll they were momentarily hidden away out of sight and out of mind. At one point, such was the mess created, this area needed to be rededicated. But it was not fruitless. God was working; several wrote their own simple but profound prayers and on Sunday evening three came and sat in our evening service. A member of the church, not knowing them, said, "Do you come here often?" They replied, with customary wit, "We've been here every night this week!" That

Sunday evening they lasted until the sermon, which means in our church services that they had been there for about one hour!

Earlier that same Sunday evening I had seen some of the BBC's Songs of Praise programme from the Hillsong church meeting in the Mermaid Theatre in London. The stunning testimonies from that remarkable church were so refreshing and direct that they seemed to blow away all the cobwebs of ecclesial traditions, replacing them with a simple and profound faith in Jesus. The week's events made me further reflect that the church in its myriad shapes and sizes is a variegated reflection of the kingdom. It spans a group of "unchurched" teenagers not yet saints sitting in Victorian pews in a medieval village church that has been there since the twelfth century to a highly urban "celeb" culture of glamorous twenties and thirties accustomed to sophisticated worship in a West End theatre. In fact, the span of church worldwide is far greater and far more various than that. It goes from a group of exiled Christians meeting under a tree in southern Sudan, in fear of attack, to a prayer breakfast in the White House where the most powerful in the world may be found; from the most destitute to the most influential. No one bit of the church has it all; none is perfect, none is doing it all right. It is easy to be mesmerised by the bigger ones and overlook the devoted service of small and vulnerable communities of Christians in hard-pressed places. Never before have there been so many expressions of faith in Christ as there are today. There is almost weekly re-definition of what it means to be church now. Young people care nothing for labels or denomination. The motto is, "If it works join it"; conversely, "If it doesn't, avoid it or leave well alone." In such a fast moving church culture we are thrown back to important insights. The first is that we are, as Christians, called to be part of God's kingdom; and the second is that the church is simply an all too human expression of what that means.

However, since we are as Christians first and foremost members of the kingdom, and secondly members of particular churches, the question we are answering in this book is: What does it mean to be a citizen of the kingdom and how do we become the citizens that we are intended to be? We will start by exploring further the connection between church and kingdom with special regard to our own culture and situation in Britain. Understandably, this may not resonate so well with the church in the global south.

Church and kingdom

The church in Britain has undergone huge change in the last hundred years. At the beginning of the twentieth century, Christians were divided into three main groups: Anglican, Catholic and Free Church. Issues that dominated political debate at that time were the disestablishment of the Anglican Church in Wales and education of Free Church children in Church of England primary schools.[1] The First World War hastened reassessment of the old world-view in which the church in Europe still occupied centre stage. In the post-Second World War era there was an Indian summer of churchgoing inspired partly by the Billy Graham "crusades" of the 1950s, which continued until the 1980s. I remember Billy Graham's rallies in 1989 in Crystal Palace, just a mile from the parish church of which I was then vicar. On three consecutive evenings we took groups of people to hear him and several found faith in Christ, in time becoming leaders in our local church. Many were inspired to go into full-time ministry from the campaigns of the1950s and are only now retiring.

In the 1960s there was the early stirrings of the charismatic renewal movement which led both to the founding of new churches, initially called "house churches", and the renewal movement in the mainstream churches as well. The founding of new churches and the vision of a church for every community (and later, in the late 1990s, a church for every network) also led to the church planting movement in the 1980s which has developed over the last twenty years. These movements of renewal both of Word and Spirit have led to powerful spiritual movements which cross most boundaries of denomination. Spring Harvest, New Wine and Alpha are the most obvious examples of these movements in the UK. Most have now been going for ten to fifteen years, born by the spiritual renewal movement in the church in the 1970s. If that thumbnail sketch is reasonably accurate as well as being encouraging it is only one half of the story, for during the same period the institutional church has continued to haemorrhage, and the overall numbers committed to institutional or organised Christianity in the UK continues to decline.

Most of us will be familiar with the broad outline of the story. The facts are that in the last fifteen years the churches together will have lost a million members, fifteen hundred buildings and a thousand full time ministers. So in the same fifteen year time span, we are confronted both with some powerful spiritual movements (as mentioned above, to name but a few better known ones from one particular tradition in the church) and, at the same time, a decline in membership of a million members in all churches together. You might well ask, "What is going on here?" Bishop Nigel McCulloch, the Bishop of Manchester, put it succinctly when he wrote, "It has long been said that there is a yearning for spirituality across our countries, but until now the evidence has largely been anecdotal. What the 2001 census has shown is that a huge majority of our population, in the privacy of their own homes and without any external pressure have expressed a personal allegiance of some kind to the Christian faith. Unfortunately, as the trends noted in this book ably demonstrate, there is a seeming inability on the part of most Christian churches to understand and engage with that opportunity."[2] With this issue in mind he wonders whether the Church of England could disappear in a generation or two, echoing George Carey's famous statement that the church is always only one generation away from extinction. Our own Bath and Wells Diocesan Missioner (Canon Roger Medley), at a recent conference entitled Changing Lives, said that there were now more Christians outside of church membership or church attendance than in membership or regular attendance. There are certainly new studies coming out of people with a churchless faith, in which a significant number of people have left all kinds of churches but continue their faith in small informal groupings.[3] So with a profoundly anti-institutional culture prevailing in the UK does this mean that the prevailing culture strongly militates against membership? This dilemma has led in turn to a deeper theological questioning of what is church anyhow. And we must turn to that question now.

The Reformers had a neat definition of church. It was the place where the word of God was preached and the sacraments were faithfully administered. It is a good working definition but perhaps it is not Calvinist enough in that it focuses more on what ministry must be performed rather than on the grace of God that must be experienced. For surely it is God in Christ who brings the church into existence by the work of the Spirit in the hearts of people using the powerful seed of his word in our lives. So an even simpler definition might be that the church is formed wherever Jesus is at work. Church is now no longer regarded by many as a noun defining a group to belong to or a place to go to, which is how the word has been basically regarded for a thousand years, but is regarded as a verb in which God, by the action of the Spirit and in conjunction with the Word, brings into existence a body of believers. So people ask how do you "do church" where you are? In fact to be fair to this latter definition we cannot "do" church but we can allow God to "do" it where we are and then recognise and shape the particular way he does church in our locality. The language may seem ungainly but it emphasises a more dynamic rather than static way of being church today. What has become quite clear is that "the old is passing away and the new is coming." Or has it?

The old that is passing away is Christendom, as we once knew it. The roots of Christendom lay in the adoption of the Christian faith by Constantine around 312AD. The previous three hundred years saw the progress of the gospel through apostolic preaching, great persecution, and tireless missionary endeavour and doctrinal defence against heresy which sought to destroy the essence of Christianity, until the eventual baptism of the church into state sponsored religion by Constantine himself, who made Christianity the religion of the empire. Ever since then Christians have viewed that event with deep ambivalence, rejoicing at the opportunities to reach all people through the organs of the state but aware of the corruption and mixed motives which pervaded Christian profession subsequently.

Since this Constantinian settlement, the Christian faith has faced four main assaults. They are: internal corruption through either false teaching or errant behaviour; persecution by the state, whether motivated by another religion or ideology —as in the case of Islam or Communism, which is still the case today, for instance in Indonesia (Islam) or China (communism); persecution by individual tyrants who wish to have no other centre of power apart from their own rule —for instance Idi Amin in Uganda; and secularisation from a culture in hock to human creeds such as rationalism, or man-made spiritualities. These appear to be the main forms of assault upon the church. In Europe until the late twentieth century the church was profoundly important to the fabric of the society, but the reality now is that, although there are vestiges of that relationship between church and state still in existence, much of the relationship is, more than anything, the outworking of tradition. If, on the one hand, the extent of Christendom has declined hugely in the twentieth century, and is still declining and may be yet further diminished, there are still on the other hand many examples of fresh expressions of church today as well as many vigorous expressions of old ways of doing church too.

Occasionally, you may hear it said by local clergy, especially those of the Church of England, that they are off to do their bit for Christendom. This might be shocking; but what is meant is that they will perform those functions of their role, granted by virtue of being the parish minister of the church by law established. This traditionally has involved "hatch, match and despatch" or baptisms, weddings and funerals. Because they emanate from Christendom, that is the tie up between church and state, it does not mean that they necessarily lack meaning or significance, but the minister knows that such occasions arise partly because of the institution of the Church of England. But then, as said earlier, 72% of the population do own up to believing in God. However, it is now a comparatively motivated person who will seek out a minister for a wedding or baptism, although when it comes to death perhaps there is greater demand! What is clear from all the statistics is that Christendom on the local level is also decreasing and will be yet further diminished.

The signs are clearly to be seen that whether in terms of congregational numbers, full time stipendiary ministers, numbers of church buildings, national or parochial influence, the age of Christendom in Britain is on the wane. And as Philip Jenkins says, the leadership of the next Christendom has moved south to Lagos, Kampala, Seoul and Sao Paulo, with the notable exception of the United States. He writes, "While traditional Christianity is weakening in large sections of the North, it is indeed being reinforced and reinvigorated by Southern churches, by means of immigration and evangelisation. And the Christianity spread by such means has a predictably Southern cast, conservative and charismatic. How this process develops over the coming century is enormously significant, not just for the future shape or religious alignments, but also for political history. The success of the prophets of Africa – and of Asia and Latin America – will determine exactly what kind of North will be confronting a rising South."[4] Behold the new is coming! But there are other kinds of newness.

In recent years there has been a plethora of thinking, books and activity around the concept of "emerging church", or new ways of "doing church". We have moved quickly from Christendom to Liquid

Church (the title of a book by Ward), or emerging church. These forms of church take cognisance of changing culture, the emergence of networks of relationship branded by their own culture. A myriad of cultures are identified by age, ethnicity, leisure likes and dislikes, music, economic grouping, so that planting churches is no longer simply about placing an identifiable church in a specific geographical area but doing church in a particular network which may have no geographical centre. So here we see church responding to shifts in culture and the simultaneous demise of Christendom. Is this to be the shape of things to come? It is far too early to say. If the old is passing away and the new is coming, the rate of decline or change will almost certainly be extremely uneven. In some places Christendom may thrive locally for at least another generation, possibly much longer, and emerging church will no doubt emerge through many false starts and dawns. So perhaps we must, as Archbishop Rowan Williams has said, be prepared to live for some time to come in "a mixed economy" of church expressions. A thousand years of church history is unlikely to be cast off in a day but the challenge to the institution which provides continuity, accountability and future leadership is to seriously change its patterns of ministry to take account of changing culture. But for the purposes of this book we must state that all forms of church, however they are done, are in the end merely pale and mostly inadequate expressions of the kingdom of God.

According to the Gospels, Jesus rarely talked about the church, but he did talk ceaselessly about the kingdom. The church is an expression of the kingdom, but unless it is conformed to the pattern of the kingdom it will lack any authenticity. As Dr William Abraham pointed out in his important book *The Logic of Evangelism*, becoming a true member of the church involves incorporation into the realm of God's rule. This carries both requirements and benefits.[5] There is no doubt that Jesus' world-view was defined by the kingdom of God. That kingdom and living in it was his consuming passion. It is time to consider his world-view alongside ours.

The kingdom of God: the Jesus world-view
We humans are a contrary lot, swinging from one extreme to another. A brief history of the Western world-view shows that we do swing from one pole to another: from the anarchy of marauding hordes which characterised the period of Goths, Visigoths and Vandals, to

the beginnings of medieval Christendom under Charlemagne with its emphasis on order and form; from the overarching monolith of the medieval church to the breakout of rationalism in the days of Rousseau, Voltaire and the Encyclopaedists; from the age of Enlightenment and the scientific rationalism, with its brief homage to communism, to the new so-called "new age" movement and post-modern thought. One world-view succeeds another like an ever-rolling stream of human history and perspective. Each world-view is formed by a combination of prevailing social conditions, recent scientific or technological invention, contemporary accepted patterns of thought, and controlling fears for the future. Current world-views prevailing in British society have been well documented in recent years; in each of them something of the Christian world-view may be found, but through the half-truth they enshrine they lead only into a spiritual cul-de-sac or a literal dead-end.

The curious thing about the predominant world-view found in Britain today is that two fundamentally opposing world-views are found in tension. This is indeed odd, because the one ought to undermine the other, when in fact people are seemingly able to hold the two together. There is rationalism along with superstition; materialism with the need for a spiritual explanation of life; and the scientific with the credulous. The basic reason for this is that as a society we are in revolt against the strict tenets of scientific materialism which do not of themselves offer a satisfying explanation for our existence, whilst at the same time we want to find a spirituality which is on our own terms and is not too demanding. As always we want as humans to have our cake and eat it!

As already said, bits of this spiritual search are right in so far as they go, their wrongness lies in placing too great a trust in things or beliefs that cannot ultimately bear such faith; they were simply not meant to do so. For instance, "materialism", in a narrower sense, is present in the gospel. Arguably, Christianity is the most "materialist" of faiths. The incarnation or God taking on our material form means that, more than in any other world religion, Christianity hallows the material life. God became a man; he lived a human life, was born, became part of a community, laboured with his hands, ate bread and drank water. God hallowed the material, but it was given its rightful place— to be used rightly, not abused, but not worshipped either. And yet, as we see from Jesus' conversation with Nicodemus, our material existence cannot contain the kingdom of God; for that to happen another ingredient must be added to the mixture —one which was lost and must be regained.

Or again, Christianity recognises that God made everything, as John says in his famous prologue to his Gospel, "Through him all things were made; without him nothing was made that has been made" (John 1:3). But recognising that everything was made by him does not warrant worshipping those things which he created, which so often new age spiritualities tend to do, so confusing the Creator with the created. No, the created points to the Creator. The vital distinction must always be kept between the Creator and the Creation. The pantheist and pagan want us to worship the creation, while the great monotheistic religions rightly distinguish between God and what he has made. The reason for so many in modern society wanting to worship the created order is that in such religion there is little demand that we should change or be accountable morally in our lives, apart from possibly our treatment of creation itself. We can simply do as we choose. So if we find what we do helpful, then we should do it —this is the only criterion applied. If it does me good and is not a problem for others, it is legitimate and cannot be gainsaid. It is, if you like, religion on our terms, and as such is very appealing.

Alison Morgan in her succinct analysis of modernism and postmodernism writes, "The problem about modernism is that it leaves things out. In stating that the foundational value of society is human reason, it follows that everything which is not susceptible to human reason is marginalized. When we value the material over the spiritual, we also value thinking over feeling, analysis over creativity, fact over intuition, and technology over art. "How" becomes more important than "why", knowledge more important than belief, structures more important than relationships, and money more important than everything. Religion retreats into the private realm and becomes a purely personal matter, and progress becomes the ultimate goal. In modernism fundamental human needs that cannot be, and were not meant to be, addressed with the tool of rational thought remain unidentified and unmet. And so reality loses its relational and spiritual dimensions."[6] Equally, post modernism leaves other parts out. In short it has become besotted by image at the cost of substance, overboard on feelings at the cost of truth, and desperate to find a new, untried and reality changing experience, often drugs or sexual experience, to inject a longed for sense of mystery into life. In fact in both modernism and postmodernism there are slivers of meaning, but what is needed is to wed experience to truth, reason to spirit, and soul to body. And who better to speak about those things than the one who said he is, "the way and the truth and the life" (John 14:6).

But before considering Jesus' world-view, which was firmly based on the kingdom of God, a further word about the formations of any world-view. It results from the interplay of the private and the public. Any psychiatrist will tell you that any human world-view undergoes a progression from birth to the grave which arises out of normal development of human life. This development has sometimes been classified into five identifiable stages. Experiences in our own personal world have a powerful influence on our view of the world, so that the loss of a parent in childhood or in teenage years, a divorce, sustained unemployment in the home, the effects of alcoholism, abuse, emotional deprivation, rejection or prolonged illness, will all have far reaching effects on a person's world-view. Thus, in the case of Dickens, his father's debts and spells in the debtors prison had a continuing effect on his whole outlook. Debt, and falling into debt and into the hands of the lawyers, was a theme which was never far from most of his writings. The fear of becoming a debtor himself was one of the motivations for his prodigious literary output. So what happens to us personally, and especially in our childhood, will have a strong influence on our own world-view. That world-view will be a set of responses to the world and to others, which may in turn continue to influence our thinking and behaviour.

But our personal experiences are not solely determinative of our world-view; that depends too on the way we respond to the contemporary culture in which we are placed and the prevailing culture in our country. Every culture will have a prevailing set of world-views, and they have a profound influence on us. In a recent article about imprisonment, two cultural attitudes to imprisonment were compared. In the United States, out of 100,000 people, apparently 500 will suffer imprisonment, whereas in Japan only 37 will. (Presently in the US there are around two million prisoners.) What is the reason for that? The answer lies in the respective attitude of the culture to someone who is imprisoned. In the US it is relatively unexceptional; whereas in Japan such is the dishonour brought to a family if a member is imprisoned that, when freed, the prisoner is shunned by his own family. Asian society is so dominated by the idea of honour that someone who transgresses the accepted codes is brutally punished by their own family. Again, it is virtually inconceivable to a Western family that one family should kill another to expunge disgrace. But in certain people groups it sometimes happens, and is actually believed by some to be justifiable. In the UK such attitudes have led to many incidents of "honour killings" of women who have transgressed their community's moral code, or who have refused to take part in arranged marriages. It is often the woman who is punished, not the man, in cultures in which women may be regarded as inferior.

In Western society we have seen already that two prevalent world-views coexist. They are generally called modern (the scientific /rationalist world-view) and postmodern (the view that broadly says that what seems right to you is right). Lesslie Newbigin, something of a prophet on these matters, in outlining a Christian response to contemporary culture, writing of the crisis in Western culture, points us to an expression used by the Chinese writer Carver Yu: "technological optimism and literary despair". On the one hand he sees the unstoppable dynamism of our technology, always forging ahead with new means to achieve whatever ends, wise or foolish, we may desire. On the other hand he looks at our literature and sees only scepticism, nihilism, and despair in which life is depicted as having no point, nothing is held sacred and reverence is seen as an unworthy relic of past times. Everything is a potential target of mockery. [As I write this, Madame Tussaud's, the London museum of waxworks, has released a version of the nativity for Christmas 2004, with David Beckham and his wife Victoria as Joseph and Mary, with Blair, Bush and the Duke of Edinburgh as the Three Wise Men, so fulfilling Newbigin's words.] Newbigin notes that individuals are left on their own without respected maps and models. There is a search for personal identity, not least among the young. And without answers to that search, violence and drug abuse flourish.[7]

The expression "literary despair" we could justifiably replace with "spiritual despair". But to find this literary despair, which has shaped our society in the last sixty years, we could not do better than consider Sartre, the father of existentialism (which, in turn, became the philosophical basis for postmodernism). In his novel, typically entitled *Nausea*, we see "literary despair".[8] Nothing has a beginning or end; everything appears futile and without meaning. That is the Western world-view for many.

So the formation of a world-view depends on the interplay of the private or the personal with the prevailing cultural moods of the day. But Jesus' world-view was the kingdom of God. He literally spoke of very little else. How did Jesus come by such a world-view, which he then came to speak about unceasingly? What does it mean? Did it arise from both understanding his own identity and the purpose of God as already displayed in history? It is time to look at the background to this idea of the kingdom of God about which Jesus was so eloquent, and compare it with the world-views of his own day, before looking at how anyone might enter it.

Rumours of the kingdom in the Old Testament

Most of the great themes of the Bible are prefigured in the Old Testament before reaching full clarity in the New Testament. The sacrifice of Jesus on the cross is foreshadowed by the sacrificial system laid out in the first five books of the Bible. The temple built in Jerusalem prefigures the church, a temple not built with hands. The prophets of the Old Testament promise the Messiah in various ways but it is Jesus who dramatically and unexpectedly brings together their images of the Suffering Servant and the mysterious figure of the Son of Man found in Daniel. What is true of these fundamental themes, namely of redemption, sacrifice, the identity and role of Jesus and the function of the church, is also true of the kingdom of God. They are all trailed in the Old Testament and brought to fulfilment in the New. What takes centre stage in the New Testament, and above all in the teaching and actions of Jesus, is shadowy in the Old Testament but nonetheless present. What is embryonic in the Old Testament is fleshed out in the New. The kingdom is a rumour in the Old Testament but it becomes a firm promise in the New.

Before looking at the promise of the kingdom and how Jesus demonstrated what it is all about, we must piece together the rumour of the kingdom in the Old Testament. The rumour is based on four strands present in the narratives, prophecies and inspired reflections of the Old Testament. These strands are, in turn, a brilliant but flawed king, a mad emperor, two prescient prophets and inspired poetry. We shall look at each in turn.

After the settlement of the Promised Land under Joshua, a period

28

of intermittent warfare against the neighbouring Philistines followed, so that the Israelites wanted a king. Although God was their king, they wanted to be like the surrounding nations with a king of their own. Despite Samuel's warnings they persisted, "No.... We want a king over us. Then we shall be like all the other nations, with a king to lead us and to go out before us and fight our battles." Despite Samuel's reluctance, God said, "Listen to them and give them a king" (1 Samuel 8:19-22). Saul, the first king, although promising at first, eventually failed. The second king, David, became the prototype for a future ideal form of kingship or rule. There was no mistaking that David was a brilliant individual with uncommon gifts —the shepherd boy turned king. He was a charismatic military leader. Perhaps the same could be said of David as Wellington once said of Napoleon, the greatest European commander since Alexander, that his (Bonaparte's) presence on the field of battle was worth 10,000 soldiers! David was able to unite the kingdom, to found its capital at Jerusalem and site the temple on the threshing floor of Araunah the Jebusite. (See 1 Chronicles 22:1ff; 2 Samuel 24:24f.)

But he was not only a military commander, a statesman and a leader, he was also sensitive and reflective; a writer, poet and musician who expressed the profoundest spiritual aspirations and depressions ever penned by man. But, for all his undoubted kingship, his rule was flawed. For a time his rule over Israel and neighbouring states was legendary, as expressed by the writer of the Chronicles. But he grew overconfident and lazy allowing himself to commit adultery with Bathsheba and murdering her husband to cover his sin. He was, like many human rulers, brilliant but flawed. Nonetheless, in the providence of God, it was through his line and descendants that a future king would come. "Of the increase of his government and peace there will be no end. He will reign on David's throne and over his kingdom establishing and upholding it with justice and righteousness from that time on and forever. The zeal of the Lord Almighty will accomplish this" (Isaiah 9:7). David provided a model of kingship which prefigured a later king who would surpass him. David was a leader, a shepherd to his people, a warrior, a teacher, and a priest.

Nevertheless what was present but imperfect in him would become fulfilled and perfected in his greater son. The kingship of David was the first rumour in the Old Testament of a type of king and kingship still to come. For the second rumour of another kingdom we must fast forward in history from this point nearly five hundred years, to the words of a mad emperor, who figured largely in Judah's history and was not, in a certain respect, unlike our English king George III.

Nebuchadnezzar is a name to conjure with and it sounds highly exotic. Just as Cyrus was later the instrument whom God used to free the Jews from their captivity in Babylon so Nebuchadnezzar was the instrument whom God used to punish his people for their repeated failure to follow him. Babylon for a time vied with Egypt to be regional superpower. For a while it was Egypt which was in the ascendancy, but in 605BC Babylon reasserted its power, defeating the Egyptian army at Carchemish on the Euphrates some 100 km north east of Aleppo in present day Syria. Jehoiakim, the king of Judah who had allied himself with Pharoah Neco of Egypt, was punished. Jerusalem was sacked in 597 on the 16th March, the second day of Adar, a date which brought about the culmination of years of prophecy by Isaiah and Jeremiah and began the period of exile in Babylon. The captives were marched off a month later into exile in Babylon and were to remain there for a minimum of seventy years. Some families remained in exile for 150 years. Nehemiah did not return to Jerusalem until 445BC. At first glance the notion of kingdom seemed to be over. David's line appeared to have come to a crushing end and the monarchy was never to be restored as an independent monarchy again in Judah or Israel; and yet the idea of kingdom was not lost. As with many other parts of their theology it was reworked in exile, as exile became place of renewal.* Nebuchadnezzar not only was the conqueror of Israel but he was also a highly religious man, although pagan and Gentile. The early chapters of Daniel tell of his recognition of the God of Daniel (see Daniel 2:29). His eclectic attitude towards divinities showed that he was prepared to acknowledge a god of power wherever he discovered one. This attitude of reverence towards Daniel's God was however turned to something deeper through an episode of madness. Falling into a fit of boasting he is judged with a bout of madness that lasted either seven months or seven years. (Daniel 4:32). During this time he lived outside, grazed like the animals, and his body itself was changed. At

---

* Although this must be a theme for another book, the idea of exile and renewal being interlinked is an important one, not least for the church in the West as it feels increasingly exiled from a society in which formerly it had such an important and powerful role.

the end of this period he appears to have received a revelation both about his own state and that of God's kingdom for, surprisingly on the lips of a former pagan ruler, the one chosen to judge Judah, were these remarkable words,

> His dominion is an eternal dominion;
> his kingdom endures from generation to generation.
> All the peoples of the earth
> are regarded as nothing.
> He does as he pleases
> with the powers of heaven
> and the peoples of the earth.
> No-one can hold back his hand
> or say to him: "What have you done?"
>
> *Daniel 4:34b, 35*

It is easy to pass over the great significance of this confession and the recognition in it of a kingdom which is over all. In a very real way this was the precursor for a later confession by another ruler, Darius, who succeeded Belshazzar or Nabonidus in a velvet revolution in Babylon, when the Babylonian Empire imploded and was overtaken by the Medes and then soon after that by the Persians. But what is clear is that there was a growing conviction amongst the rulers of these successive empires, Babylonian, Mede and Persian, that the God of Daniel was the ruler of an eternal kingdom. So it is ironic that the notion of kingdom took a new step forward at a time of exile when Judah seemed at its most vulnerable and weak, and was acknowledged not by the Jews themselves but by the non-Jewish rulers to whom they were subject. But, as we shall see, such is the nature of the kingdom of God breaking out where you least expect it. And doing so not as a result of God's people's endeavour but through his sovereign power at work through the agency of a faithful person. Two of these faithful people who took forward the notion of kingdom were Isaiah and Daniel.

Although many of the prophets looked forward to the coming of God's kingdom,* the two men with the most sustained understanding of a coming kingdom were Isaiah and Daniel. Isaiah's prophecy covers a long period, from 740BC to 540BC, and has often been

---

*E.g. Jeremiah, Ezekiel, Nahum, Habakkuk, Micah and Zechariah.

thought to be the work of several prophets of similar vision edited under a single name. Whatever the truth about this, the content of the prophecy is remarkable for the scope of its vision, the unique portrayal of the Messiah as the Suffering Servant, the yearning of the prophecy as well as its hope for the future. At times the kingdom is portrayed in mouthwatering terms, not least in chapter eleven when we are told,

> The infant will play near the hole of the cobra,
> and the young child put his hand into the viper's nest.
> They will neither harm nor destroy
> on all my holy mountain
> for the earth will be full of the knowledge of the LORD
> as the waters cover the sea"
>
> *Isaiah 11:8f*

The figure in Isaiah who will bring this about is both the shoot from the stump of Jesse and the Suffering Servant depicted in the centre section of the book. This unique figure, whom Jesus would identify as himself, would usher in this kingdom. Isaiah prophesies a coming kingdom of utter harmony and peace, brought to pass by the shoot from Jesse and Suffering Servant who will see the suffering of his soul and be satisfied. (See Isaiah 53:10-12.)

Alongside Isaiah, the other "prophet" to glimpse most clearly this coming kingdom was Daniel. We have already seen from the story of Nebuchadnezzar the growing awareness, in both Daniel himself as well as some of the Gentile emperors he served whilst in captivity, the hope of a coming kingdom unlike any other. This vision was further confirmed by Daniel's extraordinary vision of successive empires waxing and waning. These included the Babylonian, Medes and Persians, Greek and Roman. Taken together, these empires lasted very nearly a thousand years, from the fall of Jerusalem in 597BC to the fall of the Roman Empire in 410AD. As a prophetic vision of history it is unsurpassed in the Bible (see Daniel chapters seven and eight), and no wonder at the end of the vision and its explanation by Gabriel, Daniel, "...was exhausted and lay ill for several days" (Daniel 8:27). However in the midst of this vision of successive empires another new and powerful figure emerged, described majestically by Daniel as follows, "In my vision at night I looked, and there before me was one like a son of man, coming with the clouds of heaven. He approached the Ancient of Days and was led into his presence. He was given authority, glory and sovereign power; all peoples, nations and men of every language worshipped him. His dominion is an everlasting dominion that will not pass away, and his kingdom is one that will never be destroyed" (Daniel 7:13f). The point could not be clearer. Unlike all other empires and kingdoms, here was a kingdom that would increase and never pass away. All human empires will be destroyed. But the figure who will be given authority to receive and inaugurate the kingdom is the Son of Man, Jesus' favourite title for himself. So between Isaiah and Daniel a picture is emerging of a kingdom growing through the shoot from Jesse, the Suffering Servant and the Son of Man. Isaiah and Daniel between them are given the outline form of this kingdom, the pieces that Jesus himself will pick up, identify in himself and fulfil in his life and ministry. Before turning to think of the way Jesus did this, there is one more strand in the Old Testament to appreciate: the psalms of kingship.

Perhaps the greatest of these psalms, pointing to a kingdom in which God will reign completely over his people, are those in the later part of the Psalter. These promises of a future king who will reign unchallenged with justice and compassion are linked both to David's throne and to a coming Messianic age. So the psalmist speaks of a king, initially referring to David but being fulfilled by the coming Messiah:

> He will call out to me, 'You are my Father,
> my God, the Rock my Saviour.'
> I will also appoint him my firstborn,
> the most exalted of the kings of the earth.
> I will maintain my love to him for ever,
> and my covenant with him will never fail.
> I will establish his line for ever,
> his throne as long as the heavens endure.
>
> *Psalm 89:26-29*

The theme of the reign of God is a consistent one in several of the psalms in the 90s, so we read,

> The LORD reigns, he is robed in majesty;
> The LORD is robed in majesty

> and is armed with strength.
> The world is firmly established;
> it cannot be moved.
> Your throne was established long ago;
> you are from all eternity.

Psalm 93:1f

and in Psalm 95,

> For the LORD is the great God.
> The great king above all gods.
> In his hand are the depths of the earth,
> and the mountain peaks belong to him.
> The sea is his, for he made it,
> and his hands formed the dry land.
> Come let us bow down in worship,
> let us kneel before the LORD our maker;
> for he is our God and we are the people of his pasture,
> the flock under his care.

The persistent theme of these psalms is the Lord is king and he reigns. The kingship of God first modelled by David and the early years of Solomon is to be fulfilled in great David's greater Son.

So these are the main strands in the Old Testament which when woven together make an emerging tapestry of the kingdom of God: the establishment of a monarchy in Israel which reaches a peak in God's covenant with David; the acknowledgement of this kingdom by non-Jewish rulers whose own empires would pass away; the proclamation by the prophets, especially Isaiah and Daniel, of a coming kingdom linked to a messianic age; and lastly, the announcement of this kingdom in psalms of worship. Together these strands made for a powerful emerging picture of a kingdom to come. It was when Jesus burst onto the scene after the witness and preaching of John the Baptist that this kingdom was finally announced and displayed. But the style and horizons of the kingdom Jesus announced took all the kingdom or Messiah watchers by surprise; indeed many were highly offended having their own ideas of what this kingdom would look like challenged, but there was no doubt that the kingdom had come and was coming, for those who had eyes to see, for as Jesus said: "The kingdom of God is near. Repent and believe the good news" (Mark 1:15b).

Jesus and the kingdom

It is amazing how wrong we can get things. Never was this truer than in Israel's misunderstanding of what the kingdom of God would be like, and subsequently the church has been busy misrepresenting the kingdom too. The only template for the kingdom of God which we have is the ministry of Jesus; what he said and did, and perhaps especially what he did. The actions and words of Jesus are the lodestar for what the kingdom is all about.

There was an expectation of the kingdom of God in Israel which was that God himself would come and rule over Israel restoring the land, the covenant, the temple and the Torah. But the only conceivable way in which it was envisaged that this could come about was through the military overthrow of the occupying power, which was the Romans. The expectation was that the Messiah would usher in this rule of God and that he would lead a revolt against the Romans, and probably with this in mind Simon the Zealot joined the disciples and the people tried to make Jesus king. (See John 6:15.) But, as we shall see, Jesus' kingship was not of this world. (See John 18:36.) From the outset Jesus came proclaiming this kingdom, and in one way or another each of the Gospels presents this declaration of the kingdom at the outset. (See Matthew 4:17; Mark 1:15; Luke 4:16-20; John 2:7-11.) For Matthew and Mark it was a simple declaration of the arrival of the kingdom, with the presence of Jesus connected to a call to repentance; with Luke it was the fulfilment of Isaiah's prophecy in Isaiah 61:1f, and with John the recording of Jesus' first miracle at Cana of Galilee, where Jesus turned the water into wine —a highly symbolic miracle in which the inference must be that the water of the Old Covenant had run out and that, through Jesus, a new age or covenant had begun which surpassed anything before, as wine is better than water or mature vintage wine is better than *vin ordinaire*! The old had passed away and the new was coming. The nature of the kingdom is what we must explore next before seeing how Jesus demonstrated it in his words and actions.

This has been a long opening chapter and before moving on to consider the nature of this kingdom, it might be worth briefly summarising what we have covered. The kingdom of God is not the same as the church. The kingdom creates the church; the church should bear witness to the kingdom. The problem for the church in the old countries of Europe and the Near East where the church has existed for nearly 2000 years is that very often the dynamic of the kingdom is obscured by the institution of the church. We need to recapture the dynamic of the kingdom so we know what it is we are called to bear witness to. For Jesus the idea and indeed reality of the kingdom of God made up his world-view. His life, teaching and ministry were a living manifesto of this kingdom. His death and resurrection were the entry point for people into this kingdom as the dying thief dramatically discovered. Indeed the thief's entry to the kingdom was expressed in the language of it. Nor was this kingdom unknown to the Jews, as we have seen there were rumours of the kingdom scattered in the Old Testament and therefore in the narrative of Jewish history. Jesus uniquely gathered the strands together in his own life and presented the reality of the kingdom of God, in a way which was utterly surprising and indeed shocking to his contemporaries and to others ever since. The temptation to the church has always been to institutionalise the kingdom and to remove or diminish its essence which is the dynamic rule of God over human life and the cosmos. So with the message of the kingdom Jesus exploded onto the scene in around 27AD —"The kingdom of God is near. Repent and believe the good news." It is time to consider more carefully the kingdom that was being announced.

Chapter Two

THE NATURE OF THE KINGDOM

I am writing this chapter in early January 2005; at the time of writing one of the most significant events of recent years has just taken place, namely the earthquake and resulting tsunami in South East Asia. Along with 9/11 it will shape the world-views of a generation. From the point of view of the Westerner, especially the gap year student or holidaying family, there may never be such a glad and innocent morning on a South East Asian beach again. The forces of nature have unleashed a wave of mass destruction greater than any terrorist could perpetrate. For the shoreline inhabitants of around nine Asian countries there is now only an inexorable climb out of infinite loss with regard to family, housing, livelihood and security back to normality, which may take a decade or more. No wonder many are re-examining the roots of their faith to see how such a catastrophe can be reconciled with a loving and almighty God. The old dilemma is posed that if such events occur in a world of which he is in charge then either he is not loving or not almighty —he surely cannot be both? The question we are left with is one about the nature of God's reign, if such things can occur in his world. If anything, the tsunami is more difficult to explain than 9/11, because at least 9/11 has the element of human evil which has resulted from an evil choice. But these natural tragedies sharpen the question: what is the nature of this rule or kingdom of God which can allow such things to happen? In one sense, this whole book is an answer to this question.

If it is not too much of a leap, the place where we are going to begin to answer this question, as well as to define the nature of this kingdom of which Jesus constantly spoke, is in a conversation between Jesus and the Roman governor Pilate in the last hours of Jesus' life, just before his crucifixion. This conversation takes us to the heart of the definition of this kingdom.

The kingdom on trial   John 18:28 – 19:16

In John's Gospel there is little talk of the kingdom. Unlike the synoptic Gospels, where every page is filled with Jesus' teaching about the kingdom, especially in his parables, the kingdom in John's Gospel is more implicit, demonstrated through the seven signs around which the Gospel is built, which show Jesus' authority and power. Only in his conversation with Nicodemus, which we shall look at later, together with this almost philosophical conversation with Pilate, at the very end of Jesus' earthly life, is there any sustained teaching about the kingdom in St John's Gospel. But in this interview with Pilate shortly before the crucifixion, discussion about the nature of Jesus' kingship and kingdom is centre stage.

From the outset, the line of questioning that Pilate pursued with Jesus in this quasi-judicial interview is about Jesus' claim to be a king. "Are you the king of the Jews?" he asks as his first question in his interrogation of Jesus. Jesus replies, "My kingdom is not of this world. If it were, my servants would fight to prevent my arrest by the Jews. But now my kingdom is from another place." (See John 18:33-37.) To the annoyance of the Jews, Pilate persists in referring to Jesus as a king, even to the point of having the famous inscription "Jesus of Nazareth, the king of the Jews" fixed to the wooden upright of his cross. (See John 18:39; 19:14f and 19.) To what extent this was sincere or a further mockery of Jesus, who was later taunted by the soldiers as a king, we cannot be sure, but there does seem to be more than a hint of deference in Pilate to Jesus' authority, even though he could not have truly understood Jesus' allusion to the source of that authority as being "from above". The idea of Jesus' authority not being of this world was one which Pilate must have found hard to understand. He knew his own authority or *imperium* (right to rule) came from Caesar, but from who did Jesus gain his evident authority? In the end, Pilate's political expediency prevailed over any nascent recognition of Jesus' authority ("...my kingdom is from another place") and, cajoled by the mob, he unconvincingly punished him as a usurper.

In his replies to Pilate, Jesus did not deny that he was a king. He also recognised that his kingdom was quite unlike any earthly kingdom. His authority was derived "from another place". And from this place all authority proceeded, as Jesus made plain to Pilate with the words, "You would have no power over me if it were not given to you from above" (John 19:11). Of this kingdom Jesus spoke throughout his entire ministry, as well as demonstrating its reality through many miracles. It was fitting that the nature of this kingdom should come up at his trial, for it was the central part of his teaching and actions. It is time to explore what lay at the heart of this kingdom for which Jesus was prepared to die.

The meaning of "kingdom"

Wherever the word kingdom occurs in the teaching of Jesus we would do well to replace it with the word "rule". The kingdom of God is to be found where the rule of God is. In the Old Testament the expression "the kingdom of God" does not occur, but the idea is found throughout the prophets. God is frequently spoken of as king both of Israel and of the earth. Eldon Ladd has pointed out that, despite its being true to say that God is now king, the Bible also refers to a future time when he will be ruling the people of God. A distinction is made between the sense in which he is king over all and the distinctive way in which he is king of his own people, the latter being partially a future reference. So the prophetic hope is for God to govern not only Israel but the whole earth.[1] Indeed John Bright defines the kingdom of God as the rule of God over his people, and particularly the vindication of that rule in glory at the end of history.[2] So the kingdom of God is simply where the rule of God is.

In the Old Testament the Hebrew word *malkuth* is used to denote this authority to rule, so the psalmist writes,

> The LORD has established his throne in heaven,
> and his kingdom [*malkuth*] rules over all.
>
> *Psalm 103:19*

However, the same word denotes not only the "reign" of God but also the realm – the place where that reign is exercised. (See 2 Chronicles 20:30; Esther 3:6; Daniel 9:1, 11:9; Jeremiah 10:7.)

So in the first instance the kingdom of God is the actual rule of

God, and secondly it is where that rule is found, whether in the hearts and wills of people or on the earth or the world that he has created. As Jesus said in his conversation with Pilate, this power or right to rule is given from "another place" —meaning God himself.

This idea of power, or the right to rule, being conferred on another was familiar to Jesus' hearers, for he uses it in the opening of the parable of the ten talents or *minas* (a *mina* being about three months' wages). Luke prefaces the parable with the comment that Jesus told the parable because, "...he was near Jerusalem and the people thought that the kingdom of God was going to appear at once" (Luke 19:11). But the people's idea of the kingdom and Jesus' idea were very different, since they thought that it would mean the certain overthrow of the Romans, whereas for Jesus his crucifixion and resurrection were the unavoidable events which would throw open his kingdom to all.

His followers' other mistake was to think that the kingdom of God would be fulfilled at once. In fact it would not be fulfilled for ages, so Jesus told a parable the main teaching point of which was faithfulness and accountability during a period of extended waiting for the fulfilment of the kingdom. The parable begins with a little vignette which is both historical and instructive. Jesus prefaces his story with the sentence, "A man of noble birth went to a distant country to have himself appointed king [or receive a kingdom *basileia*] and then to return" (Luke 19:12). This had in fact happened. Archelaus, Herod's son, in 4BC, had gone to Rome following his father's death, to have his kingship or "right to rule" confirmed by the emperor Augustus. This had happened although he was opposed by fifty Jews who had also gone to Rome to contend his appointment. However, his kingdom or "right to rule" had been confirmed and his opponents had been killed.[3]

In summary, the "kingdom of God" primarily refers to the rule of God and his Christ; secondly, it refers to where that rule is acknowledged and received, which is his realm. It is a rule that comes from "another place" conferred on Jesus by his Father, giving him authority to overcome his enemies and to bring in the rule of God. What became clear from the outset, when Jesus' ministry exploded in Israel, was that this rule of God, which was coming with him, was quite unlike any other form of government or rule ever seen on earth. Again as Jesus said to Pilate, "My kingdom is not of this world." For the rest of this book we shall see how his rule or kingdom is different from all other, worldly, forms of government, and is the one which shall outlast them all.

The style of government

For Christmas, two years ago, I gave our eldest daughter, who like her grandfather and myself studied history at university, amongst other less serious presents a book entitled "A History of Humanity". It is one of those remarkable publishing triumphs which chronicles simply through text, maps and charts the succeeding empires which have governed human affairs in East and West, North and South (The Times Compact History of the World). It covers most of recent human history from 10,000 BC to present day. Empire succeeds empire, whether it is Egyptian, Persian, Roman, Greek or more recently Turkish, Russian, British and now American.

The characteristics of each empire are quite different, from the sudden bursting forth of the Mongols under Genghis Khan in 1206 to rule half the northern hemisphere from the Pacific Ocean to the Caspian Sea to the more settled rule of the Ottomans in the West from 1453 to 1918. In any survey of empires there are two points to draw out: firstly, that each empire came to an end as either it crumbled from within or was overtaken by another superior force; and, secondly, that every empire or rule had its own special style or character.

The Roman Empire was one of the longest lasting, continuing for around five hundred years in the West; although it was to continue in the East as Byzantium until the fall of Constantinople in 1453. The present day American "empire", which is not a territorial one principally – as its territorial rule is in fact kept to the United States – but more one of culture and commercial influence, might be dated from the Japanese attack on Pearl Harbour, from which military reversal the United States became the greatest superpower the world has seen. It spends more on defence than the next seven nations put together. And although we cannot envisage it now, presumably its ascendancy will be at some stage surpassed, and the only possible rival at present seems to be China.

The first observation from this short overview of human history is that every human empire comes to an end. But contrastingly the kingdom of God does not. When Jesus was born, the angel said to Mary, "He will be great and will be called the Son of the Most High.

The Lord God will give him the throne of his father David, and he will reign over the house of Jacob forever; *his kingdom will never end*" (Luke 1:32f, my italics), so fulfilling the prophecy in Daniel of a Gentile emperor, Darius:

> "For he is the living God
> and he endures for ever;
> his kingdom will not be destroyed,
> his dominion will never end."
>
> *Daniel 6:26b*

If the first great distinguishing feature of the kingdom of God, compared with all other human empires, is that they all wax and wane but the kingdom of God only grows, as we shall see later, the other great distinguishing feature of the kingdom of God is that its style is quite unlike any other, and that is what we must consider now.

The nearer you live to any government the more aware you are of its style, so that in the UK in the last twenty years different political administrations have been attributed very different styles. The closing years of the Conservative administrations, which in all lasted from 1979-1997, almost twenty years, was characterised by one word— "sleaze". Whether that was a fair way of characterising the administration of John Major, history will tell, but memories of brown paper bags full of cash being sent round to a minister to ask questions in the House of Commons was one of those defining perceptions of a government, together with the cruel phrase used by a resigning Chancellor that the Prime Minister was in office but not in power. Equally, in more recent times, the New Labour administration has been characterised by one word— "spin"; a political art form learnt in opposition then applied in government, reaching its denouement in the period leading up to the Iraq war, where selective use of facts and language was made to convince the British public that Iraq was a threat to the UK. The failure to clarify the impression given by a government dossier that Iraq had strategic weapons capable of mass destruction and of being deployed in forty-five minutes, when what was in fact referred to in the intelligence briefing were battlefield weapons of no strategic significance, was the nadir of such political chicanery. Every government has its style, and the closer you are to that government the more aware of that style you become. Some governments are so notorious that you know their character from afar. The style results from the personalities at the centre of the government, the way they seek to handle power, and the policies they wish to pursue.

For a glimpse of the style of Jesus' kingdom, we will return to his conversation with Pilate before Jesus' execution. The person at centre stage was Jesus, standing seemingly helpless before the envoy of the Roman emperor, Pilate, having been scourged by Pilate's soldiers. Pilate recognised an authority in Jesus that he wanted to acknowledge but did not want to endorse, so he took, in his mind, a kind of middle way, condemning him to death on the one hand, thereby placating the Jews who sought his death, and obviating any charge that he was not Caesar's friend, but fixing a notice to the cross that he was "Jesus of Nazareth, the king of the Jews". Pilate was fearful of the claim that Jesus was the Son of God (John 19:8), was in awe of Jesus' remark that, "You would have no power over me if it were not given you from above" (John 19:11), and so Pilate said to the Jews, "Here is your king!" (John 19:14b, see also vv. 15b, 19). The style of Jesus' kingdom could not be more different from any other. At his crucifixion, the king hung naked on the cross. Unlike all other kings, he came not to be served but to serve. His use of power was dissimilar to all others, and his kingship was so well disguised in the overalls of humanity that very few seemed to see it. But a thief dying next to him on a cross said, "Jesus, remember me when you come into your kingdom", and was told that he would be with him in paradise. Here was a kingdom which was not extinguished by death and therefore could never end, and whose style was completely different to the sleaze, spin or tyranny of human government. Throughout his ministry, Jesus was at pains to explain the nature of his kingdom and he did so through his parables, his actions and his teaching. We must turn now to the way this kingdom works, its preoccupations and its driving force.

PART II

THE WORKING OF THE KINGDOM

Chapter Three

THE GOVERNMENT OF GRACE

In this section entitled the working of the kingdom we shall see how Jesus said this kingdom, this rule of God, functions in relation to human lives and the destiny of the world. Jesus explained these weighty matters through homely stories or parables. Whenever he spoke to the crowds he used them; often he explained them to his own disciples. Most of his recorded teaching appears to be done through them. Only in John's Gospel, which is set out quite differently from the synoptic Gospels, is the teaching conducted through discourses —that is either long conversations or monologues. Here we will look over the sweep of Jesus' teaching about the kingdom in his parables. I have clustered them in four main categories, each of which looks at one aspect of the kingdom of God. In brief, these categories are parables about grace, parables about discipleship, parables about growth and parables about the coming crisis. These four categories seem to catch at least 90% of the parables that Jesus uttered. These parables taught in a memorable way – and sometimes a brain teasing or spirit teasing way – the main things we need to know about the working of this kingdom of God, which is his just and gentle rule. Thus we can only become subject to that rule and all its benefits through grace. Our aim as subjects, under that rule, is to become warm-hearted disciples, constant learners. Then we may be assured that we are part of a growing kingdom not, to use modern parlance, part of a failing organisation or state; so we should be humbly confident. Lastly, the kingdom moves to a climax, a point of crisis which will be either a denouement or triumph for all concerned. With this overview in mind we can turn to see that only through grace can we enter this kingdom. In C.S. Lewis, Narnia speak, grace is the wardrobe whereby we enter a kingdom in which the Son reigns.

I once served in a church where there was a memorial plaque on one of the church walls which simply read, "Grace died in this parish on June 22nd 1746, beloved by all who knew her"! No doubt it was a sad day when she died, but how much sadder a world or church without grace. Too often in the church we have all too readily succeeded in burying grace. As the much-quoted poet George Herbert wrote, with a sigh no doubt, "Ah, what a thing is man devoid of grace." Grace lies at the centre of our message, but too often the impression the church gives about its life is that it is more to do with rivalry, jealousy, suspicion, judgement and, not to put too fine a point on it, self-righteousness rather than grace, faith and love. And, as John Newton the eighteenth century converted slave trader understood, our best and correct impression of this grace is most probably our first. As he memorably wrote, "How precious did that grace appear the hour I *first* believed." It was this totally unexpected grace, which also continually amazed Paul when he considered that God had chosen him as his chief apostle who hitherto had been vehemently persecuting the church, which lies at the very heart of God's government of his kingdom. In this section of the book we are looking at the fundamental policies which operate in the working of the kingdom. First and foremost of these is the operating principle of grace, which is God's undeserved love for us humans. (Ephesians 3:7f.)

Too quickly we Christians forget and, like the Galatian Christians, abandon the one who called us by grace. (See Galatians 1:6.) Often, we need to summon up our first understanding of grace in order to recapture our first love of Christ. What is unmistakeable in both the actions and parables of Jesus is that the government of the kingdom is one of grace, and this is what we must concentrate on now in surveying Jesus' stories about this basic operating principle of his kingdom. And, as always with Jesus, what he talked about in his parables, he demonstrated in his life.

As the scholar Jeremias pointed out in his book *The Parables of Jesus*, the context for most of these stories or parables about grace in the kingdom of God is the provocation of the Pharisees by Jesus' own lifestyle. So we find at the beginning of Luke 15 a statement about Jesus' conduct which had firstly provoked the Pharisees, whose reaction in turn provoked Jesus to tell a series of parables about grace! Luke tells us, 'Now the tax collectors and "sinners" were all gathering round to hear him. But the Pharisees and the teachers of the law muttered, "This man welcomes sinners, and eats with them"' (Luke 15:2). Those same words could in fact be said with a totally different inflection in the voice, giving rise to an opposite meaning. The Pharisees quite clearly thought Jesus' lifestyle and fraternizing with sinners a cause of complaint, but the sinners found in it a cause for celebration. It simply depended on your self-understanding and what you perceived Jesus was offering.

On another occasion, Jesus had a terrific feast at the house of Levi the tax collector, also called Matthew, the apostle and author of Matthew's Gospel. There are accounts of Levi's call in each of the synoptic Gospels. Mark records the event as follows, 'Once again Jesus went out beside the lake. A large crowd came to him, and he began to teach them. As he walked along, he saw Levi son of Alphaeus sitting at the tax collector's booth. "Follow me," Jesus told him, and Levi got up and followed him.

'While Jesus was having dinner at Levi's house, many tax collectors and "sinners" were eating with him and his disciples, for there were many who followed him. When the teachers of the law who were Pharisees saw him eating with the "sinners" and tax collectors, they asked his disciples: "Why does he eat with tax collectors and 'sinners'?"

'On hearing this, Jesus said to them, "It is not the healthy who need a doctor, but the sick. I have not come to call the righteous, but sinners"' (Mark 2:13-17; see also Matthew 9:9-13; Luke 5:27-32). Jesus' call of Levi, or Matthew, a despised tax collector, who himself clearly fell into the category of "sinner" (since he followed a proscribed job in the eyes of the Jews) incensed the Pharisees and provoked the comment from Jesus indicating that he had come to call sinners to repentance, not "the righteous". (See Luke 5:32.)

Sinners were carefully categorised by the Pharisees and the teachers of the law. They were people who either had a disreputable lifestyle, like prostitutes and swindlers, or who belonged to an inferior or "dirty" occupation, like shepherds, excise men, tax collectors, donkey drivers, pedlars and tanners.[1] They were not on any account to be associated with; in fact, a sign of a true man of God to the

Pharisee was knowledge of a person's morals so that the immoral could be avoided —such was their point at the party given by Simon the Pharisee. (See Luke 7:36-50.) If Jesus was truly a prophet or man of God he would not fraternize with such a woman who gatecrashed the dinner, unfurling her hair, anointing his feet with perfume and washing his feet with her tears. Here the situation was reversed, in that Jesus was dining with the right kind of host, according to Pharisaic convention, but there was an undesirable guest whom Jesus welcomed!

The invitation to Jesus to come to dinner this time came from Simon, a hospitable Pharisee. All was going well at the dinner party until an embarrassing incident happened. A woman burst into the room. She was carrying a jar of perfume. Her hair was let down, symbolising her profession of prostitution. She was weeping. Falling at Jesus' feet still crying, she wet his feet with her tears and then proceeded to wipe them with her hair, kiss them and then pour this expensive perfume over them. The whole thing was very un-English and also very un –Jewish, at least in the right circles! What was worse, thought Simon to himself, was that if Jesus really was a prophet or a man of God he would have known that this woman was a "sinner" and would have shown her the door. (Luke 7:39.) But once again Jesus' reception of a sinner sparked a reaction, in this case in Simon who in turn provoked Jesus to tell him a story about forgiveness. "Simon," said Jesus, "I have something to tell you…. Two men owed money to a certain money-lender. One owed him five hundred denarii, and the other fifty. Neither of them had the money to pay him back, so he cancelled the debts of both. Now which of them will love him more?" The point was the more a person knew that they were freely forgiven the more they would love God. This woman's love made her do the very things which Simon in his formal reception of Jesus could never do. She washed Jesus' feet with her tears, wiped them with her hair, kissed him as a greeting and poured oil over his feet. The whole incident was a parable of the kingdom in which grace and love meet. It was a further illustration of the Pharisees' judgement of a penitent sinner provoking Jesus to uphold the sincerity and acceptability of what, in this case, this unnamed woman had done.

However, what we also notice about this and other incidents is that Jesus' parables about the kingdom often arose out of his actions not only as a defence of what he was doing but also as a further illustration that his conduct was all of a piece with his Father's governance of the kingdom. Almost certainly if Jesus were with us here in person today he would shock us by the people he would associate with. He might not be attending swanky Christian conventions in well-appointed hotels. Perhaps he would rather be amongst the asylum seekers, in the prisons, the gay bars, with the addicts and with women who, for whatever reason, have found themselves in places of exploitation. For sure he would be with the sinners, his teaching would be in face-to-face meetings with the "immoral". We have hardly begun to truly understand, even though two thousand years have elapsed, what it means for Jesus to be the friend of sinners. And we continually want to put him back into the safer box of being friendly only with the righteous. I imagine that if he were here now we would be in for a considerable shock! Many today would want him to address the United Nations, but perhaps he would eschew that for the back streets of one of the mega-cities of the world, for the Son of Man came to seek and to save the lost.

Here follow some of the familiar stories that he told about what might be legitimately called the operating system of the kingdom.

Lost and found

It appears that God is on a perennial treasure hunt, always looking for those who are lost. And finding the lost gives him singular joy. To express this joy in finding lost people, Jesus told three stories, one about a shepherd who had lost a sheep, another about a woman who had lost a coin and the third about a father who had lost his son. They are put together by Luke in chapter fifteen of his Gospel to rebut the Pharisees' criticism of Jesus eating with "sinners". To start with, we shall look at the first two parables before coming on to the most substantial of the three about the loving father. (Luke 15:4-7; Matthew 18:12-14; Luke 15:8-10; Luke 15:11-32.) In the first two, God is compared to a shepherd and to a housewife, so what we are being shown about his nature is represented in both male and female characters. Both are looking for something which is precious but lost.

The shepherd in Jesus' story had a hundred sheep, a medium sized flock; three hundred would be unusually large, with 20-200 being a common size.[2] The shepherd normally counted the sheep before nightfall. On this occasion one is missing, so he leaves the 99 in the charge of another shepherd, with whom he would probably be sharing the overnight fold.

Apparently on one famous occasion the young goatherd Muhammad ed-Deeb, having unusually counted his flock in the morning because he had failed to the night before, went looking for his lost goat, putting the rest, 55, in the care of two companions. It was while searching for the lost goat and throwing stones at a hillside above Qumran at the Dead Sea that one of the stones hit a stone jar in a cave which led to the greatest archaeological find of the twentieth century, the Dead Sea Scrolls which had been deposited in the jars around two thousand years previously. Such is the aridity of the area that they were perfectly preserved. If a search for a missing goat led by accident to the greatest archaeological find since Carter opened the tomb of Tutankhamen in Egypt, for our purposes it is enough to note that it was still good practice for a shepherd in the 1940s to leave behind the rest of his flock to go after the lost one.

When a shepherd finds a lost sheep he brings it back to the flock; generally, when a sheep has got lost and separated from the flock, it lies down and waits: "When a sheep has strayed from the flock, it usually lies down helplessly, and will not move, stand up or run. Hence there is nothing for the shepherd to do but carry it, and over long distances this can only be done by putting it on his shoulders i.e. round his neck."[3] So the good shepherd leaves the secure sheep to find the lost one, and in finding it receives great joy. This demonstrates the action of God whose rule or government is more concerned to find the lost than just tend those who are secure. It must mean that his heart is more concerned with those outside the fold of the church than in preserving the church just as it is.

In the second story the main character is a housewife who has lost one of her twelve drachmas, a coin valued at about a day's wages. They may have been kept in an embroidered headdress, as Palestinian women were accustomed to doing. However they were kept, the loss of one coin of such value was a great anxiety. Her house is dark with little fenestration, she lights a candle to see better, she brushes the floor with a palm-twig "...because in the dark the room may make the coin tinkle on the stone floor."[4] When she finds the coin, then her joy and relief are great —it is reason for rejoicing.

In both these parables a number of truths become clear about the gracious government of God of his kingdom. He is more concerned with the lost than the secure, more exercised over the missing than the sheltered, more prepared to give energy to the search than time to the preservation of the found. And consequently he is, like the shepherd and the housewife, delighted at recovering what was lost. "In the same way", (see Luke 15:7,10) is the link phrase from the story in the parable to the emotion in the heart of God that these stories illustrate. And just as the fellow shepherds and neighbours are called together by the shepherd and housewife to rejoice with them, so God calls the angels together to rejoice over any sinner who repents.

But the third parable in this sequence recorded by Luke, though sharing some common features with the first two, takes us deeper into the heart of the Father in relation to two sons who, in different ways, have rejected his love. More than any other parable it is the supreme demonstration of the Father's grace which governs this kingdom. It is time to re-consider it now.

The parable of the Father's love

There have been several titles given to this famous parable which perhaps more than any other depicts what I call the basic operating principle of the kingdom of God. Generally, it is called the parable of the Prodigal Son, but that gives scant attention to the older son. Sometimes it is called the parable of the two sons, but that ignores the critical role of the father. The one I prefer is the parable of the father's love, for he is the central figure of the story and his love its main revelation. The watching, running, embracing father is what it is all about. In Henri Nouwen's lovely book, *The Return of the Prodigal*, which is an interpretation of the parable in the light of Rembrandt's picture of the same subject, the picture dwells on three aspects of the father's love which unlock the meaning of the parable. These aspects are the father's grieving, forgiving and generous love. With these three keys we shall unlock the treasures of this parable again and, in so doing, rediscover this love. It is a love or grace which Jesus was at pains to explain to the Pharisees who objected to him eating with sinners and for whom this parable was told.

The father's grief is in fact twofold; we often think it is singular. It is for both the younger and the older son. The younger son demands his one third share of his inheritance which was due to the younger son. This may be paid over in the lifetime of a father, but if so the father in Jewish law normally held the right to the interest.[5] At any rate, the younger son wanted to get his inheritance immediately, so this precipitated an early division of the inheritance between the two sons. For other commentators such is the vehemence of the younger son's request that it might be read as the younger son saying to his father, "I wish you were dead so that I might get my inheritance!" It was a demand for independence, distance and "freedom". We know the result of this request. The prodigal faced starvation, was without friends and was degraded, feeding unclean animals. He eventually comes to his senses. But all the while the father is grieving for his son who was lost to him and was away from home. Likewise, the father grieved over the older son for different reasons. This time it was over the resentment, jealousy and bitterness of the older brother. So much so that the father, "...went out and pleaded with him" (Luke 15:28). The father grieved over the rebellion of the younger son and the estrangement of the older son. Nouwen has written powerfully and movingly of the boundlessness of God's love revealed in the forgiveness shown here. The magnitude of human sinfulness is so very great that it moves one to grieve.[6] The rebellion of the younger son and the alienation of the older son together work the grief of the father. But he is always looking for the first flicker of return, the first inkling of a thaw. In the case of the younger son his waiting was rewarded, his grief would turn to joy.

The second aspect of the father's love is his forgiveness. The essence of grace is to treat us as we do not deserve; and the core of this treatment is forgiveness. For what is now a classic exposition and description of grace, I would especially recommend Yancey's *What's so Amazing about Grace?*[7] Such grace resulting in such forgiveness is unbelievably lavish and extravagant. To our minds, so conditioned by getting what we deserve, it also borders on the unfair and morally irresponsible. Presumably this is exactly what the older son thought of the father's reaction to the younger son's return. After all he complained of exactly this when he replied to his father, "When this son of yours" [not 'my brother'!] "who has squandered your property with prostitutes comes home, you kill the fattened calf for him!" The underlying theme is: How irresponsible can you get, treating this son of yours like this. It is scandalous, but then forgiveness can seem quite scandalous.

The younger son had planned what he would say, "I will set out and go back to my father and say to him: "Father, I have sinned against heaven and against you. I am no more worthy to be called your son; make me like one of your hired men" (Luke 15:19). When the moment came for his carefully rehearsed speech, there was only time for half of it. For his father, breathless from running – something that no self-respecting father would ever do in the Middle East – listened to his words but immediately, "...threw his arms around him and kissed him", so providing a picture of the Father's love which endures. His father embraced him, throwing his all too forgiving arms around his returning son. It was Irenaeus who said that the arms of the Son on the cross were stretched wide the better to embrace his wayward children. Forgiveness was offered freely and extravagantly. It lies at the heart of the message of the kingdom and we will return to this theme later.

The third aspect of the Father's love as shown in this parable is demonstrated by generosity, a hallmark of Christian love. Nothing could be more generous than the father's love for both his sons. To the younger he refuses to hear anything more of his confession, sure as he was of the repentance of his heart. He reclothes him with the best robe to be found, a ring signifying his restitution to his place within the household, and sandals signifying his restored dignity after the long journey away from home. And he kills the fatted calf for a feast with music and dancing! Nothing could be more generous for none of it was deserved; they were not celebrating a brilliant set of exam marks, a promotion at work, a marriage or a birth, but the return of someone who had been lost. But although he did not understand it the father was equally generous to the older son. In some ways it would seem harder to be generous to him: there was no motivating factor of a beloved child's return, the older son was angry, sullen and bitter —but it does not stop the father saying in great generosity to him, "My son... you are always with me, and everything I have is yours" (Luke 15:31). If the father's love toward the prodigal is obvious, he is no less loving to the older son whose response is so unattractive.

The Father's love is supremely demonstrated in this parable. It shows that the kingdom of God is governed by a love which grieves over human independence, that forgives at the first glimpse of repentance, and that generously lavishes undeserved favours upon us. But Jesus had not exhausted his description of God as a grace-filled Father; he also described him as a generous employer. To see this

55

we move from the context of a home to one of a labour exchange or market place.

The parables of the good employer and the two sons
It is Matthew who records Jesus' parable of the generous employer. (Matthew 20:1-16.) Once again the main focus is not so much on the labourers as the employer. It is perhaps better described as the parable of the generous employer. The parable is probably familiar. The owner of the vineyard needs labourers for the vintage and the pressing. The work appears to be urgent. Five times the owner goes to the market place, where men have gathered to be hired for work. Firstly he goes soon after sunrise, "early in the morning", and hires an early shift, agreeing to pay them a denarius, which is the normal day's wage. He then returns at the third hour, nine o'clock, and hires more. He returns again at midday, the sixth hour; and again at the ninth hour. But so urgently must the work be completed that he returns finally at five o'clock, just an hour before sunset, and hires further workers. Although there is an underlying theme to the story of the employment of workers who otherwise would be idle, standing around and gossiping with no meaning or significance to their lives that day, the fundamental point of the story, of course, lies in the payment.

It is at the end of the day that the surprise comes; and the content of that surprise is what makes the kingdom of God different, or unlike any other exercise of authority. The labourers are gathered at sunset. Those who came to work last at five o'clock were paid first; they are given a denarius, equivalent to one whole day's wages for nearly twelve hours' work! It was very generous but it was also an exciting moment for those who had worked all the day. They anticipated, wrongly as it turned out, that they would be paid more! They thought that they would be paid proportionately more but they were in fact paid the same. At first they grumbled, thinking it unfair, but they had not bargained for the mathematics of grace.

The mathematics of grace is that the least deserving appear to be paid proportionately the most; and the most apparently deserving get no more. Those who have least get most, and those who think they have most think they get least, but that is because their estimation of themselves is wrong and their estimation of what they need is wrong, too. Jesus has a neat way of summing it all up by saying at the end of the parable, "So the last will be first, and the first will be last" (Matthew 20:16). As there is no one who is fundamentally more deserving than anyone else in the kingdom of God, everyone receives the same. But throughout the Gospels, Jesus' extravagant form of mathematics catches out his disciples and the crowd repeatedly.

So, when faced with a hungry crowd of men, Jesus assures a sceptical Andrew that five (three barley loaves and two fish: "... how far will they go among so many?") into five thousand goes beautifully with lots left over. (See Luke 9:13; John 6:7-11; Mark 8:4,5; Matthew 14:15-21.) Again when faced with an embarrassed host who has run out of wine at a wedding feast, he produces from water enough wine satisfy an entire village. (See John 2:1-11.) When telling Peter how often he must forgive, he says 70 x 7. When reinstating Peter after his resurrection at Galilee, the disciples catch 153 fish after a fruitless night's fishing. (John 21:11.) All of this could be called the mathematics of grace: unbelievably generous; beyond everyone's wildest imaginings. The mathematics was therefore mostly multiplication, occasionally addition, but very little division, since what was on offer was essentially indivisible as it is salvation. It was a question of all or nothing. This was the point in the story of the good employer or the labourers of the vineyard. The wages had been agreed at the start of the day, and at the end it was the same for everyone. One denarius, the normal day's wage for each person, was given whenever they started work. The denarius represented salvation, grace, and eternal life given to each —not because they were entitled to it but because the owner chose to give it to them. The punchline is, "Take your pay and go. I want to give the man who was hired last the same as I gave you. Don't I have the right to do what I want with my own money? Or are you envious because I am generous?" (Matthew 20:14f.)

The generosity of God's grace is sometimes met with envy, feelings of unfairness and even resentment. It was so with the older brother when his brother was feted on return, "...The older brother became angry and refused to go in so his father went out and pleaded with him" (Luke 15:28). Likewise the labourers who had worked all day muttered when the late arrivals were paid the same as them. "When they received it [the denarius], they began to grumble against the landowner. 'These men who were hired last worked only one hour,' they said, 'and you have made them equal to us who have borne the burden of the work and the heat of the day.'" The reason for this grumbling or resentment is that it is hard for us to get accustomed to the economy of grace; we are so used to getting what we think we deserve, and others getting what we also think they deserve, that we cannot sometimes abide someone getting what patently they don't deserve! Again, Yancey has commented on the amazing way in which Jesus, through such parables, calls people to move into the divine kingdom where his grace rules.[8]

Likewise, Miroslav Volf writes of the primacy of grace (which we do not deserve) over what is deserved in terms of strict morality.[9] That is what the elder brother and the early-day labourers thought was unfair but in fact, given that no one had a right to any employment in the vineyard in the first place, it was the fairest or most gracious contract – or should I say covenant – of all.

The conclusion that Jesus draws from his own story is, "So the last will be first, and the first will be last" (Matthew 20:16). He means that the self-evident sinner who knows his own faults only too well comes easily to repentance and new life, while the self-righteous or self-satisfied find it hardest to reach the fountain of grace. Amongst that group are to be found the rich, the religious, the moral and the well educated. In Jesus' own day they were the Pharisee, the scribe, the Sadducee and the power brokers —they would be the last to enter his kingdom if they did at all. But the sinners, the prostitutes, the tax-gatherers and some Gentiles, like the centurions and the Syro-Phoenician woman, came running in. Just a few chapters later in Matthew's Gospel, Jesus told another story of a vineyard. This time the workforce consisted of two sons. The first was asked to go and work in the vineyard, but he refused and then changed his mind and went. The other son did the reverse. Jesus asked, "Which of the two did what his father wanted?"

"The first," they answered.

The conclusion was the same, "I tell you the truth, the tax collectors and the prostitutes are entering the kingdom of God ahead of you" (Matthew 21:28-32). Repentance, a change of heart and mind, as with the Prodigal in the far country, was the key to entering the kingdom as it is always met with the mathematics of grace. Nowhere is this more clearly put than in our final parable in this section, the parable of the Pharisee and the publican.

The Pharisee and the publican   Luke 18:9-14

It could not have been a more shocking story to his audience. As Jeremias says, "To its first hearers the parable must have seemed shocking and inconceivable."[10] Of all Jesus' parables this may have seemed the most improbable. The story is well known: two men went up to the temple at the hour of prayer, the one a very devout Pharisee, the other a tax collector. The Pharisee could not have been more diligent in observance of the law. Indeed, in certain respects, he went beyond it. While the law prescribed only one annual fast on the Day of Atonement, he fasted twice a week, on Mondays and Thursdays. Whereas the law (*Torah*) legislated that on the seed of the land, on the fruit of the trees and on flocks and herds, a tithe should be paid (Leviticus 27:30-32), this Pharisee tithed everything that he got or bought, although a tithe would have already have been paid by the producer! His diligence was startling. He would have been revered in the community for his apparent holiness and yet the clue to his deficient spirituality was given in the parable: He stood up and prayed about [or to] himself; and his disdain for the tax collector, also praying in the temple, of whom he said, "God I thank you that I am not like other men.... or even like this tax collector," was a give away as to his feelings of self-righteousness. So he perfectly demonstrated the characteristics evident in some people who, "...were confident of their own righteousness and looked down on everyone else" (Luke 18:9). By contrast, the tax collector was a despised member of the community, working for the occupying power, raking off money for himself and a virtual social outcast. He kept his eyes lowered, beat his breast and cried out, "God, have mercy on me, a sinner!" which echoes the opening words of David's great penitential psalm in which he went on to state that,

> "The sacrifices of God are a broken spirit;
> a broken and contrite heart,
> O God, you will not despise."
>
> *Psalm 51:17*

The staggering punchline of Jesus' story, which reversed all previous misconceptions about true spirituality, was that this despised tax collector went home "justified", whereas the apparently laudable Pharisee did not! The shock of this judgement must have reverberated through the crowd of listeners. This statement about justification – being accounted righteous – also precedes all Paul's great teaching about justification by faith, and shows this cardinal part of Pauline teaching firmly located in Jesus' parables about grace and mercy. This teaching was a revolutionary thought to the prevailing mindset of Judaism, that counted observance of the law as the only way to righteousness. It was not. The justified person is the one who throws himself or herself on God's unmerited grace.

Taken together, these parables, which may often have been repeated to the crowds, were a sustained onslaught on the prevailing world-view of the Jews and especially the Pharisees. Theirs was a view in which observance of the Torah was the way to remain distinct from surrounding paganism and pollution, and by which also to gain righteousness. As Tom Wright argues, the Pharisees, "...faced with the social, political and cultural pollution at the level of national life as a whole, reacted by concentrating on personal cleanness."[11] The purity laws, and by extension tithing and anything that maintained their national, social and religious distinctness, were both a form of non co-operation with the Romans and thought to be a way of becoming righteous. But Jesus stood all this on its head. Again and again his parables showed that mercy and grace were at the heart of God's dealing with people. It was a grace which was uncommonly generous, seemingly unfair, and triggered by the slightest (but genuine) display of repentance. At that point of repentance which is a change of heart and mind, this mercy would come running towards you, embrace you, and celebrate your return. It would give you the new-minted coin of salvation and declare you righteous. It was truly the operating principle of the kingdom, but at the same time this mercy and grace would demand that you become a follower and a citizen, and it is to this teaching in other parables that we must now turn. But no one can rightly understand the kingdom of God and its reign in human hearts and affairs unless the starting point is to grasp this offer of grace to all. This is where Jesus started at his home synagogue in Nazareth when, taking the scroll of Isaiah, he began to read,

"The Spirit of the Lord is on me
because he has anointed me
to preach good news to the poor.
He has sent me to proclaim freedom for the prisoners

and recovery of sight for the blind,
to release the oppressed,
to proclaim the year of the Lord's favour."

Luke 4:18f

"Favour" meant grace. It was scandalously generous; but if the entrance fee to the kingdom was nothing (for it is entirely at Christ's expense) the annual subscription was everything.

Chapter Four

A NEW WAY OF
FOLLOWING

If grace is the chief operating principle of the kingdom of God which Jesus was at pains to explain in the parables we have looked at, the response to that grace, which Jesus was looking for, was becoming a disciple or submitting to his just and gentle rule. His oft-repeated command was, quite simply, "Follow me". Many of the parables Jesus told, as well as many other pithy sayings, were about the nature of this following and this is the focus of the present chapter.

I had an appointment one morning to meet a woman who was going to talk to me about a plan of evangelisation for our city. It was a bold and exciting plan, consequently she was making the rounds of the ministers of our city to get their support and listen to their views. But when I opened the door to welcome her in for the meeting she was in tears! I may have that effect, but this was before the conversation had even begun! But she was as surprised as I was! It transpired that the cause was a conversation she had had with another minister she had met earlier that morning, in which he had shared both his burden to reach people who were "without hope in the world" and his sense of aloneness. It powerfully affected her, and in that frame of mind she arrived on our doorstep. In our subsequent conversation I said that in our culture many people took some time before they were able to believe. She said that her conversion, contrastingly, was dramatic, sudden and life-transforming, and it was as though she had had a meeting with each member of the Trinity. The truth is that some people search for ages before they find, while others stumble and hit on what hitherto they have not been looking for. Jesus spoke in two of his parables about these two ways of finding the kingdom. In one a merchant in pursuit of fine pearls finds one of inestimable value and sells everything to get it, and in the other story a farmer accidentally finds treasure in a rented field. (Matthew 13:44f.) In both cases they sold everything to secure the pearl or the treasure. It is worth looking at these two parables about discipleship a little more closely.

Throughout this period, pearls were highly sought after. "They were fished for especially in the Red Sea, the Persian Gulf, and the Indian Ocean, by divers, and used for adornment. We hear of pearls worth millions. Caesar presented the mother of his subsequent murderer Brutus with a pearl worth 6 million sesterces. Cleopatra is said to have had a pearl which would now be worth £2,500,000."[1] The merchant in Jesus' story, although looking for fine pearls, was nevertheless surprised to find one of such value. Likewise the man who found treasure in the field, presumably when he was ploughing or digging it, was equally surprised to find treasure of such value. They both sold everything to possess what they had found. Jeremias says that the key phrase in the parable was "in his joy", mentioned in the treasure story and implied in the pearl merchant story. The effect of this joy of discovery was such that it enabled both to make the necessary sacrifice (the one selling his previous pearl collection, the other buying the field) to embrace a kingdom and a new way of life. "When that great joy," says Jeremias, "surpassing all measure seizes a man, it carries him away, penetrates his inmost being, and subjugates his mind. All else seems valueless compared with that surpassing worth. No price is too great to pay. The unreserved surrender of what is most valuable becomes a matter of course. The decisive thing in both parables is not what the two men give up, but the reason for their doing so; the overwhelming experience of the splendour of their discovery. Thus it is with the kingdom of God."[2] Joy, surrender, selling everything are marks of this discipleship. It begins with an about turn, and it is far from comfortable. In his celebrated autobiography *Surprised by Joy*, C S Lewis memorably wrote of the moment when he came to faith alone in his room. He describes himself as the most reluctant convert in England. For him the joy did not come immediately. It was preceded by that reluctant surrender, as well as by a time in which he had counted the cost.

The cost of discipleship

Just as Jesus told parables about the joy of discovering the kingdom of God, he also told short, sharp parables about the cost of following him. To do this he employed pithy, memorable sayings and images which must have been both perplexing and shocking to some of his hearers.

At one point when large crowds were following him, he turned to the crowds and said something which must have sounded outrageous, on first and even second hearing: "If anyone comes to me and does not hate his father and mother, his wife and children, his brothers and sisters – yes, even his own life – he cannot be my disciple. And anyone who does not carry his cross and follow me cannot be my disciple" (Luke 14:25–27). This new kind of following was to be total. Of course Jesus did not mean his followers were to hate their parents. Otherwise it would have contradicted the commandment "Honour your father and mother", but Jesus meant "hate" in the sense of not preferring them or other members of the family to him. His will must come first, and their expectations and demands were to come second.

Jesus went on to teach his disciples that before embarking on discipleship they were to consider carefully what they were getting themselves into. They were to be like a builder estimating the cost of building a tower before starting to construct it. Otherwise they would start the building and then leave off when the process becomes too difficult or costly. Again none of us knows what life has in store and what difficulties we will face on the way, but at the outset we should realise that discipleship is for the whole of life. For, as Stott memorably expressed it, "the Christian landscape is strewn with the wreckage of derelict, half built towers —the ruins of those who began to build and were unable to finish."[3] As I write, Dame Ellen Macarthur has returned from her epic and record making single-handed circumnavigation of the globe. Only she knows the true extent of the difficulties she faced, but before she left Falmouth, seventy-one days before her successful and triumphant return, she must have spent many an hour assessing what the cost might be to her. And presumably in the calculation, however fleeting, she must have been prepared to lose her life. The same could be said of many great endeavours. Jesus is no less demanding. Before embarking on discipleship, we are to count the cost.

We recall another of his shocking images, "And anyone who does not carry his cross and follow me cannot be my disciple" (Luke 14:27). The metaphor used here could not have been a more striking image. He was asking his followers to follow him literally to possible death, and very many did and do still around the world. But in another sense every Christian must – spiritually – crucify the flesh. So Paul writes, "Those who belong to Christ Jesus have crucified the sinful nature with its passions and desires" (Galatians 5:24). This involves an ongoing putting to death of those instincts and desires which would lead us into sin. It is painful, and can be done only with the help of the Spirit. (See Romans 8:13, and my first work in this trilogy, *Becoming Fully Human*.) To be seen carrying a cross in 1st century Palestine, which under the Romans must have been an all too common sight, was to be on your way to crucifixion. So to be asked by Jesus to take up your cross and follow him was to put oneself into the position of a condemned man on his way to execution. For some Christians it will literally mean to put yourself in the way of death for his sake; for all Christians it means the rather less fashionable teaching today of mortifying – putting to death – the desires of our self life. This too is an inescapable part of discipleship.

Counting the cost, crucifying the self, preferring Jesus to the demands of family or selfish ambition or social convention, may well be too high a demand for some, as it was for the three individuals who talked about discipleship as Jesus resolutely set out for Jerusalem. (See Luke 9:57-62; Matthew 8:18-22.) However Jesus also explained, in the context of discipleship, the great paradox of following him, which is that, "...whoever wants to save his life will lose it, but whoever loses his life for me will find it. What good will it be for a man if he gains the whole world, yet forfeits his soul?" (Matthew 16:24-28). The truth of this is well and powerfully illustrated by the famous words of the American missionary Jim Eliot, who said, "He is no fool who gives what he cannot keep to gain what he cannot lose." Indeed, he gave his life in 1956 whilst on missionary work in South America, when he and his colleagues were speared by South American Indians on the banks of a river. He gave his life but also found it for eternity; but not only did he find it, but so did many other South American Indians, who had killed him. He fulfilled his discipleship as it came to its earthly conclusion and to its point of heavenly reward.

Discipleship involves joy; it involves cost, but next it involves crossing boundaries to fulfil the command of God to love both him and neighbour. Nowhere was this more memorably expressed by Jesus than in his parable of the Good Samaritan.

Crossing boundaries: the Good Samaritan   Luke 10:25-37

What is quite certain, from reading the Gospel narratives, is that Jesus consistently broke many of the social or religious boundaries in the society of his day. As Alison Morgan makes clear, he was prepared to meet anyone at their point of need; "He had a long conversation with a Samaritan woman whom he met at a well, and he had no hesitation in healing the servant of a Roman centurion. Far from avoiding tax collectors, he seemed to seek them out, calling one, Matthew, to be his disciple, initiating a conversation with another, Zacchaeus, and accepting hospitality of both —in flagrant and immediately controversial defiance of the rule which forbade table fellowship between the clean and unclean, righteous and sinners. He did it again in the house of Simon the Leper. On another occasion he allowed a sinful woman to pour perfume over his feet, and on another gently released a woman caught in adultery from the vengeful condemnation of an angry crowd."[4]   And so it went on, barrier upon barrier came crashing down, a whole iron curtain of prejudice and bigotry came tumbling down, to the consternation of those who had set themselves up as the guardians of religious convention. The gospel Jesus had brought was indeed wild beyond their wildest imaginings. Jesus taught that if you follow his ways you will receive eternal life; it was teaching that provoked questions.

One day, a religious leader stood up to question him, asking, "Teacher... what must I do to inherit eternal life?" He was a serious man, and he showed that he had been listening to Jesus, for where else would he have found the phrase "eternal life"? He wanted to obtain it. So Jesus answered a question with a double question: "What is written in the law? How do you read it?" The lawyer, who was well taught in the Torah, answered perfectly, "'Love the Lord your God with all your heart and with all your soul and with all your strength and with all your mind'; and, 'love your neighbour as yourself.'" But this man wanted to prove himself, so asked a question he might possibly have lived to regret, so shocking was Jesus' reply. He said, "And who is my neighbour?"

67

It was a risky question to ask Jesus then, as it is now. Indeed, who is our neighbour? The UK government pamphlet entitled *Rough Guide to a Better World* reminds us that our neighbour (in the sense Jesus used it) could now be anywhere in the world. The booklet has a preface by Bob Geldof, who draws our attention to many of the desperate things we are now so familiar with: the deaths of so many people in the world from preventable causes; those trading relationships which are so often unfair, and detrimental to the well-being of the world's poor; the excessive exploitation of natural resources. What is brought to the fore in all this is that it is all about people, not just abstract ideas. Our "neighbour" may be too weak to be heard, but he or she is there— in so many places, throughout the world, and we need to heed our neighbour.[5] As Jesus taught, anyone who is in trouble and who we come across is our neighbour. Does this now mean that those of whom we learn from television in our living rooms are now are neighbours? Surely they are.

At the time when this lawyer's question was asked of Jesus there was no common definition of neighbour or friend. The Jews generally said it was only necessary to love other Jews and proselytes; some Pharisees thought it was required to befriend other Pharisees. Indeed the pharisaic community was itself split between Hillel and Shammai. The Essenes, who were hard-core ascetics living in the desert of Judea, required that one hate "sons of darkness". There was a rabbinical saying doing the rounds at the time which ruled that heretics, informers and renegades should be pushed into the ditch and not pulled out. So the issue at the root of the questioner's question was how far should his or our love extend —if love itself is defined as extending oneself in compassionate action for another. What are the limits of this kind of loving? Jesus told a story to show what fulfilling the command in the Torah actually meant.

A man went on a journey from Jerusalem to Jericho. As he went along he was attacked by muggers who stripped him, beat him up, robbed him and left him by the side of the road to die. He was naked, wounded and robbed. Two religious men who held office in the institutions of Judaism passed by on the other side, either because they were on their way to Jerusalem to worship and did not wish to become ritually unclean or because they were either fearful or lazy and did not want to become involved. The hearers of Jesus' story fully expected that the third person to come along would have been another religious of some sort. Jeremias points out that according to the triadic form of popular stories, the audience would now have expected a third religious character (who might have been a Jewish "layman") after the priest and Levite. Thus the story would have had an anti-clerical slant. But it would have been shocking and totally surprising to hear that the third person to appear in the story was a Samaritan. For Jews had no dealings with Samaritans. There was an ongoing feud between Jews and Samaritans. Some time between AD 6 and AD 9, during a Passover and at midnight, some Samaritans had defiled the temple court by spreading dead men's bones there, greatly increasing the animosity between them. A Samaritan was *persona non grata*, but here he is the hero of the story, exhibiting the true love which should be at the heart of true discipleship. The Samaritan, with all his supposedly defective view of God, was the one who did what was right whilst the other two who had all the outward religious orthodoxy did not fulfil the command of Torah which they purported to follow. What an important lesson this was about true and loving discipleship!

The Samaritan's love involved him in doing three things (among others). Firstly he crossed the road. It was a simple action in the story yet it spelt out the difference between him and the priest and Levite. The essential point this simple action illustrated was that the neighbourly love of this Samaritan compelled him to cross boundaries. There is no doubt that there are huge barriers or boundaries to be crossed in most communities. But whereas the priest and Levite were unwilling to cross either the boundary of their own fear of involvement or the ritual boundary of uncleanness (because the man lying in the road might be dead), the Samaritan was prepared to cross the Jew/Samaritan divide to help a person in obvious need.

He crossed the road. There are many roads to be crossed if communities are to be healed, and it requires either unusual courage or compassion to do so. Occasionally such people arise who are inspirational boundary-crossers. Nelson Mandela is such a man, willing to cross the boundary of AIDS by speaking publicly about the death of his remaining son from the disease, so focussing the attention of his people upon the needs of the AIDS sufferers in his country. On a personal note, I think of my wife's godson, Tom Hurndall, who was crossing the street in Rafa to help a young Palestinian child in danger of being killed by gunfire from the IDF, and was shot in the head, a wound from which he would not recover. Many people have "crossed over" to help another or others in great need, whom they perceived to be "neighbour" to them. In so doing they are following the example of neighbourly love; that was the first thing that the Samaritan did, and without that motivation or intent the rest could not have happened.

Secondly, what Jesus offered was costly. The Samaritan gave up a good deal. It is thought that he may have been a merchant travelling from Jerusalem to Jericho, leading a second donkey carrying wares of oil and wine which he used for the victim. The Samaritan was prepared to go out of his way, give some of his wine and oil to disinfect and bathe the victim's wounds, and then take him on his own donkey to a nearby inn where he gave the innkeeper two denarii which is the equivalent of two days' wages —and twelve times more than a night's board and lodging cost. So he was generous, too! The Samaritan's neighbourly love was costly in time, money and effort, and possibly in reputation since his people had no dealings with Jews.

Thirdly, his love was unconditional. At the end of the parable, Jesus returns to his earlier method of teaching, asking the expert in the law a question. The lawyer's whole approach to the question of neighbourly love was: What is the limit to my responsibility of loving? —or, to put it another way: Where does the responsibility to love end? It was a lawyer's question and approach, seeking to define a theoretical boundary to love beyond which he need not go; seeking to put in place some conditions which would excuse the obligation of loving. But Jesus makes him look at it from the other end: Who was neighbour to the one who fell amongst thieves? Or who needed help? And then, who met that need for help? Answer: the Samaritan, as he acted in a neighbourly way. So to act in a neighbourly way is to give help wherever it is needed, without conditions. The Samaritan's love was an unconditional love, and to such love the disciple of Jesus is called. To follow Jesus is to follow in this way. Another way of describing this kind of discipleship is to point out that it blends together both obedience and humility. So with the help of two other parables we shall look at these qualities of discipleship.

Parables about table manners   Luke 14:7-11

In the teaching of Jesus, the path of discipleship, which is the proper response to the government of grace in the kingdom, is marked by many qualities. But high on the list of the things Jesus looked for in his disciples was humility. This is made clear in the parable Jesus told about table manners —or seating at a feast. Luke tells us that one day, while having dinner at the house of a prominent Pharisee (see Luke 14:1, 7ff), Jesus noticed how the guests took their seats. Some took the best seats – the places of honour – first. The parable which followed from this observation pointed both to the guests' overestimation of their own importance and to the risk they ran of being humiliated by being asked by the host to move to a lower place. It was the tradition for the most important guests at a feast to arrive last and so take the honoured seats, asking anyone sitting in their place to move to the inferior places at the table, because by then all the intermediate ones were occupied. The conventional wisdom as expressed in Proverbs was,

> Do not exalt yourself in the king's presence,
> and do not claim a place among great men;
> it is better for him to say to you, "Come up here,"
> than for him to humiliate you before a nobleman.
>
> *Proverbs 25:6f*

Jesus taught us to take the lowest place, so that when your host comes he will to say to you, 'Friend move up to a better place' (Luke 14:10). The conclusion that Jesus draws is that, "...everyone who exalts himself will be humbled, and he who humbles himself will be exalted" (v. 11). In other words, the disciple was to be like his master. As he was "gentle and humble in heart" (Matthew 11:29b), so should they be; as he was willing to serve, so should they be. (See Mark 10:45.) If he was prepared to give up the majesty of heaven, they should be prepared to be servants. As we shall see later in this book, the way up is the way down; and this parable about table manners was a manifestation of this general teaching. Humility is integral to both discipleship and leadership.

The other quality associated with discipleship is obedience. This is made clear in the parable of the servant's reward (Luke 17:7-10). In it the disciples are asked to imagine the unimaginable, namely that a boss says to his servant who has come in from a hard day's work in the field, "Come along now and sit down to eat." Jesus then asks them, "Would he not rather say, 'Prepare my supper, get yourself ready and wait on me while I eat and drink; after that you may eat and drink'?" Likewise, the disciple must be obedient to his master, doing his bidding. Obedience is another vital characteristic of true discipleship.

These two parables, with their encouragement to humility and obedience, further characterise the path of discipleship which is the ongoing response of the true disciple to the government of grace in God's kingdom. Since God's rule is one of grace, our response should be one of true discipleship. The path of discipleship involves a wholehearted response, for Jesus makes it clear that disciples are to live in complete surrender. This was further typified in the saying that, "No-one who puts his hand to the plough and looks back is fit for service in the kingdom of God" (Luke 9:62). It has been pointed out that, "The very light Palestinian plough is guided with one hand. This one hand, generally the left, must at the same time keep the plough upright, regulate its depth by pressure, and lift it over the rocks and stones in its path. The ploughman uses the other hand to drive the unruly oxen with a goad about two yards long, fitted with an iron spike. At the same time he must continually look between the hindquarters of the oxen, keeping the furrow in sight. This primitive kind of plough needs dexterity and concentrated attention. If the ploughman looks round the furrow becomes crooked. So whoever wishes to follow Jesus must be resolved to break every link with the past, and fix his eye only on the coming kingdom."[6] As we learn from another parable, which concludes the Sermon on the Mount, active obedience to the words of Jesus is the rock on which to build the house of discipleship. (See Matthew 7:24-27.)

This is demanding discipleship and it is not possible without ample provision, so we must now take a look at some parables about that provision.

Provision of grace and justice
Perhaps two parables suffice to show the provision God has made for this costly discipleship: the story of the friend at midnight, and that of the unjust judge. Both are about response to prayer and both are about provision —either of spiritual strength through the Holy Spirit or of justice through the courts.

The parable of the friend at midnight is sandwiched amongst Jesus' most protracted teaching on prayer in Luke's Gospel. (Luke

11:1-12.) It all began with the disciples asking Jesus to teach them to pray as John had taught his disciples. The result was the Lord's Prayer, which is the kingdom prayer, and which we shall look at in the final section of this book. But Jesus must have sensed that they needed more encouragement to pray, for he then gives to them a whole raft of encouragements both to pray and to trust their heavenly Father. He does this with a series of vivid stories, amongst which is the parable of the friend at midnight. There are few more vivid and amusing parables than this one in the Gospels. Anyone privileged to have seen the theatre company Riding Lights perform their version of it will never read this parable without recalling the humour inherent in this little story.

We can imagine the scene: a family has retired to bed in a first century Palestinian village. The house would have been in darkness except perhaps for the weak glow coming from a small oil lamp. The door had been locked and bolted with a wooden or iron bar fixed to it. To unbolt the door would be a nuisance and rather noisy. We are to think of a simple one room house, in which the whole family, parents and children, would have been asleep on a mat in the raised area. The whole family would have been awakened if the father had to get up and unbolt the door. So, in the parable, "can't", as is often the case, means "I won't". ("I can't get up and give you anything" —see verse 7.) Notwithstanding the inconvenience involved, there is a greater imperative at work which will make the householder get up and give his neighbour what he needs. Here we see the binding rule of hospitality at work.

Jesus is in fact playing up to this cultural imperative of hospitality in the way he tells the story and the way in which he introduces it to his listeners. The manner of its introduction is something like this: Can you imagine a situation in which a neighbour goes to another neighbour at midnight, having just had a friend arrive and for whom he has no bread in the house, and the neighbour tells him not to bother him, because they were all in bed, so they could not get up and give him anything? Can you imagine such a situation? Of course not, it is impossible! Of course the neighbour will get up and will provide the bread. It is unthinkable that he would stay in bed when his neighbour had such a need. He will get up not only because of the neighbour's boldness and persistence but also to help his neighbour fulfil the laws of hospitality; failure to do so would be shaming for him and the rest of his household who preferred to sleep in bed. So, just as the disciples see that the neighbour will arise from bed and give what is needed, how much more will God give what is needed by his petitioning children. He will provide for his disciples what they need for their discipleship. So ask, seek, knock; for you will be given, you will find and the door will be opened to you. Jesus is teaching that God is much more willing than the reluctant neighbour in bed, and even more aware of your true needs than the affectionate parent on earth. He provides this inner grace of the Spirit to enable your following. But also he provides final justice, as our other parable of provision suggests— the parable of the unjust judge, found in Luke 18:1-8.

Once again, the context is prayer. The widow who is petitioning the judge might be quite young, as a marriageable age in those days of a much shorter life span could be as low as thirteen or fourteen. She was poor so she could not give the judge the customary bribe. The case may have been about an unpaid debt which she was seeking to reclaim. But the judge was lazy, and insensitive both to her claim and the religious laws under which he operated. Nevertheless she kept bothering him, and her incessant petitioning eventually wore him down so that he said, "I will see that she gets justice, so that she won't eventually wear me out with her coming!" (Luke 18:5.) The parable is essentially what we call an *a fortiori* construction, meaning that if this unjust judge was worn down with the petitioning of this woman and eventually gave her what she desired and was owing to her, how much more would God answer the prayers of his people for justice. So Jesus says, "And will not God bring about justice for his chosen ones, who cry out to him day and night? Will he keep putting them off? I tell you, he will see that they get justice, and quickly...." Inherent in the parable is therefore a promise of provision of justice.

The provision of justice for God's people, or indeed for anyone, is problematic. We know that many live their lives with little experience of justice and some are unjustly treated for very long periods of time. What does the speedy handing down of justice mean? In some societies where Christianity is a minority religion, justice may take years or indeed never come in this life. However, recent history shows that although injustice or persecution may last for years it tends not to last for generations (except in some intractable situations as in the Middle East), if that is any comfort! But even if justice is not always speedy in this world's courts, the hope of final vindication is strong enough to maintain hope in testing and unjust circumstances. I read of a case recently about a man who died in 2005. He was a Czech called Rudolf Pernicky, who opposed the Nazis during their occupation of Czechoslovakia. He worked during the 1940s, with a number of exiles, to weaken the Nazi regime. Together with fellow resistance fighters, he was able to assassinate the leading Nazi Reinhard Heydrich, head of the Nazis in Czech lands. But after the war and the onset of communism in 1948 he was arrested and sent with others to a labour camp in the uranium mines of Czechoslovakia. While he and others worked there they never gave up hope that communism would pass and they would be freed. Released from that servitude in 1963, he was only allowed to take a job as a labourer. Only after 1989 was he eventually liberated and vindicated. It was only two months before his death, at the age of ninety, that he was awarded the highest Czech decoration, the Order of the White Lion. For him vindication was a long time coming, but it eventually came.

God rules his kingdom with grace. To live in the kingdom, to welcome that reign of God in our lives, is to become a disciple. Subjects in the kingdom are disciples, essentially learners and followers. This discipleship may begin either through a long search or a surprise discovery. Supremely, the disciple is called to love in an unprejudiced way without any of the religious, racial or social barriers which human beings are so adept at creating. It is a lifetime's work to dismantle these barriers, and in most of our lives they are never fully taken down. However, in following this path of obedience and humility, we are assured of provision for the journey: the continuing strengthening of the Holy Spirit, and the hope of justice both for ourselves and for others who cry out day and night.

Above all, this discipleship is a daily business —daily we pick up the sustenance we need, daily we pick up the cross and daily we are filled with the strength of the Spirit. To contemplate discipleship in any other way than a daily walk can result in our becoming either overladen with cares or provisions, so that we are too encumbered to follow, or too overwhelmed by the magnitude and demands of the journey. Later we will look at other teaching Jesus gives for the disciple to follow about what we should invest in. How should we regard the future? What should we set our sights on? Whom are we really serving? As we will see, this is all further instruction about being a disciple in the kingdom of God. Suffice to say now that, in response to God's government of grace, each of us must learn to live as a disciple in the assured knowledge that we are part of a growing kingdom, and that it will one day be fully manifest —if only at a time of global crisis.

Chapter Five

THE ASSURANCE OF GROWTH

At any moment in time a school, church, business, nation, government or organisation is either in a state of growth or one of decline. Likewise, an individual may either be growing physically, morally and spiritually or he or she may be in a state of decline: physically weakening, their gifts atrophying and their prospects becoming more circumscribed. At any moment a person or a community is either waxing or waning. This seems to be a common feature of life in this world. The point which emerges through the further cluster of parables we shall look at in this chapter is that, whatever the outward appearances, the kingdom of God is on an assured path of growth, and in this we may have boundless confidence.

Jesus taught this repeatedly. If the kingdom is governed by grace and its citizens are known as disciples, the assurance they are given is that they will be part of a kingdom which will inexorably grow through the ages. This was the vision that Daniel was given during his exile in Babylon; "In my vision at night I looked, and there before me was one like a son of man, coming with the clouds of heaven. He approached the Ancient of Days and was led into his presence. He was given authority, glory and sovereign power; all peoples, nations, and men of every language worshipped him. His dominion is an everlasting dominion that will not pass away, and his kingdom is one that will never be destroyed" (Daniel 7:13). Such a mighty vision is brought to fruition through what looks like a fragile and vulnerable process, and Jesus made this clear both in his own life as in his teaching. This paradox takes us to the heart of the "way" or "being" of the kingdom, and to the kernel of many of the parables about growth in the kingdom.

In many human societies expansion comes through force of arms, like the sweeping victories of the Assyrians or the Babylonians or, later, the Greeks and Romans. In more recent years expansion has been brought about by technological ability, natural resources, and economic muscle which have given, for instance, the US pre-eminence as the world's only superpower. In other words, power and dominion is brought about through the exertion, often through brilliant leadership, of economic, military or technological strength; historically this seems to have been the case. But in his ministry Jesus speaks about a kingdom which will expand out of the very opposite things. It will come out of weakness, vulnerability, defencelessness, and the absence of aggression; although it will have power it will look completely different from the power structures with which politicians or rulers were or are familiar. The kingdom of which Jesus spoke will come from insignificant beginnings; it will have deceptive appearances. It will succeed through many apparent failures. It will be both quietly pervasive and subversive. It will grow to gigantic proportions, and there will be, for a time, both the genuine and the counterfeit. At some point in the future there will be revelation of its true reality which for the most part, presently, lies hidden and unseen. All these things will occur in the course of the growth of the kingdom.

Insignificant beginnings, overwhelming endings

The dynamic growth of the kingdom is nowhere more vividly put than in the parable of the mustard seed. (Mark 4:30-32; Matthew 13:31f; Luke 13:18.) Of the three synoptic accounts of this parable Mark's is the fullest, with its slightly longer introduction of, "What shall we say the kingdom of God is like, or what parable shall we use to describe it?" The parable contains a vivid contrast, which is that in the kingdom small or even tiny beginnings give way to great results. It has been rightly pointed out the meaning of the parable is that, "...out of the most insignificant beginnings, invisible to human eye, God creates his mighty kingdom, which embraces all peoples of the world."[1] The birds in the parable were a traditional Jewish representation of the Gentiles.

78

It is generally true of both human and natural life that "great oaks from little acorns grow". There are countless examples of this, for instance the growth of the computer industry from Babbage's binary number theory or the growth of one of the largest software companies in the world from initial thinking about a comprehensive operating system. An analogy may be drawn between such processes of invention and production with what Jesus talks of here about the kingdom; from unseen beginnings great works of God may grow. And the agent that stimulates and energises this in his kingdom is the word of God, repeatedly described as a seed in these parables. The word of God is like the tiny mustard seed —almost invisible, vulnerable and seemingly insignificant, but within it lies the power and force to produce, in terms of this parable, the largest domestic shrub in the kitchen garden. The parable of the mustard seed has therefore become synonymous with dynamic growth in the kingdom of God. And the kingdom of God is all about the greatest from the least.

Looking over the history of the growth of the church, which is a visible if very uneven expression of the kingdom in the world, we can see the truth of this parable. Allowing for the fact that in the "branches" of the visible church there is room for all kinds of people to "nest" – a point we shall look at further in the parable of the wheat and the tares – there is nonetheless remarkable growth. In his important book *The Next Christendom*, Philip Jenkins charts the movement of global Christianity from the North to the South, with the exception of North America. He shows that in many of the poorest societies in the world Christianity is becoming strong and encultured with the result that from seemingly insignificant beginnings large churches are forming. One such example is the Dalits, whom we might commonly know as the "untouchables". It is estimated that there are anything between 150-250 million of them in India. "Although legal discrimination against these people has been outlawed since 1950, Dalits still suffer from appalling persecution and violence, and there are regular stories of murder, lynching, torture and rape."[2] Around 2.3% of the Indian population is reportedly Christian, with a significant number of them being Dalits. This means that there are 23 million Christians in India; that is ten times more practising Christians than in the UK. Dalits represent 90% of the Protestant church in North India. At the same time, fears amongst the Hindu population that Christianity might make greater inroads into this caste led to an upsurge in violence against Western Christians, and in 1999 Graham Staines and his two young sons were burned to death in Orissa.

Growth often comes from the most unlikely situations. The beginning of Protestant evangelisation of South America in the eighteenth century could not, on the face of it, have had a more inauspicious start. Allen Gardiner and his companions who went to share the gospel with the people of Patagonia found themselves starving in a boat on the tip of Tierra del Fuego. Having converted no one, and all having died, it seemed that mission had been a failure. But Gardiner's diaries were found, and the effect of his published diaries had such an impact on Victorian England that a stream of missionaries went to South America, and the South American Missionary Society began its fruitful and enduring work.[3]

Time and again, the parable of the mustard seed is re-enacted. The seed of God's word is invisibly received into a heart of faith and from that germination a work of God is born which in time becomes visible, and in some cases can become a work of very significant proportions. But as the companion parable in Mark's Gospel – the parable of the sower – shows, such success is by no means certain. There may be much wastage and mishaps along the way but, as we shall see, despite the many frustrations a harvest is assured.

The parable of the assured harvest

There are few parables with which we are more familiar than the parable of the sower, which maybe would be more aptly named the parable of the soils. But perhaps it should in fact be called the parable of the assured harvest. It is included in all three synoptic Gospels (Matthew13:3-23; Mark 4:1-20; Luke 8:5-15), and it has been used as the standard text on the ministry of the word and the difficulties that the word encounters in the hearts of people in the struggle to be fruitful. There are three levels to the interpretation of this parable and its accompanying teaching. Firstly, in the context of telling it, Jesus gives an explanation to his disciples, repeated in each of the Gospel accounts, as to why he used the method of parable telling at all. Secondly, there is the aspect of the parable which demonstrates the unrewarding nature of sowing the word, as so much of its life force is overwhelmed by the various types of inhospitable soil. And the third aspect is that, despite everything, there is an assured harvest. We shall look at each of these facets in turn. I well remember our university lecturer, Professor Kingsley Barrett, at Durham University when lecturing on Mark's Gospel, trying to explain to his students the meaning of the words Jesus spoke to his disciples:

"The secret of the kingdom of God has been given to you. But to those on the outside everything is said in parables so that,

> "'they may be ever seeing but never perceiving,
> and ever hearing but never·understanding;
> otherwise they might turn and be forgiven'"

Mark 4:11f

At first glance it seems that Jesus deliberately spoke in parables so that the secrets of the kingdom of God would be obscured from the crowd and therefore they would not be able to be forgiven. The difficulty of Jesus' teaching here is that he appears to have the intention (reflected in the causal "so that") of teaching in parables so that they could not understand the nature of the kingdom and so turn and be forgiven. However, if this were the case, the resulting apparently self-contradictory implication would be that Jesus was actively preventing the crowds receiving the very thing that he had come to bring, namely forgiveness of sins, by teaching in parables! But surely Jesus is not teaching that it was his intention that they should fail to grasp the message of the kingdom —but rather that the spiritual blindness in which they shared, and which Isaiah predicted would be theirs as a matter of fact, prevented them from receiving forgiveness, or the secret of the kingdom. Therefore the telling of a parable only confirmed what was already true, namely they were unable to understand. So the parable, once it was told, had the effect of exposing their spiritual blindness.

To use an analogy, we may go to a hospital thinking that we are quite healthy, although complaining of an irritating pain, but when we are given tests we discover the gravity of what is there. In the event the parable, like the test, shows the patient more clearly what is in fact the case —that he is gravely ill. It is very important to be aware that being unable to understand the significance of the parable reveals spiritual blindness. We reiterate that it is not Jesus' intention to prevent the hearer from receiving forgiveness; rather, the parables, which have a power of their own, confirm or reveal the already existing condition of spiritual blindness, so something further will be needed to take people from darkness to light.

On the other hand the disciples had the meaning of the parable explained to them, and although they may have understood that meaning at a superficial level, it would not be until after the resurrection and Pentecost that they truly saw the full meaning of Jesus' teaching. They too were partially blind, even with the explanation. And the beauty of the parables as a teaching vehicle is that they could be progressively understood.

The second level of meaning of this parable – and this is its commonly held interpretation – is that it is all about the reception the word gets in the various types of soil. We are familiar with these soils. The first soil, if it can be called that, is a hard pathway on which the seed alights but never takes root, so it is easy prey for the birds representing the evil one who snatches it away. Matthew tells us that Jesus said this was like the message of the kingdom not being understood, so never penetrating the heart and being able to grow. (See Matthew 13:19.) The second soil is the rocky one, where the seed can get no proper root because the soil is thin and shallow. This soil, although initially receptive, provides no opportunity for root structure so that when "trouble or persecution comes along" it quickly shrivels up and dies. The third soil is one full of weeds which choke the plant. They hear the word, "...but the worries of this life, the deceitfulness of wealth and the desires for other things come in and choke the word, making it unfruitful" (Mark 4:19b). In the space of a few phrases, Jesus sums up in memorable language the things which choke the growth of the word. They are consistently the anxieties or worries of life, the deceitfulness of riches and the desire for things. In a consumer society, which is predicated on acquisition, these weeds have become much stronger now even than in the days of Jesus. But the final soil, the good soil, produces a harvest. There is no doubt that this is a brilliant description of the struggles the word has in human hearts to become fruitful; nevertheless, it is still not the primary point of the parable.

The overriding point of the parable is that the harvest is assured. Despite all the problems, the difficulties, and the things which oppose the kingdom encountered along the way, God's promises will be fulfilled. If doubt in the outcome of the kingdom existed in the minds of his followers – especially when Jesus during his ministry increasingly made it clear that he would not take Jerusalem by force and lead an insurrection against the Romans – a parable with an ending like this one made it abundantly clear that this kingdom would increase and grow. Once again, Jeremias puts it so well: "From a dreary fallow land grows a field of waving corn, with a yield that surpasses all prayer and understanding. As so often the dawn of the kingdom of God is compared to the harvest. The abnormal harvest tripling, presented in true oriental fashion, of the harvest's yield (thirty, sixty, a hundredfold) symbolizes the eschatological overflowing of the divine fullness, surpassing all human measure. To human eyes much of the labour seems futile and fruitless, resulting apparently in repeated failure, but Jesus is full of joyful confidence: he knows that God has made a beginning, bringing with it a harvest of reward beyond all asking or conceiving. In spite of every failure and opposition, from hopeless beginnings, God brings forth the triumphant end which he had promised."[4] The church in western Europe needs a large measure of this joyful confidence which may be gained by reflecting on these parables of growth, but also through sharing in the abundant harvest already existing in Africa, south east Asia and South America. In other words, we need to keep our global perspective which more than bears out the teaching of this parable; and which instils confidence in the word which, in the way of the kingdom, will always finally be fruitful.

The parables looked at so far in this chapter are all out about growth, whether it is growth from insignificant beginnings as in the parable of the mustard seed, or whether it is to point out the pervasive effect of the kingdom, as in the parable of the leaven, in which the yeast spreads throughout the dough. (Matthew 13:33; Luke 13:20.) The final triumph of the kingdom, despite all the struggles and vulnerability of the word in the different types of soils or lives, is assured. But there is a problem which we must turn to next: the growth is very mixed or uneven. There are wheat and tares in the same field. There are fish of all kinds in the net, so there will be an eventual sort out. Expansion does not come without difficulty or tension. Although the kingdom is not the same thing as the church, the teaching of Jesus suggests that there will still be those ostensibly under God's rule who will be cast out of the kingdom.

Sorting out the harvest

If I have said it once I have said it a hundred times: there is no such thing as the perfect church. My own local church is certainly not perfect, although it is very encouraging. Nor will your church or mine ever be, this side of the parousia! And while we are on the subject, nor is this minister (or your minister) perfect! This is not an excuse for laziness, nor is it an excuse for not using any form of discipline to hold back sin or corruption in the church. Anyone who knows just a little of the church's history will know that it is full of failure. That point is inescapable. However, theoretical knowledge of this truth (that perfection of church life does not exist on earth) does not prevent Christians in each succeeding generation riding off into the sunset to try just one more time to set up the perfect church! The hope is commendable, but the reality is normally disappointing. Nonetheless, the yearning still burns ever brighter in the breasts of Christians, that their church will be the one to defy historical experience. Such a hope, while laudable, is unrealistic and does not take account of the teaching of Jesus in two parables: the parable of the wheat and the tares and the parable of the seine net. (Matthew 13:24-30; Matthew 13:47-52.)

These two parables in Matthew's Gospel demonstrate that in the initial stages of growth in the kingdom good and bad, genuine and false, will be found. The essence of the teaching of these two parables is that the detection of the false, with the consequent uprooting or throwing away, is so disruptive to both the good and the genuine that it can only be done by God himself at his judgement. Is it therefore a policy for *laissez faire* or studied inaction? It seems so. But this truly presents us with a dilemma. On the one hand there are many occasions in the New Testament where action is enjoined on leaders of the community to deal with obvious cases of immorality, or false teaching or error (see 1 Corinthians 5:6; Galatians 1:9; 2 Peter 2:4-22; Jude 1:4), whilst in these parables there is an acknowledgement that error and immorality will be in the church until the day of judgement. The outcome of this teaching is therefore a combined approach. There will sometimes be an absolute necessity to deal with issues of immorality, error and false teaching now as best we may; but there also needs to be an acknowledgement that it will not be possible to build a pure or perfect church here on earth. It will always have its imperfections. So to try and uproot these things by judicial process may prove counterproductive.

The history of the church is littered with attempts to purify it here and now. Straight after the period of the Reformation, the Counter-Reformation used the Inquisition, admittedly the instrument of the Roman Catholic Church, for the imposition of her teaching. Many would argue it was an attempt to tear up the wheat rather than the tares! Equally in Calvin's Geneva, the courts were used to try Severus for heresy and condemn him to be burnt. The religious wars in the sixteenth century used punishment and war to enforce their differing interpretations of the faith. The use of judicial violence in the resolution of religious dispute between churches was commonplace up until the nineteenth century, and only then did the principles of religious toleration take root. Both sides used power and force to impose their beliefs. Were the parables of the wheat and tares and seine net given by Jesus to avoid just this eventuality, so that the record of such violent enforcement of "purity" might not besmirch the witness of the church thereafter?

From the overall teaching of the New Testament it appears that we need to combine both vigilance over the teaching and conduct of the church and especially its leaders with a degree of acknowledgement that the church will not be pure in its faith and conduct until the Lord sorts out the weeds from the wheat and the good from the bad fish at the judgement. In recent years the sexual abuse scandals in the Roman Catholic Church, especially in Ireland and the United States, and the controversy over the appointment of practising gay clergy to positions of leadership in the Episcopal church in the United States and the Anglican church in Canada, are cases where discipline has been needed. Not all sorting out can be blithely left to the final judgement. Either civil law or church discipline demands action now.

It is very easy for one part of the church to be judgemental of another, but we must know that in every part of the church or kingdom wheat and tares grow together, good and bad fish are in the same net (or under the same roof). The religious right in the US have their fair share of "televangelists" who have gone off the path. Parts of the church which are known for their biblically orthodox teaching may nonetheless find that some of their leaders have feet of clay. Let the denomination, church or Christian community which is without sin throw the first stone! The fact of our own church's culpability is not a reason for doing nothing and so not taking appropriate action to discipline where needed, but it is a powerful argument for recognising our own weaknesses rather than trumpeting our own strength, success or imperviousness to the presence of sin in our church life. There are few more sickening things than the smug identification of the speck or grit in a fellow Christian's eye while ignoring the plank that is in one's own.

The parables of the wheat and the tares and the seine net are, in fact, joyful reminders that God himself will sort out his kingdom or church. Ultimately, in God's time, the good will be separated from the bad. God's people will one day be pure. Until then, we must be vigilant but patient, assured that God will bring about the fulfilment of his kingdom.

Nearly all of these parables are a call to confident patience, and to this we must now turn.

Patience

If the growth of the kingdom is assured, and in the end there will be a great sort out or separation of good from evil, genuine from false (more of which we shall see in the next chapter), then the qualities these struggles demand are patience and confidence: patience, because the timescale is long and the growth is not always apparent or perceptible; confidence, because the outcome is assured. This confidence and patience is evident in two final parables that Jesus told, which we shall look at now. They are the parables of the patient farmer (husbandman) and the barren fig tree or patient gardener. (Mark 4:26-29 and Luke 13:6-9.)

The first parable is about the growth of seed, almost irrespective of what the farmer does. "Night and day, whether he sleeps or gets up, the seed sprouts and grows, though he does not know how." To the first century farmer who knew nothing of the science of DNA or the process of germination it was both a miracle and a mystery that tiny seeds planted in the ground should of themselves ("all by itself") grow and bear fruit. However, the farmer saw, year on year, that, despite stony ground, weeds, pests and the hot sun, the seed did produce a harvest. So he became confident of the result and patient while the process of growth occurred. This was the same in the kingdom. The seed, the word sown in the hearts of men, would in the end produce a harvest, and of this those in the kingdom could be assured. This was not an argument for complacency or laziness in Jesus' book, but it was one for patience and confidence. Although in the global South there is evidence of great harvest, presently, in the North this is generally not so. Just because the evidence of harvest is not so clear in the global North is not a reason for despair —though it may and should instil a deep longing in the hearts of all God's people for the growth which is seen elsewhere.

The other parable is specifically about the patience of God. A fig tree bears no fruit. The landlord looks for three years and finds no fruit. He grows impatient at the tree taking up room in his vineyard and asks for it to be cut down. The gardener who actually looks after the place advises patience and perseverance. The landlord agrees to it being allowed one more year. The gardener, determined that it should have the best chance of bearing fruit, digs around it, fertilises it and says, "If it bears fruit next year, fine! If not, then cut it down" (Luke 13:9). Some trees take time to fruit. I bought a fig tree at our church plant sale, and after two years there is little sign of fruit. I once planted a mulberry tree which after twenty years has not yet fruited, and it will be years before it will fruit! But that is mulberries for you; you need to be patient. Tantalisingly, we are not told the outcome, and maybe that does not matter since the point of the parable is that the patience of the gardener gives it another chance to fruit. Likewise we are to expect fruit but also to be patient until it comes. Many works of God require that combination of expectation and patience. Patience must not be a mask for complacency, and expectation should not degenerate into anxiety. As Christians we should regularly inhabit the "last chance saloon", knowing full well God's immense patience with us.

In conclusion, this cohort of parables reminds us of the unstoppable growth of the kingdom, and assures us that despite all the wastage, setbacks and disappointments the growth will continue. Wherever the seed is sown there will be growth and in the end a harvest. In the meantime there is call for confidence and patience.

So far we have seen in the first cluster of parables about the kingdom that it is governed by grace. Where that grace is received, and God's just and gentle rule accepted, each citizen becomes a disciple, always learning about what it is like to live in this grace filled kingdom where justice and love are supremely valued. The citizen has the assurance that, despite appearances, this kingdom will grow and grow. Its growth is assured. But it is a kingdom which inexorably moves towards a crisis. By far the greatest number of parables that Jesus told were about this aspect of the kingdom, and how in the light of it citizens of this kingdom were to be vigilant, ready and wise. We shall look at these parables next and the qualities they call from the citizens of the kingdom.

Chapter Six

THE COMING CRISIS

There hardly has been a time when humans have not lived with a sense of impending crisis. When Augustine began writing *Civitate Dei* in the North African city of Hippo it was precipitated by the impending fall of Rome to the Goths. A world which had been relatively stable for nearly five hundred years was about to change for ever. It is hard to gauge the magnitude of that moment now. More recently, in the twentieth and now in the twenty-first century, crisis has never been far from the politicians' or world leaders' minds. The late Victorian and Edwardian sense of permanence and optimism was suddenly and abruptly changed by the military massacres of the First World War. The brief mood of luxury and frivolity for a few in the twenties was suddenly punctured by the Great Crash of 1929, followed by the depression of the thirties. And following the Second World War, with its enormous loss of life and genocide, half the world lived with the real threat of a nuclear holocaust engulfing it, a threat reflected in the work of many novelists and film makers. For a few days in 1962 the world held its breath whilst President Kennedy negotiated with Khrushchev for the removal of Russian nuclear missiles from Cuba. The crisis, as we know, was averted, but nuclear war was widely feared.

However, the demise of the Cold War in 1989 was soon followed by another sense of crisis, brought on by the September 11th 2002 attack by Al Qaeda on the World Trade Centre. We are now told that this threat may continue for at least a generation. Finally, the

BECOMING A CITIZEN OF THE KINGDOM

south east Asian tsunami of Boxing Day 2004 has underlined the environmental threat to human life. Part of that threat is caused by the effect of global warming, about which we can do something; the other part of the threat is from the inherently unstable nature of the environment itself, with its shifting continental plates, its frequent hurricanes and earthquakes — all of which the world indiscriminately suffered in 2005. Even as I write, plans for an early warning system to protect the world from earthquakes, tsunamis and asteroid strikes are being drawn up for the British government by Professor Sir David King. Crisis is therefore never far from the thoughts of the human family. Nor was it far from the teaching of Jesus about the kingdom of God. Indeed, it may be a surprise to some that by the far greatest amount of Jesus' teaching to the crowds was about a coming crisis for which they should be prepared. The nature of this teaching appears to fall into three categories: its spiritual origins; its demand on us for preparedness; and the final accountability it places on us for the way we live our lives now. We shall look at each in turn.

The origins of crisis
Only one of these crisis parables is common to each of the synoptic Gospels, and that is the parable of the wicked husbandmen or, to make it more up to date, the tenants (Mark 12:1-11; Matthew 21:33-44; Luke 20:9-18). Unlike many of Jesus' parables, this story is much nearer to an allegory, in which there are corresponding spiritual realities to many of the images or characters in the story. So the vineyard is Israel, as in the song of the vineyard in Isaiah 5:1-7. The tenants are the leaders of Judaism. The owner of the vineyard is God. The messengers are the prophets. And the son is Jesus. And as such it was patently an attack by Jesus upon the conduct of Israel's leaders over the years and especially in the age of the Messiah. The leaders of the people who were in earshot when Jesus first told the story rightly recognised it as an attack upon themselves. In the parable Jesus made it quite clear that insofar as the leaders of Israel acted in character with those tenants – that is, those who gleefully said to each other, "This is the heir. Come, let's kill him, and take his inheritance" – they, too, would face crisis and judgement.

So Jesus goes on to say, "Therefore, when the owner of the vineyard comes, what will he do to those tenants?"

"He will bring those wretches to a wretched end," they replied, "and he will rent the vineyard to other tenants, who will give him his share of the crop at harvest time."

It could not be clearer that part of the judgement on Israel and her leaders would be that the tenancy of the vineyard would be taken away from the former tenants and vested in others who are Gentiles. This does not mean that no Israelite had any future rights of tenancy in the vineyard, to use the terms of the parable, but that as Paul argued in treating this important theme in Romans, "...not all who are descended from Israel are Israel" (Romans 9:6); or, to put it another way, true Israel is faith-ful Israel, that is Israel which has a faith in the Messiah. (See Romans 3:29-31.) For Paul, Israel is not simply defined by ethnicity (i.e. birth, or belonging to a race) but is defined by trusting in God's promises, from Abraham onwards. So once again Paul says in a much-overlooked verse, "A man is not a Jew if he is only one outwardly, nor is circumcision merely outward and physical. No, a man is a Jew if he is one inwardly; and circumcision is circumcision of the heart, by the Spirit not by the written code" (Romans 2:28f).

However, our chief purpose here is not to define faithful Israel so much as to show, through Jesus' teaching in this parable, that the rejection of the Messiah by the leaders of Israel precipitated a change of "tenancy in the vineyard" which was brought about by the actions of their leaders. The Gentiles, too, could become tenants of the vineyard and enjoy its produce and benefits. Judgement fell on those leaders who handed over the Messiah to crucifixion. It was Jesus himself who said – and he is *the faithful Jew* – quoting Psalm 118:22f, "Have you never read in the Scriptures:

> "'The stone the builders rejected
> Has become the capstone;
> The Lord has done this,
> And it is marvellous in our eyes'?"

"Therefore I tell you that the kingdom of God will be taken away from you and given to a people who will produce its fruit. He who falls on this stone will be broken to pieces, but he on whom it falls will be crushed" (Matthew 21:42-44).

What could be clearer or more dramatic than these words of Jesus meaning that the kingdom of God is now to be given to "a people who will produce its fruit". This "people" will be capable of producing the fruit of the Spirit, through the grace of God creating the obedience of faith, which befits this kingdom. No ethnic group has a prior claim to this kingdom; it is for all nations! In the economy of God, the rejection of the Messiah by Israel has brought about the inclusion of the Gentiles.

The first crisis to which the ministry of Jesus was moving, therefore, was his own rejection by his own people, as John says so memorably in his own Gospel prologue: "He came to that which was his own, but his own did not receive him" (John 1:11). This is not in anyway to be anti-Semitic, as some have said (wrongly, I think), but it is simply to acknowledge that this was part of the divine plan. And anyhow, in a deeper theological sense, all of humanity were accomplices to his death, requiring his atoning sacrifice for all our failings.

The consequence of the death and resurrection of Jesus was that through these events the whole world was made accountable to him and, as Paul taught by his preaching at Athens, God had put humankind on notice of judgement to come by raising him from the dead. (See Acts 17:31.) Again and again, Jesus taught that we should be ready and prepared for this eventuality, and this was the coming crisis for which all should be prepared.

Be ready, be prepared
Jesus unambiguously taught that there would be a crisis between the partial coming of the kingdom of God in this world and its final coming and fulfilment. (See Revelation 11:15.) As we shall see later in the book, there is a sense in which the kingdom has come, and also another sense in which it has not fully come, nor can it until after the second coming of Jesus. This crisis, which Jesus anticipated in so much of his teaching, would involve the return of Christ to the world as the visible and undisputed king, and a general resurrection from the dead (John 5:25-30) followed by judgement.

All of these orthodox teachings are declared in the Apostles' and Nicene creeds in short telegrammatic sentences. The Nicene Creed says, "He will come again in glory to judge the living and the dead, and his kingdom will have no end." So anticipating the reality of this, but without knowing when it would actually be, Jesus constantly encouraged his listeners to live in the light of this forthcoming event which was sure but undated.

There are whole clusters of parables which encourage his listeners to be both ready and prepared for this eventuality whenever it occurred. These parables stress the finality of this moment: the parable of the closed door (Luke 13:24-30); the unexpectedness of this coming crisis —the parable of the burglars (Matthew 24:43-44); the necessity of preparedness —the parables of the wedding garment, the ten virgins and the door keeper (Matthew 22:11-14; Matthew 25:1-13; Mark 13:33-37 and Luke 12:35-38); and finally the need to respond to the invitation to the kingdom banquet now —the parable of the great banquet. (Matthew 22:1-10; Luke 14:16-24.) This corpus of teaching, which we shall look at in closer detail next, revolved around the theme of responding now to the message of the kingdom. And in good kingdom tradition we shall look at this final theme presented in the great banquet first!

Jesus repeatedly taught that now was the time to respond, as he made plain in his extraordinarily vivid parable of the great banquet. The emphasis in the parable is twofold: the first is that all is now ready; but the second theme is that the invited guests paid not the least attention to the gracious invitation they had received. It was not as if they had not known of the feast, for the guests had been given previous notice of it by an initial invitation; but when the supper was ready and a further invitation was graciously sent round, they all made excuses. The point was that they were all relatively wealthy people, one having just bought a field, another five yoke of oxen implying that he had at least 45 hectares and possibly much more;[1] another, if not rich, was preoccupied, having just got married, and did not want to leave his young wife! Each had their excuse for refusing the invitation although notice of the party had been given well in advance. The parable was both an allegory of the Jewish nation's response to Jesus and, in particular, an insightful account of the response of those especially who have many attractive opportunities in their lives.

With regard to the Jewish nation, the parable reads as an allegory, since on many previous occasions they had been invited to the banquet by the prophets of old and now their Messiah was here with the invitation that all was now ready, so the Son of Man issues the invitation "Come", but they would not. As Jesus most poignantly said to the Jewish leaders, "You diligently study the Scriptures because you think that by them you possess eternal life. These are the Scriptures that testify about me, yet you refuse to *come to me* to have life" (John 5:39f, my italics). When the final invitation was given they would not come. So, just as in the parable of the tenants in the vineyard, the privilege is thrown open to those who had not previously been included: 'Then the master told his servant, "Go out to the roads and country lanes and make them come in, so that my house will be full. I tell you, not one of those men who were invited will get a taste of my banquet."' (Luke 14:23f).

Although the parable can be read as an allegory of the Jewish nation's response to the Messiah, it is also an accurate measure of those too caught up with the exciting options of their own lives to either hear or respond to the gracious invitation. This could not be a more urgent and timely reflection on our Western society, in which so many are so caught up with the extraordinary opportunities available to us that there is virtually no space available to consider the needs of our soul rather than our body. The opportunities for entertainment, pleasure and pampering are such that the needs of the human soul or spirit do not get a look in! Although not everyone in our society may share in this prosperity, it is now the experience of the majority. In this parable, for fields read houses and their purchase or improvement, either in our country or abroad; for yoke of oxen, read cars or consumer products; and for a wife read any number of relationships which we may make or break in our fractious community. So enmeshed are we in the web of our living that we do not even have the time to consider the invitation, let alone reply! The sheer range of opportunities that we have has completely recast our world-view.

This was brought home to me recently when taking a family funeral in a small village churchyard. It was a burial on a windswept hill overlooking Bristol. I was asked to use the 1662 Book of Common Prayer. As I read the once familiar words, "man that is born of woman has but a short time to live and his years are full of misery", these words seemed more appropriate in films of yesteryear rather than a summary of most lives today. I could not but reflect, a little ironically, on how things have changed. The lady I was burying had nearly reached her 93rd year! And how many would say that life is full of misery in the UK? It may well be so for untold millions in the "two thirds world", and for many here who through spoilt relationships yearn for what have might been, but on the whole they are not words which many would have chosen for their funeral service! The point is that we now have so many options to choose from (and the politicians think that we need even more choice) that we often resemble the people in the story of the great banquet who refused the invitation because they thought they had better things to do! The prevailing blindness of our society is that we are so caught up with our own fare that we do not consider what might be on the menu of the banquet!

But, whatever happens, the party will be full. And it can not have escaped your notice that whereas we struggle hard to interest people in the "invitation" because there are so many others on the mantelpiece, in the "two thirds" world the invitation is received with alacrity and joy and the churches are bursting full.

If the first thing we have looked at in these parables of crisis is that now is the time to respond, the second is that, since we do not know when the full feast will be inaugurated or the kingdom fully revealed, we should be both ready and prepared. This was the constant teaching of Jesus on the subject.

There are a clutch of parables which deal with this teaching. The most obvious ones on the subject of readiness are the parable of the thief in the night and the parable of the doorkeeper; we shall look at both in turn. Once again, Matthew and Luke have the parable of the burglar or thief at night. (Matthew 24:42; Luke 12:39.) Luke places it with other teaching about discipleship in his "sermon on the plain" section, while Matthew groups it with Jesus' teaching about his return. It is quite probable that the parables were oft told stories by Jesus, nevertheless their different positioning in the Gospels show Matthew and Luke meeting the needs of their respective audiences. For our purpose we will focus on Matthew's telling of the parable of the thief in the night.

In Matthew's account, Jesus has just said that not even he, the Son of Man, knows when he will return for his second coming. "No-one knows about that day or hour, not even the angels in heaven, nor the Son, but only the Father" (Matthew 24:36). He goes on to teach that people will be so engrossed in their lives ("eating and drinking, marrying and giving in marriage") that they will not be aware of the impending crisis, just as in the days of Noah! They will not be aware of the coming division. (See vv. 40ff.) So Jesus tells his disciples to, "...keep watch, because you do not know on what day your Lord will come" (v. 42). He will come like a thief in the night or burglar.

As preachers often say, "Which burglar sends a postcard to tell you the day on which he is coming?" When living and working in south London we were often burgled, and very unnerving it can be too. Sometimes it happened when we were all asleep upstairs; once I was disturbed by a burglar during daylight hours, sometimes we had police officers in our upstairs bathroom observing a drug dealing racket across the street, and once someone was arrested in our front garden. An exciting area! On no occasion did the thief or burglar advertise their activities beforehand. It was always a complete surprise. The thief comes unexpectedly, and likewise the return of Jesus as the king to fully inaugurate his kingdom will be unexpected. And for this event we should all be ready through faith and spiritual alertness. Otherwise it will be a terrible moment.

It has been observed that when the author walks onto the stage the play has ended. By then it will be too late to choose which side we are on; we will then discover which side we have truly chosen. There is a moment in Jane Austen's novel *Mansfield Park* when the owner of the house is delayed in his return so the house party decide to while away their boredom by getting up a play without his knowledge. One day he suddenly and unexpectedly returns; the author describes their response to his unexpected return as follows, "How is the consternation of the party to be described? To the greater number it was a moment of absolute horror! Sir Thomas in the house! All felt instantaneous conviction. Not a word was spoken for half a minute!"

Jesus says, "So you also must be ready, because the Son of Man will come at an hour you do not expect." This readiness comprises an active trust or faith in God, and spiritual alertness especially evidenced in prayer and ongoing service to God in the world. A faith which is dormant, prayers which are at best perfunctory, and service which has become complacent, will not presumably elicit the response, "Well done good and faithful servant."

Two parables which urge readiness and preparedness are the parables of the wise and foolish virgins and the improperly dressed wedding guest. (See Matthew 25:1-13 and Matthew 22:11-14.) In the case of the parable of the wise and foolish virgins, the custom in Palestine was that the culmination of the wedding feast was the entry of the bridegroom into the bride's father's house. "In the late evening the guests were entertained in the bride's house. After hours of waiting for the bridegroom whose coming was repeatedly announced by messengers, at last he came, half an hour before midnight, to fetch the bride; he was accompanied by his friends, floodlit by burning candles, and received by the guests who had come out to meet him. The wedding assembly then moved off, again in a flood of light, in festal procession to the house of the bridegroom's father, where the marriage ceremony and fresh entertainment took place. Both the reception of the bridegroom's arrival with lights and the hour long waiting for the bridegroom's arrival, are frequently mentioned in modern reports of Arab weddings in Palestine."[2] The delay to the bridegroom's arrival at the bride's house could have been caused by bargaining over the quality of the presents due to the relatives of the bride! In the event, in the parable, the five foolish virgins did not have enough oil for the wait, for which eventuality they should have prepared, so that while they were buying some more the bridegroom arrived, and arriving after the procession to his house when the door had been closed and the banquet had begun they found that they were locked out. They were unprepared! Likewise, the improperly dressed wedding guest was unprepared for the feast —he was cast out. The wedding garment in the parable is a symbol of the righteousness which is given by God. It is to be taken and put on; for whatever reason, this man had refused to dress correctly in the "robes of righteousness" offered as a gift of his grace (see the earlier parable of the prodigal son) and consequently he was ejected from the feast. In both parables the kingdom of God is referred to as the wedding feast, and neither the foolish virgins, who had insufficient oil, nor the uninvited guest, who was wrongly attired, were able to share in it. They were unprepared.

Another parable Jesus told to encourage "readiness" was that of the doorkeeper. Mark and Luke have the parable in their Gospels. (Mark 13:33-37: Luke 12:35-38.) In the parable the householder (God) goes away and leaves his servants in charge of his property. Whenever he returns, the servants are to be ready to let him in. The servants are to be dressed ready for service, having kept their lamps burning. (See Luke 12:35.) These metaphors denote faith and its result of justification (dressed); readiness to serve; and prayerfulness (lamps burning). The servants are to be ready for whenever the master returns, even in the second or third watch of the night. And if the servants are so ready, then their master will reward them. (See Luke 12:37b.)

However, alongside this command to be ready was also one of being responsible for the tasks which had been assigned to you. (Matthew 24:45-51; Luke 12:42-46.) The servant may either faithfully discharge his office, giving to the household its food at the proper time, or he may use the opportunity of delay in his master's coming to abuse those over whom he has been set. If he is faithful then there will be generous reward ("he will put him in charge of all his possessions"), but if he abuses the trust he has been given, damaging or hurting those in his charge, then he will face terrible retribution.

So in these parables we have the combination of a sudden return – as with the arrival of a burglar – and the need to remain faithful until such time as the master comes back. All these parables in this section show the need for preparedness and readiness for the return of the master —dressed, ready to serve, and with lamps burning. This is the only way to meet the coming crisis, which will inaugurate a judgement of every life. The crisis will not only involve the unexpected return of the king but the judgement of every life according the standards and expectation of the king. To this final aspect of the coming crisis we must now turn, as well as to the parables which contain the prospect of judgement. There are five in all, together with a final prophetic action.

The crisis of judgement

At Christmas 2003, in her Christmas broadcast, the Queen of the United Kingdom made a memorable statement, which was that she endeavoured to lead her life in the knowledge that she was accountable to God. To put it another way, she was conscious that we must each give account of our lives before the judgement seat of God. It was a striking assertion from one who might have every reason, humanly speaking, to live life for the present only and disregard the fact that however influential or powerful we may be in this life we must still give an account of our lives. Obviously there are very many who have no such awareness, but the New Testament is unequivocal: "Just as man is destined to die once, and after that to face judgement..." (Hebrews 9:27). Much of Jesus' teaching with regard to the coming crisis is that we must live in the light of this accountability. The following parables all have this sense of accountability and judgement as their starting point: the parables of the rich fool; Dives and Lazarus; the talents; the unjust steward; and the allegory of the sheep and the goats. Lastly, we shall look briefly at the cursing of the fig tree by Jesus during his entry into Jerusalem, which was a prophetic action demonstrating his yearning for fruitfulness in his people and his disappointment at there being none.

If on the one hand Jesus prepared his disciples for the coming crisis by telling them to be ready, on the other hand he told his disciples how best to prepare for this coming kingdom by putting it first. No characters were more culpable in this respect than the rich fool and Dives. The parable of the rich fool is, as with so many of Jesus' parables, wonderfully vivid and memorable. The story is well known, if the occasion giving rise to its telling may be not so familiar.

A younger brother was despairing that his elder brother would share their inheritance with him, so he appealed to Jesus when he was in the area for adjudication, but Jesus would not oblige. "Man," he said, "who appointed me a judge or an arbiter between you?" Jesus refuses to be drawn into their dispute, but he tells a story which shows both the snares of wealth and the attitude we should adopt to money or property. It indicates clearly how little significance Jesus attached to worldly wealth. The strap line was, "...a man's life does not consist in the abundance of his possessions" (Luke 12:15). Here was the main point, and the story illustrated it. The farmer, having been blessed with a bumper harvest with too much food to eat, decided to pull down his barns and build larger ones. Canon David Cook, in an excellent series of teaching on these parables, pointed out that the rich fool mistook his body for his soul, mistook time for eternity and mistook himself for God. He neglected his soul in providing for his body, he neglected eternity in thinking only of time on earth and he neglected God in thinking only of his ego. ("I will tear down my barns... I will store all my grain and goods... I'll say to myself," etc.) His inner attitude was: "You have plenty of good things laid up for many years. Take life easy; eat, drink and be merry" (v. 19.) Unlike the Epicureans who completed the phrase, "eat, drink and be merry" by adding "for tomorrow we die", the rich fool had no thought of death, he was secure in his own complacency. "But God said to him, 'You fool! This very night your life will be demanded from you. Then who will get what you have prepared for yourself?'" (v. 20). Once again the crisis brought about here by sudden death would make all assets and holdings worthless, for you cannot take them with you!

It was Cardinal Mazarin, the worldly adviser to Louis XIII who amassed enormous wealth, chateaux and priceless *objets d'art*, who was heard muttering whilst going around his corridors of palaces, "I must leave it all behind." So Jesus concludes, "This is how it will be with anyone who stores up things for himself but is not rich towards God" (v. 21). The crisis of the kingdom is that in the new world there will not be any asset management for ourselves. This means that the priority of the citizen of the kingdom is to build up riches towards God here rather than increase any real estate or offshore assets on earth. The only real and lasting estate will be that which is really invested in his kingdom. If the parable of the rich fool shows the responsibility of the individual to store riches in heaven (see Matthew 6:19f), another of Luke's parables, Dives and Lazarus, shows that true godliness is always expressed in love for neighbour.

The parable of Dives and Lazarus comes in a section of Luke's Gospel in which the right management of wealth is given prominence. In swift succession come these parables or events: the shrewd manager (Luke 16:1-15); the rich man and Lazarus (Luke 16:19-31); the story of the rich ruler (Luke 18:18-29); the meeting with Zacchaeus; the parable of the ten minas or talents (Luke 18:11-26); Jesus overturning the money changers' tables in the temple; paying taxes to Caesar (vv. 20-26); the widow's offering (Luke 21:1-4); and the betrayal by Judas (Luke 22:1-6). This teaching was given in part for the benefit of the Pharisees, who, Luke says, "loved money", and were, "sneering at Jesus". (See Luke 16:14.) These events and parables bear testimony to the power of money. We see what Richard Foster calls its light side – the power to bring joy and benefit – but also its dark side, its power to enslave and isolate. We see, in this swift succession of stories and parallels, its power to win friends and influence people, to isolate us from the needs of others, to prevent us from following Jesus, to be gloriously overcome by grace and acceptance, to be something for which we are accountable, to overtake true worship, to fulfil our civil obligations, but not to replace our spiritual ones, to be the means of demonstrating extraordinary devotion as well as the means of stimulating the most heinous betrayal. Luke presents all this in his Gospel in a few chapters —I feel several sermon series coming on! But the parable we shall focus on now is that of the rich man and Lazarus, for once again it is a parable of crisis.

In some ways this parable seems rather Platonic, with its seeming reversal of fortunes in the afterlife. Both of the central figures are representatives of certain types. Lazarus, which means God helps, represents the pious poor —the one who has nothing, but exercises a faith in God which at the last will be rewarded. Lazarus represents the person who, in this account of the kingdom, where everything is topsy-turvy, comes out blessed and rewarded whilst the rich man, seemingly blessed in this life, ends up in hell. In a society in which clear lines were drawn between prosperity and righteousness, poverty and sinfulness, Jesus' story had once again an unexpected and almost scandalous outcome. Dives, who is not given a personal name, simply means "rich man". He has become isolated and desensitised by his wealth so that he does nothing for the poor man at his gate. After death the roles of each are reversed. Lazarus is found in the bosom of Abraham and Dives in hell, not because riches are intrinsically evil and poverty is intrinsically good, but because implicitly Lazarus expressed faith and hope in his life whereas the rich man expressed his lack of practical faith by doing nothing for the beggar at his gate, content instead to wallow in his luxury. It is all too easy for this to happen, whether it is in the palaces of the rich juxtaposed to a shanty town, suburban luxury next to sink housing, or first world affluence alongside two-thirds world poverty. So powerful is the isolating effect of money that the four brothers who are left behind in the parable, but facing the same fate as their now tormented brother, would not be dissuaded from their lifestyle, even if someone came back from the dead and warned them of what was to follow if they persisted.

These two parables, taken together, are a powerful warning that a crisis is coming, whether ushered in by death or by Jesus' return, which will be the inevitable prelude to the kingdom coming fully. This crisis will bring about a judgement of our self-centred lifestyle on earth. Although the kingdom of which Jesus speaks is real, so powerful is the blinding power of money that the rich fool does not believe that he is anything other than completely secure. Equally, Dives allows his wealth to harden his own heart both to God and his neighbour, becoming completely blind to the obvious needs of the beggar at his gate.

But Jesus not only warns us through these two vivid parables, he also instructs us further through three other parables about how we should live as we await the coming of the kingdom and so live in it as citizens now. These three parables are the parables of the pounds or minas, the parable of the unjust steward and the parable of the sheep and the goats. So far in this chapter we have considered the need to be ready for this future crisis, to live life in the light of judgement and eternity, but now in these last remaining three parables we are reminded of the need for faithfulness, shrewdness and compassion in our life now. To these parables we must now turn, and firstly to the parable of the pounds and minas.

Faithful stewards   Matthew 25:14-30; Luke 19:12-27

The word "faithful" here has a double edge. It means trustworthy but also signifies risk taking. The picture is a familiar one: a king or landlord goes away and entrusts responsibility to his servants, and in the case of this parable he gives them money. To one is given five talents, to another two and to a third servant one talent. The first two servants double their master's property, but the third has done nothing with it. The first two servants prove faithful stewards and the third proves both lazy and misinformed. He is lazy because he does nothing with it, and he is misinformed because he thinks his master is a hard man, which in fact he is not, but he still does nothing with that which has been entrusted to him. He refuses to develop or take risks with his talent, burying it in a hole, and has nothing to show his master on his return.

It is a powerful parable which teaches that with regard to all property and gifts we are simply stewards. We need to learn the art of having possessions without being possessed by them. We have but a short lease on life, and in it we are stewards of our master's property whether this is the environment in general or what we might term our personal property, whether possessions, homes, cars, assets or money. Not only that, but our "intellectual property" or personal gifts, spiritual or natural, are his investment in us as well. Of all this we are stewards, and our task as citizens in his kingdom is to faithfully develop the use of these things. This may involve risk; it will certainly involve growth. The alternative is simply burying our gifts and assets in the ground out of laziness or fear, neither of which is the result of faith. So we must go for growth, the development of that which has been entrusted to us. Again this is one of the qualities we must evidence as citizens of this kingdom. Then we will confidently be able to give account of what we have done, and be rewarded with the words, "Well done, good and faithful servant!"

The unjust steward   Luke 16:1-8

If Jesus commended faithfulness and enterprise in the parable of talents, in this most puzzling of parables, the unjust steward, he commended shrewdness and making use of money. Commentators have struggled long and hard over the ethics of the parable, in case it seems that Jesus was commending dishonesty. Ingenious explanations have been put forward, such as the suggestion that the steward was only remitting that part of the sums owing to his master which was made up of interest charges on late payments. Since interest payments were not allowed between Jews, the steward was both remitting what should not have been charged in the first place and at the same time gaining their gratitude. This is ingenious but we have no way of knowing whether it is true. It is a valiant attempt to get round any consternation or confusion about Jesus' teaching, but we should know by now that his parables are full of surprises and shock to those who think in a conventional manner.

What Jesus commends is both the shrewdness of the steward or manager and his use of money to make friends. Jesus teaches us to use our assets to make an eternal investment. These are the conclusions from a story about which, though he told it, he passed no absolute moral comment. Shrewdness and eternal investment was what Jesus was after. The point about shrewdness is on a par with his teaching to be "innocent as doves" and "wise as serpents". Christians are to be shrewd but not dishonest as citizens of the kingdom. But, secondly, they are to use money, not to pretend it is not there.

Some societies, for a time, have tried to operate a system averse to any individual ownership. This was and is especially true of communist countries. Such countries, like China and Cuba, have not yet managed such a state of affairs for longer than two generations at the most. China now has a tiger economy with its businessmen more than ever fascinated by money, expansion and profit. I read today that in 1996 China had 7 million mobile phones; in 2003 that had risen to 269 million! At the time of writing, we are being told that it uses 47% of the world's cement! The statistics of economic growth from China are endless. However, Jesus' point in the parable of the unjust steward is that we should use resources shrewdly, not denying their power, disowning them or pretending we are too spiritual to use such assets, but rather using them for the extension of God's kingdom on earth.

It is up to the Christian to use money for both godly and beneficial ends. We need to invest in the lives of people who are without good food, clean water, shelter and education whether on the continent of Africa or elsewhere. Could it be that by investing in their lives they really become our friends and neighbours, and in the final analysis we will discover this at that moment of crisis to which history moves? Could it be that the parable of the unjust steward has this eschatological meaning? Citizens of the kingdom are to be shrewd in their management and investment of money, making friends ahead of the time of crisis.

So far these parables have called humankind to faithful and enterprising stewardship, to shrewd use and investment of money; now a final parable calls us to compassionate action.

Compassionate action
The sheep and the goats   Matthew 25:31-46

Throughout the New Testament there is a healthy tension between salvation based on faith, and faith being expressed in works of compassion. So Jesus, speaking of judgement, says, "Do not be amazed at this, for a time is coming when all who are in their graves will hear his voice and come out —those who have done good will rise to live, and those who have done evil will rise to be condemned" (John 5:28f). Throughout Jesus' teaching he draws a direct link between a true faith and doing good, so, "A good tree cannot bear bad fruit, and a bad tree cannot bear good fruit.... by their fruit you will recognise them." (See Matthew 7:16-23.)

Paul teaches the same, on the one hand teaching the simplicity of grace through faith leading to salvation, and that this faith, if sincere, will produce compassionate action. So he writes, "God 'will give to each person according to what he has done'. To those who by persistence in doing good seek glory, honour and immortality, he will give eternal life. But for those who are self-seeking and who reject the truth and follow evil, there will be wrath and anger. There will be trouble and distress for every human being who does evil: first for the Jew, then for the Gentile; but glory, honour and peace for everyone who does good: first for the Jew, then for the Gentile (Romans 2:6-10).

Compassionate action following the confession of Jesus as Lord, or belief in God, is the true test of the sincerity of faith. In the same way we find in the allegory of the sheep and the goats that faith is evidenced by compassionate action as James, perhaps supremely, taught in his epistle. (See James 2:14-25.) Jesus therefore divides the sheep from the goats on the basis of what they have done; not only this but Jesus identifies himself completely, in this allegory, with suffering humanity. The goats wonder when they actually saw the Lord hungry, thirsty, an exile needing shelter, a pauper needing clothes, sick and needing caring, or in prison and needing visiting. The answer is, of course, that when they refused any of the needy they refused him, and by their hardness of heart showed their lack of true faith and their being deserving of condemnation. A true citizen of the kingdom has faith which demonstrates itself in compassionate action.

The crisis is coming and has been coming; but the issue is how should we live in the light of it. This was the question which the apostles constantly addressed. As Peter wrote, "Since everything will be destroyed in this way, what kind of people ought you to be?" (2 Peter 3:11). In these parables, told in the light of this impending crisis at some unknown time in the future, Jesus taught that we should be ready, prepared —not acting like the rich fool or Dives, who exemplified people living without thought of their eventual accountability; but, instead, living with faithfulness and enterprise like the effective stewards; with shrewdness and inventiveness, like the shrewd manager; and with a faith that leads to compassionate action, like the collective sheep. In this way we live as citizens of a kingdom which has come, and is coming more fully, under the rule of the king. He will usher in this kingdom completely after this time of crisis. And in these ways we will live as citizens of the kingdom.

****

Before concluding this section and moving on to the way the kingdom may be expressed dynamically in the present, it is worth drawing the threads of this section together. We have been looking at that body of teaching called the parables with which Jesus constantly spoke to the crowds. In fact Mark tells us that Jesus only ever spoke in parables to the crowds. (See Mark 4:10-12.) The parables were invariably about the kingdom which Jesus had himself come to inaugurate. We have grouped them together into four main themes which describe the style, government and expectations of this kingdom. Later we will look at how we may enter this kingdom in a conscious and assured way, but here we are looking at what is the distinctiveness of this kingdom, and what that means for the citizens who belong and those who have yet to enter in the future.

We have seen that this kingdom is ruled by grace —grace which is offered by a righteous King whose Son came to seek and save the lost. Citizens can only enter by grace and remain on the basis of grace. Next, the kingdom is demanding; its entry may be free but its annual subscription is everything. Discipleship is the lifestyle of the citizen. Thirdly, to be part of the kingdom is to be part of something which will assuredly grow; its very nature is growth, and although there may be wastage on the way it will, like the mustard seed, begin from tiny origins and spread, like the leaven, throughout the whole body of humanity. Such is the nature of the kingdom. And lastly it awaits a crisis at some point in the future. This crisis will be the intersection between what is experienced now and what is promised eternally. The kingdom will be fully manifest and the citizens fully revealed. Until then, qualities of preparedness, readiness, faithfulness, shrewdness and constant compassion are needed, without which faith is immature. However, in the here and now, this kingdom with these characteristics must be expressed and made known, so that it might indeed grow, not only in size but also in quality. It is to the expression, or indeed *proclamation*, of the kingdom, and how Jesus made it known, that we now move.

PART III

THE EXPRESSION OF THE KINGDOM

Chapter Seven

JESUS, THE KING

Having looked at the working of the kingdom of God, or some of the characteristics of his reign, as Jesus described it in his parables, we will now consider the expression of the kingdom, especially during the ministry of Jesus. Our starting point is Jesus himself, for he is the living demonstration of what the kingdom is like. We shall look at the ways in which his kingdom was communicated in his own person, by word and action, in this part of the book.

There are six main ways in which the kingdom was made known to the human family, both in Jesus' own earthly ministry and later through the working of his Spirit: proclamation, meaning the announcement of the "good news" or gospel; teaching; healing and deliverance; forgiveness; justice and community. To start with, we shall look at the way in which Jesus communicated the kingdom, not simply in his actual teaching (which we have considered a little in our overview of the parables) but also through individual conversations. Furthermore, the very style of his ministry further illustrated the character of Jesus' rule, and could be said to be a living parable of the kingdom itself. So it is to this conduct or manner of Jesus' ministry that we turn now, before considering the main expressions of the kingdom in the ministry of Jesus.

If we take these six expressions of the kingdom, it is still the case that different parts of the church have latched onto different expressions of the kingdom to the exclusion of others, with the result that we have a lopsided understanding of what the kingdom really is. Different strands within the church today are sometimes broadly identified as the evangelical, the sacramental and the pentecostal (or charismatic). Within each "strand" there would be a spectrum, ranging from conservative to more liberal elements. The first "strand" is best known for its strong emphasis on the centrality of the ministry of the word, the second for the high place it accords to sacraments (liturgy, and the tradition encapsulated within that), and the third for its restored emphasis on the Spirit and his work. But to suggest that each "strand" has some sort of monopoly of what it is best known for would be a massive and ridiculous oversimplification. There is a huge amount of overlap. Moreover, elements of these "strands" can be found within the same denomination. The point is that the church tends to cluster around each of those distinctives, and each has some significant bearing on God's rule.

The kingdom is in fact about teaching and proclamation based on the Scriptures —with all the struggles of rightly interpreting them; but it is also about healing and deliverance of individuals with the expectation of change. It is also about justice: fair trade or debt relief, and other moves toward justice in our world; but it is also about right sexual ethics. The kingdom spans both private and public morality; intimate concerns and structural values. It is about being open to the Spirit to direct, urge and challenge the church to be prophetic; but it is also about public truth for the whole community. It is about individual salvation; but it is also about creating a new community, a new humanity for the world to see and taste what God has to offer. It is about making known forgiveness as a result of the death of Jesus; but it is also making known the resurrection life that holds out the hope of heaven. Whereas so often we pitch our tent on one aspect of the expression of the kingdom, it is in fact limiting to do so. We make the tent too small so that only one kind can enter in. Before we look at the six major themes, we will consider some of the vital ways in which Jesus himself, through his style of ministry, expressed this kingdom to all in his day.

Quite simply, Jesus is the embodiment of the kingdom. Jesus did not only speak out the message about the kingdom, he really *is* the message. To put it another way, he is the living expression of the kingdom. And whilst he told many parables *about* the kingdom, Jesus lived out every day what it was like to live in this kingdom —showing us what it is to know the just and gentle rule of his Father in his life, and to provide the same rule for others. As John says, Jesus tabernacled among us and we beheld his glory. (See John 1:14.) Jesus' expression of this kingdom was fully human; his living out of the kingdom irradiated and enhanced every aspect of our true humanity. He was, after all, the pattern of our humanity. There are four extremely sigificant ways in which he enacted the meaning of the kingdom in his own person.

Firstly he welcomed all, especially those who were excluded by virtue of their immorality or disease, their despised occupation – like tax-gatherers or prostitutes – or their ritually unclean jobs, such as shepherds or donkey drivers. Jesus breached all the conventions that kept the religious Jew away from such people, freely meeting them. In Mark's Gospel, straight after his call of Levi, Jesus was having dinner at Levi's house. We are told that many tax collectors and sinners were eating with him and his disciples, for there were many who followed him. The Pharisees asked the disciples why he ate with tax collectors and "sinners". The answer was that he had come, "... to seek and to save what was lost." (See Luke 19:10.) Again and again in the Gospels, Jesus demonstrated that he had come for those who were excluded: the woman who was unclean by virtue of her haemorrhaging Jesus cured and called her "Daughter" (Luke 8:48); the leper whom no-one would touch, he met and healed (Mark 1:40-45); the children who were too insignificant, and who the disciples wanted to shoo away (Mark 10:13-16), he welcomed; and although all women in Judaism were not permitted to give evidence in court, Jesus showed himself first of all after the resurrection to a woman, Mary Magdalene. She, therefore, became the first witness of the resurrection. All of these were included, welcomed, and enjoyed hospitality with Jesus. The kingdom is therefore a community where no one is excluded on grounds of previous immorality, gender, race, sickness or disability. All are welcomed in on equal terms of repentance and faith. (See Luke 5:31.) This is a vital point about the kingdom of God. It is a place of welcome and change. How little our churches properly reflect this!

Secondly, Jesus treated all whom he met as having dignity and worth. This does not mean that he did not challenge them. Sometimes he did so unflinchingly, as with the rich young ruler. (Luke 18:18-23.) He gave everyone the significance of taking them seriously, but in the context of total love. Again and again this was repeated

111

with the characters he met as recorded in the Gospels. (See my book entitled *Meetings with Jesus*.) As Augustine said, "God loves each one of us as if there was only one to love." But his love had within it the ability to see what an individual could become. He always looked for potential, knowing that each had been made in the image of God and, with his help, was on the path to becoming fully human, fully themselves, with all their abilities fully functioning under his discerning leadership. (And this theme is explored in my book which is the first in this trilogy, entitled *Becoming Fully Human*.) Perhaps this was most notable in the case of Simon Peter. On first meeting him he said, "'You are Simon son of John. You will be called Cephas....'" (which, when translated, is Peter)' (John 1:42b). Both "Cephas" and "Peter" meant 'rock'. He saw his potential and later reiterated his calling on Peter's life by saying that he was the rock on which Jesus would build his church. (See Matthew 16:18.) To follow in the steps or ways of Jesus, his followers should do likewise. He bestowed dignity and gave hope.

Years ago, in the days of apartheid in South Africa, in the 1950s, Archbishop Tutu was walking hand in hand with his mother in their township of Sophia Town. From the opposite direction came towards them the only white man in the town. He was dressed almost entirely in black, a long flowing cassock, and on his head he was topped off with a biretta! It was Trevor Huddleston. When he drew level with Tutu's mother, he took off his hat and greeted her —an unheard of gesture in those days. Desmond Tutu never forgot it; later, he too became a Christian. And, as they say, the rest is history! Like his master, Huddleston not only saw all people as made in the image of God and worthy of great dignity and respect, he also saw their potential in the hand of God.

Thirdly, Jesus empathised with people. This empathy was shown in words, touch and emotion, and it was to that extent holistic. He was not distant or indifferent. This resulted in both touch and tears. He allowed others to touch him, apart from Mary Magdalene after his resurrection (presumably then because his state of being had changed and he was weaning his disciples off his physical presence and to rely on him spiritually —that is, to depend on him by faith and not by sight.) When Jesus healed people he often touched them, as in the case of the leper who knelt at his feet and said, "If you are willing, you can make me clean." We are told that Jesus was filled with compassion. He, '...reached out his hand and touched the man,' and said to him, "I am willing.... Be clean!" (See Mark 1:40f). Likewise, Jesus took Jairus' daughter by the hand and healed her; and the deaf mute he healed by putting his fingers in the man's ears and saying, *"Ephphatha"*, meaning "Be opened!" (See Luke 8:54; Mark 7:33). Again and again Jesus touched those he healed —not always, but frequently.

Many of us grew up in a generation not good at touch. I remember in my own family physical touch was fairly limited, and maybe it was not until my father was dying, two years ago, that then for periods of time I held his hand, possibly for the first time as an adult, when all other forms of communication except hearing had passed. We learn in the Gospels that Jesus engaged with those around him in a total way, in which both words and touch were central. We need only consider, for example, his dealings with Thomas at the end of John's Gospel, to see the truth of this. It was not that he was just dispensing teaching, he was always giving himself.

The other demonstration of Jesus' emotional engagement was his tears. He was not afraid to cry. As we all know, the shortest verse in the Bible is "Jesus wept." Jesus stood outside the tomb of Lazarus his friend and wept; moved, no doubt, by the mourning of Lazarus' sister Mary, who had fallen at his feet in her distress and said, "Lord... if you had been here, my brother would not have died", as well as by the weeping of the other Jews who came with him to the tomb. He may have been distressed by the pall of death itself so groaning in his spirit, but he was also overwhelmed by the loss of a friend whom he loved. Or again, when Jesus looked out over Jerusalem, knowing both its rejection of him and its eventual judgement, he wept, saying, "If you, even you, had only known on this day what would bring you peace —but now it is hidden from your eyes", and, "...how often I have longed to gather your children together, as a hen gathers her chicks under her wings, but you were not willing." (See Luke 19:42 and Matthew 23:37.) Jesus was not afraid to show his emotion, whether it was of deep sadness or foreboding. His ministry involved his total being. His commitment was of heart and mind.

Finally, Jesus ministered as a servant king. Repeatedly, Jesus showed that his kingship was not of this world. (See John 18:36.) His style of kingship was marked by humility and righteousness. (See Matthew 11:29.) He was the just and gentle king and, as Isaiah foretold,

> "Here is my servant whom I have chosen,
> the one I love, in whom I delight;
> I will put my Spirit on him,
> and he will proclaim justice to the nations.
> He will not quarrel or cry out;
> no-one will hear his voice in the streets.
> A bruised reed he will not break,
> and a smouldering wick he will not snuff out,
> till he leads justice to victory.
> In his name the nations will put their hope."
>
> *Matthew 12:18-21 (Isaiah 42:1-4)*

As the servant king, Jesus preferred silence to retaliation at his trial (John 19:9f); preferred love to the sword at the time of his arrest (John 18:11; Luke 22:49-51; Matthew 26:52); and anonymity rather than fame in his ministry. (Mark 1:45; Luke 4:41; John 5:13.) As such, his ministry – although crowd-attracting – never sought celebrity status for, as John wrote, referring to the crowd who believed as a result of his miracles, "Jesus would not entrust himself to them, for he knew all men" (John 2:24). From washing the disciples' feet to cooking a breakfast for some of them on the shore of the Sea of Galilee, Jesus' ministry, from first to last, was servant-shaped. (See John 13:2-5; John 21:9-12.) This can never be emphasised too much.

In these ways Jesus, in the style of his own ministry, demonstrated what the kingdom of God was like, what are its innate values — promulgated not in some shiny prospectus of what the kingdom would do in the future, but in the way Jesus conducted his ministry. This cannot be over-stressed, especially as we go on to consider the way, apart from this style, that Jesus made known the kingdom. He made it known by proclamation or teaching, by healing and deliverance, by forgiveness, by bringing forth justice, and by forming a community around the sure hope of the resurrection. We shall look at each of these in turn; they make up the integrated whole of how the kingdom is made known, and to neglect any of them is to fail in the continuing task of making known the kingdom in our own age. We will begin with Jesus' proclamation of the message of the kingdom.

Chapter Eight

PROCLAIMING THE KINGDOM

There is no doubt that a large proportion of Jesus' time was spent preaching. And indeed, at the inauguration of his ministry at the synagogue in Nazareth, reading from the book of Isaiah, he said that he was anointed to preach good news to the poor. (Isaiah 61:1 and Luke 4:14-21.) We have already seen that whenever he spoke to the crowds he did so almost entirely in parables, although it is fair to point out that the Sermon on the Mount was also preached to crowds (Matthew 5:1) and contained mostly what we might call straight teaching with just a few scattered metaphors or mini parables. (See Matthew 5:13-16; 6:19-24; 7:13-14; 7:24-27.) When he spoke to the disciples on their own, Jesus explained further what he had previously taught the crowds. If the activity of preaching was one way – but not the only way – of making known the kingdom of God, what must concern us are these questions: What did Jesus preach? What did he tell his disciples to preach? And how did he go about it? Furthermore, at the end of this chapter we must consider the appropriate way of preaching in our own age, and how the church and its ministers should set about it.

What we are contending in this part of the book is that the making known of the kingdom comprises several basic elements, each of which is important for the proper manifestation of the kingdom. Too often the church, whose task is to make known the kingdom, is like a golfer with only one or two clubs in his bag, determined to go around a difficult course with either just a putter and a wood, or just a few irons but no putter or wood! Whether or not you play golf, the point is that Jesus, having given his disciples a number of activities to manifest the kingdom, does not expect us to restrict ourselves to one or two ways only, on the grounds that we think that "the course" does not warrant any more! Or, as some Christians wrongly suppose, that some "clubs" have been withdrawn from circulation, presumably on the grounds that the game no longer requires them! Any look at the ministry of Jesus shows that he preached, healed and delivered, forgave, proclaimed justice, and built a community whose values illustrated what the kingdom is like. Surely he does not expect us to do anything less? So we begin, in this chapter, by looking at his preaching, before looking at others of his ministries, which were ways of expressing the kingdom or making known the rule of God, in turn.

Jesus' preaching

The synoptic Gospel writers Matthew, Mark and Luke all show us that Jesus was a dedicated and consummate preacher. At the very beginning of his ministry, Matthew tells us, "Jesus went throughout Galilee, teaching in their synagogues, preaching the good news of the kingdom, and healing every disease and sickness among the people. News about him spread all over Syria, and people brought to him all who were ill with various diseases, those suffering severe pain, the demon-possessed, those having seizures, and the paralysed, and he healed them." We are told that large crowds from Galilee, the Decapolis, Jerusalem, Judea and the region across the Jordan followed him. (See Matthew 4:23-25.) Likewise Luke tells us, as does Mark, that after a full day's ministry in Capernaum, including teaching in the synagogue and healing many, including Simon Peter's mother-in-law, Jesus got up very early the next day and then told those who wanted to detain him for longer in Capernaum that he must go on to other towns and villages that needed to hear his message. (See Mark 1:38f.) He said, "Let us go somewhere else — to the nearby villages — so that I can preach there also. That is why I have come." The mission which he had come to fulfil was to preach the message of the kingdom in communities of that region. Quite clearly, Jesus placed a very high premium on the preaching of the kingdom. What we must look at more closely now is the style and content of this preaching.

The content of the proclamation

When Matthew and Luke tell us that Jesus preached the gospel of the kingdom, what did they mean and what was the content of his preaching or proclamation of the kingdom? In essence surely the message of the kingdom that Jesus preached was quite simple and straightforward, it was that this kingdom, of which the prophets of the Old Testament had often spoken, was here in the person of Jesus himself. The rule of God was amongst them in his person and presence. As we know from the style of Jesus' teaching, he would not have said baldly: I am the king you have all been waiting for; join the kingdom! His proclamation was illustrated clearly by his actions and life, as well as being explained by his words. The illustration of what the kingdom was like lay in the actions of Jesus, while the words of Jesus were an explanation of his actions. There is in fact an invisible boundary between his words and actions; indeed, to borrow the language of the fourth Gospel, both words and actions together demonstrate the Word made flesh. Indeed, John tells us that he received both words and actions from his Father. (See John 5:19 and John 14.)

It is an obvious point to make that the gospel of the kingdom which Jesus himself preached did not contain either the events of the crucifixion or the resurrection; these events were still to happen. Although Jesus often spoke about both his death and resurrection privately to his disciples, predicting (although they for the most part did not understand), understandably he did not speak about these future events (probably unimaginable to almost all his general audience) in his preaching of the kingdom to the crowds. The preaching of the kingdom that Jesus and his disciples gave to the population of Israel was that the kingdom, for which they had been waiting, was here. The actions of healing, deliverance, forgiveness and the formation of a new community demonstrated the presence of this kingdom. So Jesus' words were an explanation of its presence. This being the case, his preaching was along the lines of "this is that"; meaning "this" – the demonstration of the kingdom – is "that" of which the prophets of old spoke; and now it is here amongst you! The gospel was therefore that "God's rule" is here and that Jesus is the bringer of that rule to all who will repent (re-orientate their lives on that basis, and believe). As Tomlin puts it: "If Jesus' ministry centred upon the coming of the kingdom of God in his own person, then perhaps the early Christians got it right when they summarised the heart of the gospel with the pithy catchphrase, "Jesus is Lord".[1] If this was at the heart of Jesus' message, that the reign of God is here in the person of Jesus, then this is where our proclamation should begin as well. "Before being told how they can respond to God, people need to know who this God is in the first place, the creator of heaven and earth, who generously provides everything for life, who loves his creation passionately, who hates all that is evil and who will one day destroy it, and in whom we find true life, joy and peace."[2]

This is where we need to start in our culture, in which world-views are largely formed by pantheism, materialism, fundamentalism and romanticism. However, in our culture people are not going to believe on the whole merely because they hear; they will probably believe because they see and then have what they see explained in words they can understand. And this is nothing new— in John's Gospel a sceptical Nathaniel is told by Philip, who says he has found the Messiah ("Come and see"). Seeing and hearing have always been integral to coming to faith. In our culture most people are asking not whether it is true (much as we think they should ask this question), but whether it works; the demonstration of something in reality, with an explanation attached, will be for many the acid test of credibility. It is not of course that the gospel is anything other than truth, but that, like it or not, many people access truth by seeing and experiencing the reality of what is being said.

This being the case, the preaching of the cross and resurrection is essentially about how we can join this kingdom and be reconciled to the king, since where there is a response of faith the cross does away with the barrier of sin and the resurrection does away with the barrier of death. Nowhere is this better exhibited than in the dying penitent thief's conversation with Jesus. Through what must have been a moment of revelation, the thief recognises the kingship and kingdom of Jesus; he is aware, despite any normal reading of the situation, that the man dying in agony next to him is a king with a kingdom quite unlike any other on earth. So he says, "Jesus, remember me when you come into your kingdom" (Luke 23:42). Jesus replies, "I tell you the truth, today you will be with me in paradise" (Luke 23:43).

Here we have it all! The proclamation is made both by deed and by word. In this case, uniquely, there is a pagan declaration by Pilate of Jesus' kingship which is attached to Jesus' cross: "Jesus of Nazareth,

118

the King of the Jews." The redemptive death of Jesus occurs even as the thief spoke, procuring forgiveness of sins. The resurrection of Jesus which was still to happen would enable the thief's own resurrection to a life of paradise. And the repentance or complete re-orientation of the thief's life in his final moments was sufficient to enter the kingdom. Perhaps nowhere in the Gospels is there a more eloquent preaching of the gospel of the kingdom. It begins with the understanding of the existence of this kingdom and who is king, and then provides, through the death and resurrection of Jesus, admission to this eternal kingdom and reconciliation with the king. Here is the message of the kingdom to be preached or proclaimed to the whole world; a message which the disciples in turn were to preach to the world.

The proclamation of the kingdom by the apostles
It is clear from the Gospels that throughout his ministry Jesus was training the disciples for the future, a future when he would not be physically present with them but when they would be making known the kingdom of God by the Spirit themselves. He used a classic teaching model of first getting them to observe his own ministry, then getting them to do what they had observed in his presence, and finally doing it in his absence. Initially they watched Jesus making known the kingdom both through words and actions, but about midway through his three-year ministry he sent out the disciples, the twelve and the seventy-two, to follow his own example of ministry. Both Matthew and Luke record the missions of these groups. What is quite clear from the instructions given by Jesus is that they were, as they went, to preach the message, saying, "The kingdom of heaven is near." At the same time they were to, "Heal the sick, raise the dead, cleanse those who have leprosy, drive out demons." (See Matthew 10:6-8.) And the instruction to the seventy-two was, "When you enter a town and are welcomed, eat what is set before you. Heal the sick who are there and tell them, 'The kingdom of God is near you.'" (See Luke 10:8f.) Clearly, then, both through their proclamation and through healing and deliverance of others, the kingdom was being proclaimed.

The message to be made known was that men and women could experience now (and not wait for the end of time) the just and gentle rule of Jesus, and that, although for a time they must live in a corrupt and unjust world, they could nevertheless partially taste the reality of another government which was faithful, righteous and loving. (This is what the theologians call realised eschatology, a bringing forward into the present what ultimately and fully lies in the future.) One day this government would fill the earth. In the meantime, "...this gospel of the kingdom will be preached in the whole world as a testimony to all nations, and then the end will come." (See Matthew 24:14.) So the apostolic church together with all subsequent generations of Christians have been charged with proclaiming the kingdom, and this is exactly what the early church did after Pentecost. Peter, in his address to the crowd gathered by the outpouring of the Spirit at Pentecost, boldly proclaimed, "Therefore let all Israel be assured of this: God has made this Jesus, whom you crucified, both Lord and Christ." Here was a proclamation of the kingdom, though put in Greek or Roman terms as well as Jewish, that Jesus was both "Lord and Christ". Peter announces in effect that the resurrection has declared Jesus Lord, or King.

The proclamation of Jesus' authority and kingship remains a theme of the apostles' preaching, so that at the very end of Acts we find Paul speaking under guard to the Jews and we are told, "From morning till evening he explained and declared to them the kingdom of God and tried to convince them about Jesus from the Law of Moses and from the Prophets." And the very final words of Acts are the moving record that, "Boldly and without hindrance he [Paul] preached the kingdom of God and taught about the Lord Jesus Christ" (Acts 28:23, 31; see also Romans 15:18f). At the centre of the apostles' mission was the proclamation of the kingdom. By that and the accompanying signs, the kingdom was made known.

****

Before considering the role of preaching in the twenty-first century church and how we can expect it to make known the kingdom of God today, we will briefly consider an overview of the apostolic teaching in the epistles, and try and answer the question: Why is there so little directly taught about the kingdom of God in their writings? Any examination of the instances of the phrase "kingdom of God" in the apostles' teaching shows that whereas Jesus used the concept continually, the apostles did so only sparingly, and any glance at a concordance shows this to be the case. There may be two reasons for this.

Firstly, the idea of the kingdom was implicit in all that they taught about the lordship of Jesus, but their task in the epistles was different from Jesus' task in his own ministry. Jesus came to announce that in his arrival and presence all that Israel had longed for was fulfilled, the kingdom was among them, and that through his life, death and resurrection this kingdom was now open to all who repent and believe (as was wonderfully shown in the last moments of the penitent thief). Naturally Jesus spoke unceasingly about the coming of the kingdom. However, the concern of the apostles in their letters was to show how it was possible to enter this kingdom and what kind of lifestyle was expected of all those who were its citizens. So Paul, in his longest and most thoroughgoing explanation of the gospel, the Epistle to the Romans, in which he explains the new life into which Christians are born, and the purpose of God through the ages, encompassing both Jew and Gentile, only once uses the phrase "the kingdom of God". And his use there is one of instruction, providing a way of resolving a potential dispute about food in a community made up of Gentile and Jewish believers. In this context he writes, "For the kingdom of God is not a matter of eating and drinking, but of righteousness, peace and joy in the Holy Spirit...." (See Romans 14:17.) So the term kingdom of God, only used once in the epistle, is used to describe the way of life and attitudes that should prevail in the community where Christ rules. That the term does not explicitly occur anywhere else in Paul's most comprehensive statement of the Christian faith is because he is at pains to show how we can become righteous (through faith in God's promise in Christ, like the faith of Abraham), what God's grand plan for the human race is – including the Jews – and what effect justification by faith has on us —that is, we become a new creation, as he explains in chapters 5-8.

To summarise, because the epistles are either issue-based (especially for example the Corinthian correspondence) or written to explain to Jewish/Gentile communities that the gospel is all about Jesus and faith in him who justifies (puts us right with God now by his death and resurrection), there is little need for language about the kingdom. Therefore, the purpose of Jesus' preaching and the purpose of the epistles (in contrast with the purpose of Acts) are determinative of the frequency of the use of the term kingdom.

The second observation concerning the use of the term kingdom of God in the instruction given by the apostles in the epistles is that, by and large, the term is used of the future rather than the present. Although we will look at this vital aspect of the nature of the kingdom – that now it is here only in part but one day it will come in full – in the final section of this book, we must note here that although Jesus preached more about the presence of the kingdom whilst he was on earth, the apostles appear to talk more about the fulfilment of the kingdom at some point in the future. So Paul frequently warns about those forms of behaviour of which, "...those who live like this will not inherit the kingdom of God" (See Galatians 5:21; also 1 Corinthians 6:9; Ephesians 5:5). Or again, in speaking about the resurrection, Paul looks forward to a time of general resurrection when the kingdom will come. (1 Corinthians 15:24.) Or again, Paul uses the idea of kingdom as the final goal to which we are aspiring and going. As he says to the Thessalonians, "...you will be counted worthy of the kingdom of God, for which you are suffering" (2 Thessalonians 1:5b). Finally, for Peter, James and the writer to the Hebrews the emphasis is on the future inheritance of the kingdom. Peter encourages his readers to make their election sure, and they will receive a rich welcome into the eternal kingdom; James asks, "Has not God chosen those who are poor in the eyes of the world to be rich in faith and to inherit the kingdom he promised those who love him?" And the writer to the Hebrews puts a little emphasis on the present as well as the future, saying, "Therefore, since we are receiving a kingdom that cannot be shaken, let us be thankful, and so worship God acceptably with reverence and awe, for our 'God is a consuming fire.'" (See 2 Peter 1:11; James 2:5; Hebrews 12:28.) In these ways, the apostles, in their writings, given the background of persecution in the early church, are looking forward to the kingdom to come. John makes no mention of the kingdom in his epistles. But those glimpses of this future heavenly kingdom, which were given to him on the island of Patmos, we will look at later, when considering the future fulfilment of the kingdom.

In summary, we can say that it is possible the apostles used the concept of the kingdom more in their spoken teaching and preaching than in their written instruction. If the Acts of the Apostles is the yardstick to go by, then the kingdom of God was wrapped up in the proclamation of the lordship of Christ, as we saw in Peter's Pentecost sermon to the pilgrims in Jerusalem, or in Paul's address to the Athenians at the Areopagus. The reason for the relative absence of teaching about the kingdom in the epistles is due both to their function and their emphasis on encouraging Christians to endure hardship and persecution with their hope firmly set on the coming kingdom. In the epistles the emphasis appears to be of the kingdom being something we are to inherit, if we remain faithful, rather than something that is among us now.

As the writer to the Hebrews puts it so cogently at the start of his epistle, "In putting everything under him, God left nothing that is not subject to him. Yet at present we do not see everything subject to him." (See Hebrews 2:8.) It could not have been put better: the kingdom is real but it is not fully manifest; it has arrived, but it has not fully come. This is the message of the apostles, which they made known in their preaching and teaching, and it is a tension we shall explore further later.

If preaching – whether in the form of heralding the arrival of the kingdom or in the form of giving instruction to the church or to a half-listening and weary world – was so much part of the way in which Jesus and the apostles made known the reality of the kingdom to their contemporaries, how should we preach today, in a society so different and in a church which has largely lost confidence in its efficacy? This is what we must turn to next.

Preaching today

It is a long time since the fine marble pulpit with ornate plaster carvings, in the church where I am Rector, has been used for preaching —possibly 25 years ago, which is about a generation. All of the children, young people and students in our church would have never seen it used, and would now find it both eccentric and quaint if it were. They might ask: is his sermon so bad that he has to go six feet over our heads? I imagine the pulpit was going out of fashion or use in the 1970s, and was in many churches either finally consigned (along with other abandoned church furnishings) to the crypt, or just left unused, like other redundant church furniture, such as the font at the west door —because church culture has changed. A preacher is now, in our church, no longer six feet above contradiction, perhaps only about eight inches, as the lectern in our church is now placed in the centre of the nave on the chancel step. For some, the eight inches is too much and pushing the lectern forward they abandon any physical height difference between themselves and their audience, finding those inches either presumptuous or distancing. And the brass eagle from which the Scriptures used to be read likewise languishes in the crypt amongst the dead, never to fly again!

A survey of church furnishings and their past and present use in a church such as ours, which underwent "renewal" of various kinds in the 1980s, would chart a typical change in theology and style, in part a response to the wind of the Spirit, and in part a response to the fast-changing culture of post 1960, when "modernity" is said to have ended.

The fact is that our society has changed remarkably in the last forty years, almost out of recognition. Authority is no longer respected; it must be won, sometimes after a prolonged struggle. The government understandably wishes to turn back the clock and rightly restore "respect", but we have spent the last thirty years systematically pulling the rug from under those upon whom authority formerly rested. With the break up of faithful relationships, and with the material satisfaction of most of our physical needs, our emotional needs have soared to the top as our pressing concerns in the West. So there has been a corresponding rise in people's wish for intimacy, as Theodore Zeldin has explained in his work entitled *A History of Intimacy*. Into this atmosphere of suspicion towards authority, the felt need for intimacy, and societies filled with communication of all kinds, comes preaching. How should we preach in the world of today if this is one of the ways in which the kingdom of God will be made known?

A question which every preacher might ask is: to whom are you preaching, and with what purpose? The answer will vary probably both from occasion to occasion and from culture to culture. In my own setting my preaching is 90% to the faithful. Very few complete outsiders will be there on a Sunday, and on average I would preach to about 350 adults a Sunday. Occasionally at a special service, particularly at the major festivals or at a service of infant baptism, there will be more who are "not yet Christians". But for much of the time most of the people are the faithful; therefore preaching is mostly teaching or instruction for them. It is teaching about how to be the people of God in our community over the coming week. And for 99% of the time it is inside a building, to people who are seated, and is part of a well-trodden liturgy. In the new churches the liturgy is possibly different in form but nonetheless it is also basically the same from week to week. If this is a fair description of the context of preaching today, then the setting is markedly different from that in which Jesus preached. Yes, he did speak when invited in the synagogues in Nazareth, Capernaum and in Judea (Matthew 4:23) as part of Sabbath worship, but at other times Jesus' preaching was in the open, on the road, in reply to questions and around the dinner table. Perhaps, therefore, only some of his preaching was actual exposition of Old Testament Scripture, in the sense of a sustained piece of exegesis, although of course he often used it explicitly or implicitly. And indeed it would make an interesting study to see just how much of Jesus' preaching was in the synagogue or in the open air, or in reply to questions —either verbalised or only inwardly thought. I suspect that his preaching in formal religious settings was a minor percentage of his total preaching time! But, for most ministers, the sermon is a set piece of teaching, either ten minutes long (despised by some as too short) or for many, like myself, twenty to thirty minutes long, and for others longer, delivered every week in the set piece of a service in the safety of our church buildings. Therefore the setting for the preaching we are doing is substantially different from that in which Jesus operated.

So, in the culture in which we find ourselves how are we to preach so as to make known the kingdom of God? There are classic definitions of preaching, like that of Ian Stackhouse: "Preaching is just the elongation of the gospel that makes it, in its most primitive form, an act of grace commensurate with the event of grace itself."[3] In my view, there are three kinds of preaching in which the community of faith should be engaged. These forms are: instructive preaching, explanatory preaching and revelatory preaching. These three classifications arise from the more fundamental distinction drawn by C H Dodd between kerygma (proclamation of the good news) and didache (the action of teaching the church). However none of these is a watertight compartment, rather they are modes of preaching which spill over into each other and only have validity insofar as they are faithful to the word and delivered in the power of the Spirit.

Most of the preaching we do is in church buildings, to the faithful, or pilgrim people of God. It is therefore instructive, it gives instruction about the content of the faith and how we are to live in response to it. However there are also increasing numbers of alternative forms of worship and teaching.[4] The venues for these meetings are as various as schools, cafés, clubs, community centres and hotels. But I suspect their preaching is still 90% to the faithful. The formats for such meetings may be different in style and structure from the standard Sunday service, but in these too there are probably times of instruction or teaching, which may be a mixture of monologue and discussion. So, whether in traditional church buildings or in other kinds of venues, there is in most gatherings of the faithful, week by week, a time of instruction based on the word of God. The length, style and interactivity of the teaching may vary considerably, but nonetheless when such teaching is based on breaking open the Scriptures to both God's people and enquirers this remains preaching of the didactic, teaching kind. For the last four years I have undertaken a midweek course of instruction based on the Epistle to the Romans, which breaks into thirteen one-hour talks, but they are frequently interrupted by questions, which invariably provoke the most interesting exchanges. Much of Jesus' teaching was of this kind when speaking to the disciples (see Mark 4:34, and the Upper Room discourse in John 13-17). In this regard we may well need to get away from cultural models of preaching, in which a man stands in a pulpit wearing special clothes, delivering a homily of a certain length, to people who remain passive for most of the time. The passivity may be true of Northern Europe, but it is not true for those in Asia, South America and Africa, nor in Afro-American settings. The efficacy of the preaching does not lie in its length, nor in the manner in which it is delivered, nor in its being uninterrupted, but in the teaching's faithfulness to the word of God, the working of the Spirit through it, and the integrity of the speaker.

Nor should we have the idea that the apostles' teaching was only a monologue. Tomlin argues that when Paul was speaking until midnight at Troas, this did not signify that he was talking for hours without being interrupted. Luke, the author of Acts, employs two words here. One is *dialegomai*, which can be translated "discuss", from which we get our word "dialogue". It is suggested that Paul was not talking *at* them but *with* them, discussing and answering questions and expecting interaction. He was of course following Jesus' rabbinic method. How much of his teaching is in fact the answering of questions?[5] So the first type of preaching is instruction.

The second kind of preaching, which is differentiated more by the content than the manner alone, is explanation of the gospel and the events in history on which it is based. The *kerygma* is the technical name for the events which form the basis of the gospel. These events are the incarnation, death and resurrection of Jesus, who is the redeemer king. It is interesting to note that, in the UK at any rate, whereas this used to be done either at a large rally or a meeting led by an evangelist, that setting now appears to be mostly (although not exclusively) a thing of the past. It may return, but it seems that, rightly or wrongly, there are not as many such occasions of such mass evangelism in Northern Europe.

In other continents this happens much more often. I well remember returning from Nigeria on one occasion when a Reinhard Bonnke mission was finishing, and meeting many of his co-workers at Lagos Airport. There were over a million people present at his meetings outside Lagos. The last time crowds of such size gathered in the UK was during a papal visit. Having been involved in arranging some large meetings supported by many churches (in London in 1980 for David Watson at the Albert Hall, and for J John in Bath in 2000), I know both the excitement and the difficulties in organising such large events. However, such occasions now seem to be going against the cultural grain, where small is beautiful and conversation is preferred to confrontation. That is not to say that in making known the gospel there is not still an implicit challenge to our modern lifestyle and a call to repentance, even if the style is different, but that people in our culture today often need plenty of time, both to have the gospel explained and questions answered, and to see the gospel in operation in the lives of those who together explain it.

In our own church we have run numerous *Alpha*, post *Alpha* (of a homemade variety using studies like *Meetings with Jesus*) and *Emmaus* courses. Undoubtedly, the formula of hospitality, talk and discussion is a brilliant one for today. It is one for our times, as people long to belong to a welcoming and loving community. Indeed, the material could well be spread over a year if true discipleship is to result, rather than a single term. The purpose of such courses is to welcome and engage with people with whom the gospel can be both shared and explained. Explanation is essential if false conceptions are to be changed and proper understanding to be given.

Whatever way the material of the gospel is presented, what is quite clear is that there needs to be plenty of explanation, plenty of prayer, and plenty of ongoing love for those who are wrestling with the issues. In our courses we have people who come, and a year later they may still be struggling with the issues; but they still come because they like the group. (And they like the food!) This ongoing explanation in the context of food is also a kind of preaching. After all, how many parables and other pieces of teaching were given when Jesus was reclining with all kinds of guests in all kinds of homes, or in private conversation with people like Nicodemus or the woman at the well, or in dispute with the Jews. (See Luke 14:1-14; 14:15-23; John 3; John 4 and 5:16-47.) And what was he doing if not explaining the kingdom, making people aware of it, and inviting people to come under his just and gentle rule? Once again we may need to change our models of preaching, formed as they are mainly in the context of church buildings and in the style of an uninterrupted monologue. But if we were to look through Jesus' teaching or preaching in the Gospels, most of it was in situations other than the formal occasion of a synagogue service, although he spoke there too.

The final facet of preaching to mention here is its revelatory nature. In fact all true preaching should be revelatory in nature, but sometimes there may be a particular edge to this. Quite simply, this is when preaching personally addresses an individual so that he or she knows and feels that they are being individually and inescapably addressed by the content of the message. We have probably heard the thought expressed: "It felt like the entire sermon was just for me." It is as though God himself is personally and directly addressing you. This, of course, is the action of the Spirit, without whose work and help preaching is fruitless. It is quite clear that in the ministry of Jesus he made great use of revelatory gifts in conversations with individuals, putting his finger lovingly on their failings —as with the woman at the well or the rich young ruler (John 4:16-19 and Matthew 19:16-22), and knowing the thoughts of his opponents' hearts reflected in their malevolent questions (Matthew 22:18), and seeing the potential of individuals when they did not realise it themselves, as with Peter and Nathanael (John 1:41; John 1:47-51) and as in his teaching or preaching (see Matthew 21:33-46). Jesus' preaching and teaching was often pointed, having within it the ability both to reveal truth to people about themselves, and to show the nature of God himself.

Since, as Calvin said, all true religion promotes a right understanding of ourselves and of God, it is not surprising that Jesus' preaching or teaching, in whatever form it came, whether in the synagogue, on the hillside, by the Sea of Galilee or in someone's house, revealed both the hearts of his listeners and the will of his Father.

Today, when it comes to preaching, we need to do a number of things. We need to take it out of the set-piece mentality in which we have frozen it. Jesus' teaching was so diverse in content, style and setting. Can we get preaching out of the church again, so that the crowds really do hear? We also need to recover confidence in the proclamation of the good news. Dr William Abraham has suggested that we need to move from the method of proclaiming the gospel in a way which is so common in much of the Protestant world: a three-part sermon read out by the preacher. The place of proclamation, anyway, is not so much in the church as in the outside world. Moreover, the message should be in terms that people of the particular culture can understand.[6] Often we hear it said that we need to recover confidence in preaching. That may be so, but more fundamentally we need to recover confidence in the good news itself. After all, preaching or proclamation is a God-appointed way of making known the news and revealing the kingdom.

If instruction, explanation and revelation interwove to form Jesus' own unique blend of preaching, then it is well to remember that his expression of the kingdom was far from word alone, but it was continuously punctuated by works of power, a demand for justice, the offer of forgiveness, and the invitation to join a new community. We must turn to the first of these, Jesus' actions of both love and judgement, which illustrated the kingdom— both what it promised and what it brought.

Chapter Nine

A KINGDOM OF POWER

In St John's Gospel they are called signs. They vary in scope and include such diverse miracles as turning water into wine, multiplying loaves and fishes, walking on water, calming storms, healing large numbers of people and freeing others who were oppressed by the devil. As Peter said later in the house of Cornelius, the first Gentile convert, in a marvellous summary of Jesus' ministry: "You know what has happened throughout Judea, beginning in Galilee after the baptism that John preached —how God anointed Jesus of Nazareth with the Holy Spirit and power, and how he went around doing good and healing all who were under the power of the devil, because God was with him" (Acts 10:37f). These miracles were largely signs of the coming kingdom, illustrations of what Jesus talked about, windows into another reality, another rule, which was coming and one day would fill the earth. The miracles of Jesus were both a testimony to who Jesus was, especially in John's Gospel (see John 20:31) and a picture of what this kingdom would be like (see John 14:11).

The question which we must face here is whether such miracles have ceased since the end of Jesus' ministry. Is the time for such illustrations on earth – of what this kingdom is like – over? Or can we still expect that God will grant glimpses of his kingdom, in the way he chooses, in the here and now?

Eldon Ladd, in his helpful book, *The Presence of the Future*, written over thirty years ago now, made this his central thesis, pointing out the way in which the kingdom of God was powerfully at work among people —in Jesus himself, and in what he did.[1] The kingdom of God, which will become evident at the end of time, has been brought forward into human history in the person of Jesus and in his continuing ministry through the Spirit in the world. Through his miracles, and especially through those that brought wholeness to human living, he displayed what this kingdom is like —that is, what this rule of God amounted to.

Did this glimpse of another coming realm cease with the physical removal of Jesus from earth at his ascension? Or are we to expect or hope for such miracles now so that further glimpses of the kingdom may be afforded to people today? Perhaps it is John who gives the answer to this by recalling Jesus' words, "I tell you the truth, anyone who has faith in me will do what I have been doing. He will do even greater things than these, because I am going to the Father" (John 14:12). What were the greater things which his followers would do, that Jesus talks of here?

There have been some biblical teachers who have contended, quite erroneously in my view, that such miracles were part of a dispensation of God's grace which lasted only as long as the apostles, and that therefore any miracles subsequently have been counterfeit. (This so-called Dispensationalism was promulgated by Darby and Scofield in the nineteenth century, passed into parts of the Keswick movement and later standardised in Scofield's Bible, which has sold two million copies and has been influential in fundamentalist circles in the US). Dispensationalists contend that the miraculous died out with the apostles, and some gifts of the Spirit died out too. However, it is plain from Paul's writings that there has really only ever been one overarching way of salvation which is promised to those who have faith in God's promise, although it is fair to say that it is divided into two stages which are before the coming of Jesus and the Spirit, and afterwards. As John writes in his prologue to his Gospel, "For the law was given through Moses; grace and truth came through Jesus Christ" (John 1:17). Paul makes this especially clear in his great statement of the gospel which is his Epistle to the Romans, where he shows that there has only ever been one way in which humankind has become acceptable or put right with God, and that is through faith in his promise —one unifying arrangement whereby humans can be put right with God: he promises, we believe, and the result is our acceptance or justification. Nowhere is this more plainly expressed than in Romans chapter four, when Paul says, quoting the Old Testament, that, "Abraham believed God, and it was credited to him as righteousness." He goes on to say, "The words 'it was credited to him' were written not for him alone, but also for us, to whom God will credit righteousness – for us who believe in him who raised Jesus our Lord from the dead" (Romans 4:3b, 22-24).

So there is one overarching way of salvation for Jew and Gentile which was fulfilled and made possible through the faithful Israelite, Jesus, accompanied by the life-changing and kingdom-making-known power of the Spirit. There is no dividing up by Paul of salvation history into different dispensations. There is one single way of salvation, first given and announced to Abraham, later fulfilled by the coming of Jesus and the Spirit. The only obvious division in God's plan is before Jesus and after Jesus.

And what Jesus began in his ministry, especially teaching or preaching, healing and deliverance, he commanded his disciples to continue —that is, both the apostles and a wider group called the seventy-two. And if the mandate to preach continues, why should not the works of power that demonstrate the kingdom continue too? What biblical grounds can there be for the continuing of one part of Jesus' demonstration of the kingdom, preaching, and the discontinuance of another expression of the kingdom, namely the ministry of healing and deliverance which the disciples were trained to expect? There seems to be no biblical warrant for saying that such works of power have discontinued. However, they are works of which it must be said that the primary intention is to exalt Christ and demonstrate his kingdom.

We will look now at Jesus' commission to these groups of disciples in relation to their commission to heal and deliver. Some way into his ministry, Jesus trained his disciples to do what they had seen him do. Matthew, in that marvellous summary of Jesus' ministry, says, "Jesus went throughout Galilee, teaching in their synagogues, preaching the good news of the kingdom, and healing every disease and sickness among the people. News about him spread all over Syria, and people brought to him all who were ill with various diseases, those suffering severe pain, the demon-possessed, those having seizures, and the paralysed, and he healed them" (Matthew 4:23-24). Here indeed was a breaking in of the kingdom of God in the here and now, a wonder-filled illustration of the presence of the future which would come in totality, as John later glimpsed in the great revelation he received on Patmos.

The context of the miracles performed by Jesus was twofold: on the one hand they were signs of who he was, his divinity, majesty and glory, and on the other hand they were also signs of the kingdom which he was ushering in. It is important to understand that the miracles of healing and deliverance which Jesus did were illustrations of the kingdom, and that they still remain so today. They are not ours by right, but they are examples of the "presence of the future", that is examples in the here and now of what God has ultimately promised, which is a time in which, "There will be no more death or mourning or crying or pain" (Revelation 21:4). The illustrative nature of these miracles of healing and deliverance was made clear by Jesus in the instructions he gave to both the disciples and to the seventy-two. To the disciples Jesus said, "As you go, preach this message: 'The kingdom of heaven is near.' Heal the sick, raise the dead, cleanse those who have leprosy, drive out demons. Freely you have received, freely give" (Matthew 10:7f). Later, to the seventy-two, Jesus said, "When you enter a town and are welcomed, eat what is set before you. Heal the sick who are there and tell them, 'The kingdom of God is near you'" (Luke 10:8f). On both occasions, the miracles of healing and deliverance were part of their mission, and the occurrence of them was illustrative of the kingdom of God being both near and present. The *word* was needed to explain their real significance, but the *deed* drew attention to the *word*. At the very end of his ministry Jesus commissioned his disciples to continue this ministry of deed and word, with no suggestion that he had changed the style of this mission, based as it was on this combination from the outset. (See Luke 4:16-19.) So Jesus said, "Therefore go and make disciples of all nations, baptising them in the name of the Father and of the Son and of the Holy Spirit, and teaching them to obey everything I have commanded you..." (Matthew 28:19f). Since Jesus had commanded both the apostles and the seventy-two to heal the sick and pronounce the presence of the kingdom, then presumably this was an instruction to be both passed on and acted upon in all future generations of mission. As with so many other things, what God has joined together – word and deed – let not man divide! Nor must our poor practice of healing and deliverance (and there is much of that around) create grounds for a "divorce" which was never originally intended.

It must be acknowledged that there have been ways of ministering healing which have been of themselves damaging, creating more problems than they solve. I well remember over twenty years ago meeting, as an impressionable and enthusiastic clergyman, a forceful Australian healer who was then working in London. His line was simply that sickness was caused by sin, and if people repented of their sins then they would be healed. It was appealing at one level, based on a half-truth, but it was also damaging. While it is true that sickness and disease entered the world because of our human ancestors' (Adam and Eve's) rebellion against God's gracious rule, it is not true that sickness is necessarily directly caused by particular sins. This is much of the point of the story of Job, whose illness and misfortune was not caused by sin, for it says at the outset that Job was, "...blameless and upright; he feared God and shunned evil." His misfortune was a great trial, but it was not the result of any sin he had committed, so his comforters were mistaken when they pressed confession on him as a cure. Likewise, the disciples learnt from Jesus that when they met the "man blind from birth" (see John 9) they were wrong to suppose that either he or his parents had sinned, so causing his condition. For, as Jesus pointed out, "Neither this man nor his parents sinned ... but this happened so that the work of God might be displayed in his life." If disease is not always caused by sin, repentance is not a fail-safe way out. To maintain such a line wrongfully could only plunge the patient into further depression or despair.

The other distortion of truth in relation to healing prayer is to say that a person is not healed because of their lack of faith. Once again there is a half-truth in the assertion that faith is essential to healing. Frequently Jesus said things like, "Your faith has made you whole" and, conversely, he said that he was not able to do any miracle in his home town of Nazareth because of their lack of faith. It is true that Jesus often rewarded faith with healing, but equally there are some instances where there was no faith and still he healed. The fact is that, as always, Jesus did not respond to people's needs with a formula, but with a response which was tailored to their own particular spiritual journey. Often, I have met extremely faith-full Christians who have not as yet received the healing that they long for. They are a witness in their sufferings, they are an example still of extraordinary trust in God in the most difficult of circumstances, they are signs of God's grace, and they have not given up hoping for and longing for healing.

But to suggest that they are not faith-full would be a travesty of the truth and only damage their trust.

As John Woolmer observed in his extremely helpful book on healing and deliverance, there are only three responses to the issue of prayer for healing: the first is to deny its efficacy altogether; the second is to say that people are not healed because either they are deficient in faith or are holding on to sin (bearing in mind that there is no such thing as a perfect Christian, anywhere on earth!) and the third is to say that any healing is a gracious but mysterious example of the kingdom, breaking into the present reality as a glimpse of that reality to come.[1] He says that we can accept that there is mystery, and we should see healing as a "sign" of God's gracious activity in our world, rather than as our "right".

The acceptance of mystery, in the sense of not being able to explain or understand God's will completely, has good biblical foundation. In a well-known part of Isaiah's prophecy, God says through his prophet,

> "For my thoughts are not your thoughts,
>   neither are your ways my ways," declares the LORD.
> "As the heavens are higher than the earth,
>   so are my ways higher than your ways
>   and my thoughts than your thoughts."
>
> *Isaiah 55:8f*

It has been said that our development as Christians can be like our development through childhood to adulthood. At first, like the small child, we may have a very black and white picture of life, with a great deal of certainty, then in the teenage years and maybe early twenties we are full of questions (although sometimes afraid to look at them in case they change our firmly held world-view), and finally we have to accept the idea of mystery in which there are many unanswered questions, such as a seemingly random response to our prayers and a seemingly unfair treatment of us.

Facing up to these issues, St Teresa of Avila once said, having being thrown to the ground by her donkey whilst on pilgrimage, "If this is how God treats his friends, no wonder he has so few of them!" She could not understand why she should be the victim of an accident in pursuit of holiness! Equally we can point to all kinds of seeming inconsistencies, like the sudden cure of a relatively unknown child, whilst one of his active servants is taken away in the prime of life by cancer. (The case has often been cited of David Watson, a very well known evangelist and teacher of the 1970s, who died from liver cancer in 1984, in his early fifties.)

Answers to prayer for healing seem so uneven. I can remember praying with little faith or expectation at a lunchtime healing service for a woman whom I had not met before. She was unwell and addicted to at least forty cigarettes a day but she left the service changed and never smoked again. Or I can remember praying in a hospital ward for a pregnant mother whose unborn child had stopped growing. After the prayer, the child resumed normal growth and was born perfectly healthy.

Contrastingly, at the same time I went to pray in the Cromwell Hospital, West London, for a young man who was the Southern African military attaché. His wife was with us in the ward but there was no change in his physical condition. He later died from cancer. Why is the result of our prayer so uneven? The answer is that prayer and God's will remain a mystery —and if we think we know why one prayer is answered in the way we hope for and another is not, then maybe we are imagining that we do not need that reassurance in Isaiah 55 that God's ways are not our ways! If we were in charge of the world then everyone would get healed, but equally if we were in charge we would have never thought to create the Leviathan of the deep or, for that matter, create the way the world is! (See Job 41:1.) In other words, we would remove that sense of mystery which is the very stuff of our existence. And as God said to Job, after 38 chapters of silence, "Who is this that darkens my counsel with words without knowledge?" (Job 38:1) and proceeds to show Job that we know only an infinitesimal part of the whole. It might fairly be said that mystery is another word for ignorance. As Paul said, speaking of love, "Now we see but a poor reflection as in a mirror; then we shall see face to face. Now I know in part; then I shall know fully, even as I am fully known" (1 Corinthians 13:12). We must all admit, whoever we are, however "used of God" we may be, that in the end we all only know in part, and to think otherwise is foolish.

There is a pattern to the healing ministry of Jesus, but there is not a formula. All too often we are interested in formulae, the "how" to achieve results, but it seems that Jesus dealt with each one uniquely, individually and without preconception. The pattern of his healing ministry was that it proceeded from compassion for individuals or crowds (Matthew 14:13-14; Luke 9:11). He looked for faith in family, friends or the sick person himself. (But not always —see Mark 2:2ff.) He was aware that in healing he was facing down the powers of darkness. His healings were signs of the presence of the kingdom; he was affected by the atmosphere around him (Mark 6:1-5; Matthew 13:53-58). The miracles fulfilled his Father's will (John 5:19-20). Finally they brought him into conflict with the authorities and the powers that lay behind them. We must now see how Jesus confronted these powers and demonstrated the kingdom by delivering captives from the dominion of darkness and bringing them into the kingdom. (Colossians 1:13.)

Deliverance

There can be no doubt that Jesus saw himself in confrontation with Satan in his ministry. In a telling short parable, Jesus said, "When a strong man, fully armed, guards his own house, his possessions are safe. But when someone stronger attacks and overpowers him, he takes away the armour in which the man trusted and divides up the spoils" (Luke 11:21f and Matthew 12:29). Jesus was the "stronger" who had come to dispossess the wrongful occupier, who had usurped God's creation. The individual deliverances were further manifestations of the rule of God or his kingdom, as Jesus made so clear. He says, "But if I drive out demons by the Spirit of God, then the kingdom of God has come upon you" (Matthew 12:28; see also Luke 11:20). So the power encounters with Satan by the superior force of Jesus led to individuals being re-possessed by God, provided that, having been delivered from the occupying forces of Satan, the latter were replaced by the sanctifying presence of the Spirit of God. (See Luke 11:24-26.) If people were not subsequently filled by the presence of the Spirit, then they were vulnerable to re-occupation by the very forces of evil from which they had been delivered. Jesus' ministry was therefore summarised by Luke with this wonderful description, "He welcomed them and spoke to them about the kingdom of God, and healed those who needed healing" (Luke 9:11b). And for healing we can include deliverance. This echoes the summary which Matthew gives us of Jesus' ministry (See Matthew 4:24) and the words which Peter spoke in the home of Cornelius, recorded by Luke. (See Acts

10:38.) Both healing and deliverance were clear signs of the presence of the kingdom breaking into the here and now.

As Tom Wright argues in *Jesus and the Victory of God*, "Thus the exorcisms, in particular, are not simply the release from strange bondage of a few poor benighted souls. (Nor are they all to be explained away with a rationalistic reductionism.) For Jesus and the evangelists, they signalled something far deeper that was going on, neither, namely, the real battle of ministry... nor a round of fierce debates with the keepers of orthodoxy, but head-on war with Satan. The belief made perfect sense within the first-century Jewish world-view that Jesus shared.... He (Jesus) seems to see himself as fighting a battle with the real enemy, and to have regarded the exorcisms – or healings of those whose condition was attributed to the work of Satan – as a sign that he was winning the battle though it had not yet reached its height."[3] The ministry which Jesus himself exercised was also one which he conferred firstly on the apostles, then to the seventy-two, and finally to the people of God in all generations of this present age. And this is what we must trace now.

Mark recalls the mission of the apostles in these words, "They went out and preached that people should repent. They drove out many demons and anointed many sick people with oil and healed them" (Mark 6:12f). Mark thus records in a more concise form what both Matthew and Luke also tell us, that the ministry of the first disciples, and later the seventy-two, included instructions both to heal the sick and drive out demons. As we saw earlier, Jesus commissioned the disciples to, "Heal the sick, raise the dead, cleanse those who have leprosy, drive out demons" (Matthew 10:8). Although there is no specific command from Jesus to the seventy-two to drive out demons, it is obvious from the results of their mission that that is precisely what they did. When they returned from their mission, they rejoiced and reported that, "Even the demons submit to us in your name." Whereupon Jesus said that he saw, "Satan fall like lightning from heaven" (Luke 10:17f), but he gently corrected them, so that they would rejoice not in what we might call the spiritual fireworks of exorcism but in the greater miracle that their names were written in heaven!

So it is clear that the ministry which Jesus himself performed he passed on to his disciples: both the smaller group of disciples and the wider group of the seventy-two. The first disciples were commanded to pass on to subsequent disciples the same missionary directives—preaching, healing and driving out demons. (See Matthew 28:18.) They did so, and records from the fourth century demonstrate that the ministry continued in the generations which followed. Irenaeus, the Bishop of Lyons and great systematiser of Christian doctrine, wrote, "Those who are in truth Christ's disciples, receiving the grace from him, do in his name perform miracles.... Some do really and truly cast out demons with the result that those who have been cleansed from evil spirits frequently believe in Christ and join themselves to the church. Others still heal the sick by laying their hands upon them, and they are made whole. It is not possible to name the number of the gifts which the church throughout the world has received from God, in the name of Jesus Christ who was crucified under Pontius Pilate, and which she exercises day by day for the benefit of the gentiles."[4] Others of the early fathers record the incidence of deliverance or exorcism in the early centuries of the church, for instance: Tertullian, Clement of Alexandria, Origen, Tatian, Cyprian and Hippolytus, to name but a few.[5]

The ministry continued in the church through its early years, and it is in the record of its spread throughout Northern Europe (see Bede's *Ecclesiastical History*), and it is evident in the Middle Ages. However, it was the intermingling of healing and deliverance with shrines, pilgrimages and relics that got these ministries a bad name as far as the Reformers were concerned. Since their task was the rehabilitation of the teaching of grace and its reception by faith alone, and their business was to distance the new protestant church from the false practices of the old, little attention was paid to the ministries of healing and deliverance at the time of the Reformation, since many had fallen into disrepute or were the outworking of mere superstition. But with the birth of the nineteenth century missionary movement, together with the start of the Pentecostal church, both healing and deliverance were once again claimed as part of the ongoing ministry of Jesus in the world today. And now, in a world which is reverting increasingly to pagan practices, magic arts, witchcraft and the occult, it is a ministry which is bound to be part of the armoury of the church. So to argue, as some have done, that healing and deliverance ministries died out with the apostolic church, seems biblically unwarranted, historically invalid and missiologically unsighted. Jesus commanded his own disciples to teach these things to those who were subsequently to believe. However, that is not to say that the practice of both these ministries has not at times been fraught with either abuse or false practice; but then, which practice of the church, through the ages, has not been sadly distorted or abused? At the time of writing, cases of child abuse under the guise of exorcism of supposedly demonised young children from Africa are hitting the headlines of the press. Equally, church leaders seeking to boost their own standing have persuaded members of their churches of miracles they have not genuinely seen. They have manipulated poor, desperate and vulnerable people. As is often said, the cure of abuse is not no use, but right use.

Precisely because both healing and deliverance affect people where they are extremely vulnerable, and often out of desperation credulous, these ministries need to be especially carefully offered. Trained, properly appointed people, gifted and skilled in these areas of ministry should be used, and at all times both ministries need to be exercised in an atmosphere of real love and dignity.

In conclusion, Jesus manifested his kingdom both through the miracles of healing he performed and by other kinds of miracles —and by relieving all those who were oppressed by the devil. In this way, Jesus demonstrated in the "here and now" that his kingdom was a place where there would be no more crying, pain and death, and that it was a place where the devil himself would be cast down. It was a kingdom or rule that was coming, and was breaking into the present through the ministry of Jesus himself or through his disciples. Jesus commissioned his disciples to continue this ministry with faith, power and love. Today we cannot guarantee that in every case the full extent of his kingdom would be shown, but we should maintain that, in the mystery that is God's will, believing prayer makes one or other aspect of the kingdom more manifest. So Jesus demonstrated the presence of the kingdom by healing, deliverance and other miracles of provision and care. He also heralded a coming kingdom which was full of justice.

Chapter Ten

A KINGDOM OF JUSTICE

There can be no doubt that justice lies at the centre of the kingdom. The rule that God as the king brings is just, gentle and true. Again and again in the Old Testament, the coming of the rule of God is seen as bringing with it righteousness and peace. The kingdom rule of God (*malkuth*) ushers in a coming righteousness or justice. The psalmist often recalls this:

> The King is mighty, he loves justice—
> you have established equity;
> in Jacob you have done
> what is just and right
>
> *Psalm 99:4*

> Righteousness and justice are the foundation of your throne;
> love and faithfulness go before
>
> *Psalm 89:14*

Here are the twin pillars of God's rule: justice and faithful (or covenant-keeping) love. So the kingdom will be made known not only through proclamation and preaching, healing and deliverance but also through the bringing of justice to the lives of the poor, oppressed and downtrodden of the world. Jesus said as much when he inaugurated his ministry at the synagogue in Nazareth when he read from the prophet Isaiah:

"The Spirit of the Lord is on me,
because he has anointed me
to preach good news to the poor.
He sent me to proclaim freedom for the prisoners
and recovery of sight for the blind,
to release the oppressed,
to proclaim the year of the Lord's favour."

Luke 4:18, quoting Isaiah 61:1f

His ministry included not only an announcement of the gospel but also the bringing of both justice and mercy.

Justice is a word that is on everyone's lips, and not surprisingly because the most glaring challenge to the world today is the discrepancy between the surfeit of the industrialised North and the poverty of the global South. Indeed the biggest paradox of our times is the material prosperity and spiritual poverty of the global North and the spiritual richness and material poverty of the global South. Sir Bob Geldof has rightly said that it is time for us no longer to accept children dying on our television screens and for us together to make poverty history. However, the gap between passing agreements at high-level summits and delivering real change on the ground is enormous. It is a gap which will require considerable time to bridge, a determination to stamp out corrupt government, forgive debt and initiate fair trade.

As I write this chapter in the summer of 2005, there is intense interest in the forthcoming G8 summit and what it may achieve both for the world's poor and for the planet itself. The planet does not look as if it is going to come off very well, since there is still unwillingness on the part of the White House to agree to the science of global warming. And any agreement on the science of global warming would contain a radical challenge to the most carbon fuel dependent economy in the world. But, hearteningly, there appears to be agreement on cancellation of debt for the world's poorest countries, which are nearly all found on the African continent. This is a signal victory for the Jubilee campaign which has gathered momentum in the last five years. The cancellation of debt must be met with a corresponding movement to good and just governance in these countries. What is clear is that issues of justice are, as ever, at the top of the agenda, and that Christians must show themselves committed to bringing in justice wherever they can, as part of their proclamation of the lordship of Christ and as part of the healing they seek to bring to those who are oppressed. We have no right to separate out what was united in the ministry of Jesus. But before looking at the way Jesus made justice a key theme of the kingdom he had come to bring, we shall look at the way in which Christians have or have not made justice part of their proclamation of the kingdom.

Christians were traditionally often categorised as liberal, evangelical or catholic, and this inadequate and largely outdated categorisation was seen as being, in part, a definition of Christians in their relation to the kingdom of God as well as to Scripture. It used to be said (and these were recognized as having been caricatures) that the liberal proclaimed a kingdom without a king; the pietist, or evangelical, a king without a kingdom; and the catholic proclaimed the church as the kingdom. Although those were never more than half-truths, and in the last thirty years there has also been a real shift in all traditions in relation to the kingdom of God, such descriptions signalled something of the tendencies, weaknesses and strengths of the various positions. The liberal, while maybe speaking of the reality of the kingdom, its values and principles, could be tempted to neglect the need for individual reconciliation to the king through repentance and faith. The pietist, who might very well be the evangelical, was seen as so concerned with individual personal salvation and personal holiness that he had very little vision for the outworking of the kingdom of God on earth. The churchly person, who might be a catholic, believes that a properly functioning sacramental church and priesthood will hasten the kingdom. The division into those old categories or "streams", superficial and inadequate as it always was in truth, lies mostly in the past, although there are some vestiges of each tendency still discernible within the life of some churches. The second half of the twentieth century saw a real shift in the previous stance of each part of the church with regard to issues of social justice. The reason for this change may be found in the church's reaction to the great world movements of the late twentieth century, namely communism, right wing dictatorships, globalisation and poverty.

The history of the twentieth century demonstrated that the church could never retreat to a merely individualistic preaching of the kingdom, nor neglect, through either pietistic withdrawal or churchly self-absorption, the society in which it is placed. The German Lutheran church as well as the Catholic Church came to rue the day when it vacated the moral ground to the Nazi party, with only a few exceptions. The Orthodox Church in Russia was caricatured by the story that leaders of the church were discussing how many fingers should be lifted in an orthodox blessing in the house next to where the Russian revolution was being planned. The Anglican Church, in England, for the early part of the twentieth century, was described as the Conservative party at prayer. But as the century wore on, neglect of issues of justice by the church in society were to be abandoned, especially in those regions of the world where there was an extremely sharp division between the dispossessed poor and a dictatorial, brutal, authoritarian regime. This was especially focussed in both South America and South Africa. In South America, in San Salvador, Archbishop Oscar Romero in the 1970s championed the cause of the repressed against the Sandanista government, which eventually led to his martyrdom. Now the new black Archbishop of York, John Sentamu, wears a cross that reminds him and others of Romero's martyrdom and the sacrifice he made. In the 1960s, John Stott drew Anglican evangelicalism in from its own self-absorption to engage with the social issues of the day, writing and preaching extensively on the need for engagement with issues of social justice. This process began at Keele and has gathered pace ever since.[1] Today a young Christian (by which I mean one under the age of forty) will easily move from praying for the deliverance of a friend oppressed by the devil, and turn in the next breath to proclaim the need for fair trade! The old partitions are coming down as we realise that the kingdom of God is as much about proclaiming the message as it is about healing the afflicted, and as it is about social justice in a deeply divided world. Again, what God has joined together in his kingdom, let not man divide!

However, there is still reluctance on the part of governments, which often include professing Christians, to follow through the themes of justice regardless of the impact on national security or economic strength. We all can be curiously partially sighted when it comes to implementing policies of justice across the board. There are a number of notable examples. Following the unprovoked attack on America on 9/11, national security became the most important political issue in the United States, understandably. It was the worst aggressive act on a state since the Second World War. It was less well signalled than the attack on Pearl Harbour around sixty years previously. Understandably, it led to legitimate reprisals against the Taliban regime in Afghanistan, which could be defended on the principles of self defence and recourse to the "sword of the state" which St. Paul expounds in Romans 13:1-7. However, the resulting detention of prisoners without trial for an indefinite period in harsh surroundings in Guantanamo Bay in Cuba may or may not be in the interests of national security (for a balance has to be struck between such an action being a recruiting sergeant for further terrorists and the possibility that such a detention either removes or intimidates other potential terrorists), but it certainly is not in the interests of justice. Justice, the right to fair treatment before the law, which is itself enshrined in the US constitution, is part of its national history and requires that all accused should receive a fair trial. The reason for the detention centre being in Cuba is because such detention would itself be unlawful in the United States. However the irony is all the greater because the United States will not trade with the regime, Fidel Castro's Cuba, from whom it leases the land for its internment centre because of its unjust rule. So here is an illustration of a country not following the cause of justice because a more overriding interest of national security demands it; and similar arguments apply with regard to the use of torture in relation to national defence. And yet it is for the self same cause of justice, admittedly on a larger scale, that the same government toppled a patently unjust regime in Iraq. Nor is national security itself a defence for detentions without trial in time of peace; indeed, other regimes in the past have been culpable for such actions and have faced the opprobrium of the international community. We cannot argue that when an individual threatens our national security we can rightly detain without trial, but when another country, with whose methods we disagree, says its national security is threatened then such detention is a violation of human rights. The law must be the same for all —that is justice.

The essential question for governments in relation to issues of social or personal justice is this: in whose interests are they to govern when they are reliant on a democratic mandate? Naturally they are accountable to their own electorate, but we are now moving to the situation in our global village where governments must govern not only in the interests of their own electorate but also in the interests of those countries which are deeply affected by their policies. To fail to notice the repercussions of the policies pursued by the global North is not only deeply damaging to the well-being of other countries but is also very short-sighted in our increasingly interdependent world. This issue faces many governments in relation to trade. In both Europe and the United States, large subsidies are given to farmers whose products are unwanted at home and are therefore dumped on world markets, so destroying the markets for other more vulnerable and impoverished countries. Whilst the principle of social justice would be accepted by many, however, its application by way of actual policies is often hotly debated. Many would say it is high time that governments and trade blocs, like the EU, moved away, over time, from policies of endless subsidy, so that there is a fair market for goods and services across the globe. Others would point to the negative effects of the globalisation of trade, such as the cost to the environment of moving produce vast distances by air, and the suggestion that it is really more beneficial for regions to be producing their own food crops. Does it make sense (and is it "just") for "global free trade" to mean that the system is structured so that people in an African developing country are economically encouraged to produce, for example, cut flowers (for UK supermarkets) in pesticide-laden plantations, when what may really be needed is the development of policies to encourage the growing of food crops for local consumption? Appropriate reform of trade, alongside the relief of debt and the promotion of good governance, is seen as the biggest need if poverty is truly to be consigned to the pages of history.

Whilst the biblical precepts of love for others and concern for advancing the welfare of the needy are perfectly clear, we have to work out what this means in practical application in a world that has vastly more complex international structures than obtained in the ancient world, and this is not always easy, given the complex effects and unintended consequences of political policies.

The advancement of justice requires a combination of campaigning for and implementing policies of social justice, but it is also about maintaining standards of integrity and righteousness in personal living. Once again, it is not a question of solely being interested in personal sexual ethics and turning a blind eye to environmental issues or the handling of wealth, as has been sometime true of "the moral majority", nor is it being solely focussed on fair trade or environmental issues with no agenda for individual faithfulness and righteousness. As with all matters to do with the kingdom, these issues are linked. The kingdom is in fact *par excellence* the example of what has been termed "joined-up" government. In his recent book *God's Politics*, Jim Wallis observed that restricting God to private space was a major heresy of twentieth century American evangelicalism. Denial of God's authority in the public arena is denial of biblical faith, constituting rejection of the message of the prophets, Jesus and the apostles. A purely private faith degenerates into narrow, excessive preoccupation with individual and sexual morality, while ignoring biblical demands for public justice. In the end, private faith can become a merely cultural religion, assuring the righteousness of people like onesself. Exclusive emphasis on private morality at the expense of engagement with the issues of local, national or international social justice can lead to collusion with other like-minded Christians who elevate private morality at the expense of public morality. The converse may also be true, of course. We cannot omit what we find hard or unpalatable; once again, what God has joined together – here referring to private morality and public morality, in terms of issues relating to social justice – let not Christians separate! The rule of Christ in his kingdom means that justice must roll on like a river, and righteousness like a never-failing stream. (See Amos 5:24.)

Having briefly considered some issues relating to justice in the modern world, we shall now look at the way the theme of justice played out in the proclamation of the kingdom in the ministry of Jesus. We shall look at the promise of justice in the song of Mary, the Magnificat; the Nazareth synagogue address; other teachings of Jesus; and, lastly, the effect of that upon the apostles, as shown in Acts and in the letters of the apostles, especially the letter to Philemon and the Epistle of James.

The demonstration of justice in the ministry of Jesus
Jesus fulfils the three great Old Testament ministries evident in the Scriptures: prophet, priest and king. He is the prophet who is heir to the great prophetic tradition of the Old Testament, the priest who offers himself as single sacrifice for human sin, and the king who is crowned on the cross with a crown of thorns. Thus the kingdom he inaugurates is a continual challenge to the culture of the world (the prophetic); it is entered only by his sacrifice on the cross (the priestly);

and its government is supremely expressed by a crucified and risen Lord— a crown of thorns and the empty tomb. In this section we note that Jesus' prophetic call was for justice brought about by repentance, and this is where we must begin.

Walter Brueggemann shows in his acclaimed book *The Prophetic Imagination* that Jesus' call to justice, in the kingdom he had come to inaugurate, was demonstrated in two ways: his solidarity with the poor, demonstrated in his whole life, and his compassion towards all those who, for whatever reason, were marginalized. We shall look at each of those manifestations in turn.

Firstly, Jesus clearly identified with the marginalized and poor, in the widest sense of that word. As Brueggemann said, Jesus, in his prophetic ministry, "...dismantled the dominant culture and nullified its claims. The way of his ultimate criticism is his decisive solidarity with marginal people and the accompanying vulnerability required by that solidarity."[2] Jesus' whole life was lived in solidarity with the poor and marginalized. He was born in circumstances of relative poverty (though not absolute destitution, as Joseph was a skilled craftsman); in his early years, his family had to go to Egypt as "refugees"; then he did not return to his home town but to Nazareth (Matthew 2:19-23); and we are told that during his ministry he had nowhere to lay his head (Luke 9:58); he was betrayed, subjected to an unjust trial, and condemned. His whole life was a demonstration of incarnational solidarity with the poor, becoming what they were in order that they might become like him. (See 2 Corinthians 8:9.) In this Jesus showed that he was unmistakably on the side of the marginalized and the poor. The inference to draw from that is not that he was against all who were rich or powerful (in fact Jesus in his ministry went out of his way to help those who were rich and influential, though some of these were marginalized too), but that he recognised the difficulties they would have in welcoming the kingdom which made their wealth of no intrinsic importance and required their power to be used quite differently. (See Luke 18:24f and Mark 10:41, 45.) So Jesus displayed his just and gentle rule by indentifying with the poor in the deepest way, by becoming like them and by making himself vulnerable.

Secondly, Jesus demonstrated his justice by showing compassion. Again, as Brueggemann wrote, "Jesus in his solidarity with the marginal ones is moved to compassion. Compassion constitutes a radical form of criticism, for it announces that the hurt is to be taken seriously, that the hurt is not to be accepted as normal and natural but it is an abnormal and unacceptable condition for humanness."[3] Compassion literally means having your innards embrace the feeling or situation of another. This was shown in countless different ways during the ministry of Jesus: to the crowds who were like sheep without a shepherd (Mark 6:34); to the widow of Nain whose only son, her only source of future security, had died (Luke 7:12f) and to the sisters Martha and Mary whose brother Lazarus had died a very untimely death (John 11:33-38). In these and in very many other ways Jesus showed compassion for people who at the deepest level had been dispossessed and marginalized —for instance by false teaching and by the hardship of life, in the case of the crowds; and by death itself in the case of the widow and the two sisters. Jesus' compassion was a demonstration of his justice; his desire that all should know his just and gentle rule bringing freedom and life.

The outcome of this solidarity with the marginalized and his compassion for them was a combination of anger and anguish: anger concerning the use of religion as a form of oppression, as has often been the case historically (see Mark 3:5); and anguish for all those caught up in denial of what he had come to bring, as demonstrated in his weeping over Jerusalem. "If only you, even you, had only known on this day what would bring you peace —but now it is hidden from your eyes" (Luke 19:41). Perhaps of all the Gospel writers it is Luke who best charts the meaning of Jesus' just rule and the resulting anguish that he feels in its rejection, which is essentially a rejection of him. So we will initially follow Luke's charting of the justice which Jesus had come to bring, before looking more briefly at the insights of the other Gospel writers.

Justice in Luke's writings and the apostles' teaching
In tracing the theme of justice, the kingdom and the coming of the new king in the early chapters of Luke, we are immediately drawn to the songs around Jesus' birth, and especially the song of Mary. At root, what Mary is singing about is a great reversal brought about by the coming rule of her God through the agency of her as yet unborn son. This is vividly expressed by the words:

"His mercy extends to those who fear him,
     from generation to generation.

He has performed mighty deeds with his arm;
he has scattered those who are proud in their inmost thoughts.
He has brought down rulers from their thrones
but has lifted the humble.
He has filled the hungry with good things
but has sent the rich away empty."

Luke 1:50-53

Brueggemann explains: "The formation of an alternative community with an alternative consciousness is so that the dominant community may be criticised. But more than dismantling, the purpose of the alternative community is to enable a new human beginning to be made."[4] The old order which is being dismantled is represented by Herod, the chief priests, the Pharisees, that is the present power brokers in the land who have everything to lose – from riches to influence – by the coming of a new kingdom in which there is a bias to the poor, a place for the excluded and an embrace for the outsider. In Luke, the shepherds, representatives of the outsiders (as we have noted, their profession was considered unclean) welcome this kingdom and king, whereas in Matthew the coming of the new kingdom is opposed by Herod, who attempts to destroy it at birth with the massacre of the innocents. So the dominant motif in the coming of the new kingdom is costly joy mixed with grief at its painful birth pangs. (See Matthew 2:16.) If the song of Mary is the trailer to the eventual ministry of Jesus some thirty years later, Jesus unmistakably builds on her proclamation and that of the prophets —especially Isaiah and Amos (see Isaiah 58 and Amos 5) in his famous Nazareth "manifesto" of Luke 4:18-21 (see above). This prophecy from Isaiah 61:1f, Jesus said he had come to fulfil. Perhaps more than any other, that text describes the kind of rule or government that Jesus had come to bring, one in which the poor (both materially and spiritually) hear good news, in which prisoners spiritually and literally find freedom, where physical sight is given to the blind (and spiritual sight to the spiritually blind), those who are oppressed are released, and the year of Jubilee and remission of debt is both proclaimed and enacted. It is a text first uttered by Isaiah and fulfilled by Jesus, announcing as it does both the kind of ministry he had come to bring and the nature of the kingdom he had come to inaugurate. It is the Lucan parallel to Mark's description of Jesus' ministry, which he summarises as follows: "After John was put in prison, Jesus went into Galilee, proclaiming the good news of God. 'The time has come,' he said. 'The kingdom of God is near. Repent and believe the good news!'" (Mark 1:14f). So, at the outset of his ministry, Jesus made it unmistakable that his ministry would usher in the reign of God's justice, which impinged both on private morality and public policy; on personal ethics as much as social justice. One could not be promulgated at the expense of the other.

The theme of justice and the kingdom first evident in Mary's song and the Nazareth manifesto is revisited throughout Luke's Gospel— and beyond, in the life of the early church, as recorded in the Acts of the Apostles. After his imprisonment, John the Baptist has momentary doubts as to whether Jesus was the Messiah that they had all been waiting for. He sends to Jesus a message from prison, seeking reassurance that Jesus was really the Messiah, and that his sacrifices for Jesus were not in vain: "Are you the one who was to come, or should we expect someone else?" (Luke 7:20). Jesus replies by drawing attention to what he is doing, by demonstrating thereby the type of kingdom he had come to bring, "Go back and report to John what you have seen and heard: The blind receive their sight, the lame walk, those who have leprosy are cured, the deaf hear, the dead are raised, and the good news is preached to the poor." Not only is this a description of Jesus' ministry but it is also, reassuringly for John, the fulfilment of the prophecy of Isaiah 29, which speaks of a day of restoration and renewal for a people who,

"..come near to me with their mouth and honour me with their lips,
but their hearts are far from me.
Their worship of me
is made up only of rules taught by men.
Therefore once more I will astound these people
with wonder upon wonder..."

Isaiah 29:13f

Justice includes the overthrow of a repressive dominion orchestrated by Satan, and the inclusion of those who are excluded. Luke's Gospel moves on, still on this theme, to the parable of the Good Samaritan, and the duty of love to provide inclusion to our bruised and excluded neighbours (Luke 10:25-37); through the reversal explicit in the parable of Dives and Lazarus, in which one state of affairs which is patently unjust is overthrown by another; and then to the persistent intercession for justice by a woman who is cold-shouldered by the judicial process in her plea, "Grant me justice against my adversary," but is eventually rewarded for her persistence, underlining God's intention: "And will not God bring about justice for his chosen ones, who cry out to him day and night?" (See Luke 18:1-8.) The themes of restoration (of the Samaritan), reversal (of Lazarus' lot) and restitution (for the persistent widow) are all themes of this justice which is part of the coming kingdom for which Jesus urges us both to pray and act.

And what is clear especially in Luke's Gospel is also present in the apostolic teachings and actions of the early church. When it came to church life in Jerusalem, it was necessary to provide for the Grecian Jews who were being overlooked in the daily food distribution (Acts 6:1) and to make provision in their community life so that there were "no needy persons among them." (See Acts 4:34.) Again in the apostolic writings Paul makes clear that we are to, "Share with God's people who are in need..." (Romans 12:13); that a slave owner, Philemon, is to treat kindly a runaway slave, Onesimus, who is being returned to him by Paul, and who should now be regarded, "...no longer as a slave, but better than a slave, as a dear brother" (Philemon 16). It is easy to underestimate the revolutionary nature of such advice to a slave owner, who in Roman law had every right to punish a runaway slave, for while Paul was in no position to campaign for the ending of slavery in the Roman Empire, he advocated the ending of slavery *de facto* in a Christian household by regarding the slave primarily as a brother and not as a chattel, by saying that the Christian owner should treat the slave in the same way as he would treat the great apostle himself. (Philemon 17.) And finally we see in James' teaching in his epistle that faith is of no value unless expressed in works —works which express the nature of God's love and righteousness. The expression of such justice for James is found in treating people impartially (James 2:1-9), in our context treating asylum seeker or benefactor the same; in speaking wisely (James 3:1-12); and in paying people what is their due (James 5:1-6). All these and other measures are barometers of justice. The apostles, whether in the ordering of the church and its mission or in the teaching they gave to the church communities, stressed the requirement of justice since it was integral to the rule of the king they set out to serve. Before leaving this aspect of the demonstration of the kingdom, we must finally consider what "act justly" might mean for our own day.

Justice today

At the time of writing, we have had a week which was one of the biggest roller coasters in British national life. Bob Geldof was playing host to a range of bands and singers in Hyde Park in the Live8 concert in aid of the Make Poverty History campaign. That was to set the scene for the G8 conference at Gleneagles, where the most powerful men on the planet gathered to consider issues relating both to the environment and the needs of Africa. Although there was disagreement on the science of global warming, there was a fresh commitment to increase aid and relieve poverty and disease in Africa. Most regarded what was offered by the G8 leaders as only a start in a very long haul. And of course, in the middle of the summit, the whole event was overshadowed by the London bombs on 7/7 in which the joy of the news of hosting the Olympics in 2012, which was heard on the Wednesday of the same week, was swiftly overtaken by sorrow for so much carnage on the streets and in the subways of London. In less than a week the aspirations of so many and the violence of a few converged to demonstrate in just a few hours the kind of world we live in. What is especially encouraging is that Jubilee Campaign of the Millennium has had such an impact on the political leaders of the world and, although we would be fooling ourselves to think that we were on an unstoppable path to making poverty history, at the very least the challenge has been clearly outlined: cancelling debt, relieving poverty and disease through aid, human rights, fair trade and good governance are all firmly on the agenda. The task is to turn well-meaning slogans into reality; that will of course be the challenge for at least one, if not several, generations of leaders. What Christians have finally woken up to is that justice is as much a part of the kingdom mandate as healing, deliverance and preaching, and this justice or righteousness has as much to do with public policy and the distribution of resources as it does with personal morality, which today is especially focussed on the issues of gay partnerships, abortion and euthanasia.

As Christians committed to a kingdom of justice, we can work towards realising the Millennium Development goals adopted in

September 2000 by the UN. These goals are practical and clearly targeted. They include: eradicating extreme poverty and hunger, halving the proportion of people living on less than a dollar a day by 2015 (more than a billion people still live on less than that); achieving universal primary education; promoting gender equality and empowering women; reducing child mortality with a target of reduction by two thirds in the mortality rate among children under five (currently 11 million children die before their fifth birthday); improving maternal health; combating HIV/AIDS (presently 40 million people are living with HIV/AIDS); ensuring environmental sustainability; increasing the numbers of people with access to safe water; and, finally, encouraging a global partnership for development including fair trade, dealing with debt and making available both pharmaceutical and communications technology.[5] There is no doubt that such goals will take at least a generation to accomplish. We are almost halfway to 2015 and there are still 350 million Africans who live on under a dollar a day. Nevertheless Niall FitzGerald, the Chairman of Reuters, in preparation for the World Economic Forum held in Davos each year (sometimes called a "beanfeast of pomp and platitude"), encouraged the delegates to focus their attention on the needs of the poorest on the planet. And despite the very considerable vested interests, there are politicians who are serious about implementing fair trade. These objectives must be pursued.

As Isaiah said,

> Is not this the kind of fasting I have chosen:
> to loose the chains of injustice
> and untie the cords of the yoke,
> to set the oppressed free
> and break every yoke?
> Is it not to share your food with the hungry?
> and to provide the poor wanderer with shelter—
> when you see the naked, to clothe him,
> and not to turn away from your own flesh and blood?
> Then your light will break forth like the dawn,
> and your healing will quickly appear;
> then your righteousness will go before you,
> and the glory of the LORD will be your rear guard.

Then you will call, and the LORD will answer;
you will cry for help, and he will say:
Here am I.

Isaiah 58:6-9

To bring in God's kingdom is to be committed to these things. Once again, what God has joined together we must not divide: justice as well as healing; private and public morality; preaching as well as acts of deliverance. Let us hold them together. The kingdom of God is about God's government becoming a reality in the affairs of humankind.

Chapter Eleven

FORGIVENESS IN
THE KINGDOM

So far, in this section, we have seen that the kingdom of God is demonstrated by a number of activities: by the declaration of the kingdom's presence and its meaning, through preaching; secondly, by the ministry of healing and deliverance which brings liberation to those who are oppressed; and, thirdly, by the pursuit of justice. Often these three things have been divided off from each other as if they were part of an *à la carte* menu from which we are at liberty to choose the one we like and want to pursue in our ministry, to the neglect of others; but a faithful reading of the Scriptures shows that these things are part of a set menu which is not to be picked over by choosy Christians. These are integrated ways of making known the kingdom of God. But these three activities are now joined by a fourth: the offer of forgiveness. Nor is forgiveness far removed from justice; in fact they are intimately related. Miroslav Volf has argued that forgiveness does not actually supplant justice; nor is it an outlet for a resentful or angry person who has been hurt. Rather, when someone is forgiven, justice is exalted, because the fact that it has been contravened is underlined even as forgiveness is released in its place.[1] Forgiveness is not a sentimental wave of the hand and saying, "Think nothing of it"; it is rather a deeply felt action in which the offended forgoes the instincts for revenge and offers the hand of friendship to the one who has deeply hurt or wounded. Forgiveness is releasing another from the guilt of their offence, pardoning them with no strings attached.

There are few more wonderful examples of forgiveness than that provided by Pope John Paul II. On May 13th, 1981 he was shot and seriously wounded in St Peter's Square. The Turkish gunman was Mehmet Ali Agca, aged 23, who has recently been freed from jail, having served his sentence. Four bullets hit the Pope at close quarters, and for a while his life was in the balance. Two bullets struck him in the stomach, one hit his right arm and the fourth grazed his little finger. After surgery to remove the bullets from the stomach, and a long period of recovery, he visited his would-be assassin in jail and forgave him. Although Mehmet served his prison term as the proper punishment for his crime, John Paul bore him no ill will, and prayed for his soul.

Twenty-four years later, on a leafy path in Berkshire, England, a young mother was pushing her twenty-two month old son, Joseph, when she was savagely attacked and stabbed in the neck. The whole nation was amazed at the mixture of courage, sweetness and faith exhibited by Abigail and Benoit Witchalls, sincere Roman Catholic Christians. Abigail was paralysed from the neck down although she is now recovering a little movement. Benoit, in an interview for television, spoke with extraordinary courage of people who had been paralysed still living wonderful lives. He did not want to pass judgement on his wife's attacker, instead expressing the desire that that person would receive help. Whilst his wife had wondered why it had happened, they had no desire for revenge. It later transpired that her attacker took his own life and the police closed their investigation. The couple thanked God that their son was unharmed. What extraordinary courage and sweetness in the face of personal tragedy! Both John Paul II and the Witchalls have been practitioners of forgiveness.

A further extraordinary case of forgiveness followed the murder of Anthony Walker in Liverpool on July 29th, 2005. He was brutally killed with an ice axe, which was embedded in his skull. Anthony, a talented and capable schoolboy and a strong Christian, had been walking his girlfriend to a bus stop when he was attacked. After the court case, in which the assailants were found guilty of a racist attack, it was reported that Anthony's mother, expressing forgiveness, quoted words which Jesus used when he forgave those who nailed him to the cross. The whole nation was stunned both by the senseless and brutal murder and the extraordinary grace of Anthony's family in the face of such appalling violence. Such forgiveness in the face of such brutality was truly remarkable. How is such forgiveness possible? We must now study more closely the principles, power and practice of forgiveness.

The principles of forgiveness

From the outset God showed himself to be a merciful and forgiving God. His love was towards a thousand generations. (See Deuteronomy 5:10; 7:9.) His love is characterised by his infinite mercy. God's love was the continual refrain of the psalmist David, who praised his love continually. It was unfailing. (Psalm 107:8, 15, 21, 31.) It endured forever. (The refrain of Psalm 136.) And nowhere was David's call on that love more urgent and intense than in the opening lines of Psalm 51, following the revelation of his sin with Bathsheba:

> Have mercy on me, O God,
> according to your unfailing love;
> according to your great compassion
> blot out my transgressions.
> Wash away all my iniquity
> and cleanse me from my sin!
>
> *Psalm 51:1f*

Just as the tent of meeting in the days of Moses and afterwards was the place where the assurance of forgiveness could be found for the Israelites, according to the rites of the sacrificial system (Leviticus 4:31), so too was the temple which was built in the days of Solomon, who prayed, "Hear the supplications of your servant and of your people Israel when they pray towards this place. Hear from heaven, your dwelling place; and when you hear, forgive" (2 Chronicles 6:21). Jeremiah prophesied about a new covenant which was coming when,

> "No longer will a man teach his neighbour,
> or a man his brother, saying, 'Know the LORD,'
> because they will all know me,
> from the least of them to the greatest," declares the LORD.
> "For I will forgive their wickedness,
> and will remember their sins no more"
>
> *Jeremiah 31:34*

And, while in exile, Daniel looked to a new, everlasting kingdom, in which the offer of forgiveness would be central. In his remarkable and passionate prayer in the first year of the emperor Darius (see Daniel 9:1ff), Daniel turned his face to the Lord and prayed, "O LORD, we and our kings, our princes and our fathers are covered with shame because we have sinned against you. The Lord our God is merciful and forgiving, even though we have rebelled against him; we have not obeyed the LORD our God or kept the laws he gave us through his servants the prophets" (Daniel 9:8-10). He concludes his prayer with a heartfelt plea, "Give ear, O God, and hear; open your eyes and see the desolation of the city that bears your Name. We do not make requests of you because we are righteous, but because of your great mercy. O Lord, listen! O Lord, forgive! O Lord, hear and act! For your sake, O my God, do not delay, because your city and your people bear your Name" (Daniel 9:18f). Daniel knew that restoration for Israel must be preceded by forgiveness; forgiveness belonged to God and was part of this coming kingdom which he glimpsed in dreams and visions, not least in his vision in the reign of Belshazzar, when he saw, "...one like a son of man, coming with the clouds of heaven. He approached the Ancient of Days and was led into his presence" (Daniel 7:13).

Some five hundred years after a succession of empires – Babylonian, Persian, Greek and Roman in the Near East – a kingdom arrived in the person of the Messiah, or Son of Man, which would daily increase and never end, but which would be neither territorial nor earthly. (See Isaiah 9:7 and Daniel 7:14.) Mary was given notice of this at the time of the Annunciation, when the angel Gabriel who had earlier appeared to Daniel (Daniel 8:16ff) said of her son, "...and he will reign over the house of Jacob for ever; his kingdom will never end" (Luke 1:33). And Zechariah prophesied at the circumcision of John the Baptist that John would, "give his people knowledge of salvation through the forgiveness of their sins..." (Luke 1:77). Jesus came, his very name signifying that he would win forgiveness for his people: "...you are to give him the name Jesus, because he will save his people from their sins (Matthew 1:21).

The ministry of Jesus was a continual mission of offering forgiveness and including within his kingdom those who, for whatever reason, had been excluded. Some of his miracles were a demonstration of his authority to forgive sins. To the shocked Pharisees who saw

162

him pronounce forgiveness to a paralytic who had been lowered by his friends through the roof to where Jesus was standing, Jesus said, "Which is easier: to say to this paralytic, 'Your sins are forgiven,' or to say, 'Get up, take your mat and walk'? But that you may know that the Son of Man has authority on earth to forgive sins.... He said to the paralytic, 'I tell you, get up, take your mat and go home.'" (See Mark 2:8-12.) The inference must be that healing the sick was easier than forgiveness of sins for Jesus, for forgiveness inevitably led him to the suffering of the cross, for, "...without the shedding of blood there is no forgiveness." (See Hebrews 9:11-22.)

Depending on the seriousness of the hurt, forgiveness may be either the simplest or hardest of things. As I have written elsewhere, it may be either a simple straightforward event or a journey or pilgrimage defining a lifetime's work. If a person has simply forgotten an appointment then presumably it should not be too hard to forgive them; if they have failed to show for a dinner party prepared especially for them it might be a little harder! If the one who needs to receive forgiveness is your best friend and has gone off with your husband, then it is harder still, and if he is a stranger who has run over your child because he is a drunk driver, then only the greatest grace could lead you to forgive them. In other words, from our own human experience we understand that the deeper the offence or hurt caused, the harder it is to forgive. In the face of our offence to God it was not possible for him just to say to us, "That's alright, you are forgiven!" Forgiveness, for God, involved him in the greatest sacrificial act. The offence caused by the human race towards God is hard for us to understand, and only in the Scriptures are we occasionally given a glimpse of the grief that our unbelief and ingratitude has caused our loving Creator. One such occasion is when we are told by the author of Genesis that the wickedness of humans deeply grieved God. We are told, "The LORD saw how great man's wickedness on the earth had become, and that every inclination of the thoughts of his heart was only evil all the time. The LORD was grieved that he had made man on the earth, and his heart was filled with pain" (Genesis 6:5f). The remedy by which God chose to demonstrate his own righteousness, to deal with the human race's wrongdoing, and to provide a way of reconciling them to himself, was the cross. It demonstrated ultimately his love for his creation and the seriousness of our rebellion against him. It provided a continual stream of forgiveness for all who placed their confidence in its power. The principles of forgiveness are simple and profound: God provides it, to his own deep cost, and we accept it as the only cure, through repentance and faith. Its power is remarkable and to this we must now turn.

The power of forgiveness

The power of forgiveness might firstly be considered from a negative point of view: what would happen if there was no forgiveness? People would remain handcuffed to bitterness and resentment, or shackled to immovable guilt. Most people would be imprisoned in one or the other, and there would be no possibility of escape. Life would become unbearable. We would be imprisoned in a cycle of revenge, despair, resentment and no hope. And for some that is exactly how life has become —for individuals, families and whole communities. In a biography of the British Liberal prime minister William Gladstone, I read that the most intractable problems he had to deal with were in Ireland, the Balkans, the Sudan and Afghanistan. Admittedly, some of the problems were of Britain's own making, because of colonial policy, but there were also either ethnic or religious divides which went back in some cases hundreds of years. Later, in the mid twentieth century, would be added the Israeli/Palestinian divide, which has seen a cycle of violence that continues today. Forgiveness and restitution, where possible, must be the only way forward, but with wounds so deep going back so long the hope for a settlement there remains some way off. And I would particularly recommend the seminal book *Exclusion and Embrace*, by the Croatian theologian Miroslav Volf, who recalls the terrible cycle of revenge unleashed in Bosnia in the Balkan war of the 1990s. He illustrates graphically the impulse for revenge following brutal attacks, and again this deeply underlines the need for forgiveness.[2]

We must cry for forgiveness with all our strength to those caught up in the cycles of violence and unforgiveness that blight our world. Who has the right to ask any defiled and abused person to forgive? The call to forgive is, of course, God's law for everyone. It can be powerful when we hear of someone who has suffered and forgiven, and found forgiveness to be the only key out of the jail of revenge.

In July 2005, the British Foreign Secretary stood on the site of the Sebrenica massacres, the worst atrocities in Europe since the Second World War, where ten thousand Muslims were killed, and apologised for our failure to act effectively against the atrocity which was committed when NATO troops were only metres away. A few days after that apology, a group of terrorists planted four bombs in London, destroying the lives of over fifty people. A colleague in our neighbourhood lost a young and very talented niece in the London bombing. In such a way the cycle of violence extends into a leafy village in Somerset.

The failure to forgive unleashes hatred, and sometimes violence. Alternatively, the power of forgiveness turns the desire for violence to peace. Receiving or offering forgiveness can bring peace and reconciliation. So far in this section, most of the examples have been from the world of international terror, with its repercussions reaching far and wide in our global village, but there are plenty of examples of unforgiveness destroying individual lives or blighting families for generations, not least because in our society there are now huge numbers of broken family relationships. But the Gospels are full of examples of those who have been forgiven and the new life it has given them. There was Mary Magdalene, a prostitute oppressed by evil, who was forgiven, and who became a leading member of Jesus' community. There was Zacchaeus the tax gatherer, working for the Roman occupying power, who rapaciously extracted money from a resentful and oppressed population, who on meeting Jesus and finding acceptance found that he was unexpectedly free to give back four times what he had stolen. (See Luke 19:1-9.) And then there was the woman who burst into the dinner party of Simon the Pharisee and anointed Jesus with oil, washing his feet with her tears and hair, and generally expressing her gratitude for the forgiveness she found. "Her many sins have been forgiven," Jesus said, "—for she loved much. (See Luke 7:36-50.) That is to mention only a few of many such instances. In each case, the power of being forgiven was unleashed in a life, bringing, as a result, a freedom, joy and purpose which previously was unknown to that person. If the power of forgiveness is so great and its consequences so beneficial, then especially as citizens of the kingdom we need to become willing practitioners of the art of forgiveness.

The practice of forgiveness

No one had practised forgiveness as Jesus did. As we know, his death enabled the possibility of forgiveness; as Paul wrote, "In him we have redemption through his blood, the forgiveness of sins, in accordance with the riches of God's grace that he lavished on us with all wisdom and understanding" (Ephesians 1:7f). But even as he was making that forgiveness possible, he was practising forgiveness on the undeserving. As the soldiers hammered nails through his hands and feet, he said, "...Father, forgive them, for they do not know what they are doing" (Luke 23:34). So although he was suffering great physical pain, an unjust punishment, the sneers of his fellow men, desertion by those who had been closest to him – indeed, what for us would have been a cauldron of emotion which so easily could have led to self pity or bitterness – he extended forgiveness to the ignorant or undeserving, and at the same time provided *the* way by which forgiveness could be found, by his dying on the cross. The forgiveness he himself gave to the undeserving he taught his followers to give to those who had hurt them.

On one occasion Peter asked Jesus how often he should forgive his brother. Peter offered the generous number of seven times. Forgiving your brother, who repeatedly fails you, seven times seemed to Peter beyond the call of normal duty. But Jesus shocked him by saying, "...not seven times, but seventy-seven times" (Matthew 18:21), and then proceeded to tell a parable about the kingdom of heaven and forgiveness. At the heart of the kingdom is an offer of forgiveness, which all who enter it can receive. Jesus compared the act of forgiveness in the parable he told to the cancellation of a debt of ten thousand talents, and this is the equivalent of millions of pounds —an unbelievable sum! By contrast, the servant in the story refused to forgive a paltry debt of a fellow-servant, for which ungenerous action he is punished. Jesus draws the conclusion from this parable: "This is how my heavenly Father will treat each of you unless you forgive your brother from your heart." (See Matthew 18:23-35.) The principle is clear: a citizen of the kingdom has received immeasurable forgiveness from God, which places upon him a corresponding obligation to go on forgiving those who hurt or offend him, as much as seventy times seven —another way of saying continually. This principle is further borne out by the request in the kingdom prayer, which we shall look at in greater depth later, in which we ask, "Forgive us our sins, for we also forgive everyone who sins against us" (Luke 11:4). So the practice of forgiveness for the citizen of the kingdom is: as much as we are "sinned against" we are to forgive; but also, and this is hard, we should be prepared to take the initiative in it.

No one said sorry to Jesus for crucifying him, not at the time; yet he offered forgiveness. He said, "...Father, forgive them, for they do not know what they are doing." In fact the soldiers were ignorant of the extent of their sin, but nonetheless Jesus prayed the Father for their forgiveness —despite their lack of knowledge and therefore penitence. With regard to the vexed question of offering forgiveness where none is asked for, no apology made and no penitence expressed, the answer must be that we are to forgive from our hearts even where no forgiveness is asked for. This is to be our response to Jesus' command to forgive and it works not just for the other's benefit but for ours as well, for not to forgive is to carry around ongoing resentment, pain and bitterness, from which we need to be released. The question is not whether they deserve it but whether we can become what we are intended to be, fully human, if we still carry around some unresolved unforgiveness. Naturally, if a person will not ask for that forgiveness by way of expressing sorrow for their failure, they also will never become what they were intended to be, and in the end that will catch up with them. But it is our obligation to offer forgiveness; it is theirs to properly receive it. If they do not do so because they are not penitent, that is upon their heads. Smedes, in *Forgive and Forget*, has likened the process to setting a prisoner free and then discovering that you yourself had been the prisoner.[3] No one said this would be easy.

This great theme of forgiveness, especially its significance in relation to the various ways we interact with those closest to us, is tackled in the work *Qualities of Enduring Love*,[4] and particularly my chapter in that work entitled *Dealing with Conflict*.

The offer of the gospel, which is in a sense truly scandalous, is that God will always forgive the truly penitent. It is scandalous because actions or words deserving of judgement are instead treated with mercy. Once again, as we have seen, the words of the penitent robber on the neighbouring cross to Jesus are testimony to this: "Jesus, remember me when you come into your kingdom" was met by the reply, "I tell you the truth, today you will be with me in paradise." (See Luke 23:42f.) Forgiveness demonstrates the nature of the ruler. He reserves the right to forgive. Alongside the proclamation of the kingdom through preaching and teaching, the illustration of the kingdom through healing and deliverance, the revelation of the kingdom as a place of ultimate justice, is this truly wonderful understanding that the kingdom is demonstrated by the offer and receiving of forgiveness. God forgives us, and so we ought to forgive one another. This understanding of mutual forgiveness is also the basis for the formation of a new community. This "community" is the last of the five expressions of the kingdom that Jesus had come to usher in. It is to the formation of this new community – indeed new humanity – through the hope of resurrection, that we must now turn.

Chapter Twelve

A COMMUNITY OF
THE RESURRECTION

So far we have seen the way the kingdom of God was both illustrated and demonstrated in the ministry of Jesus: by his teaching and preaching; by healing and deliverance; by his prophetic concern for justice and righteousness; and, lastly, by his insistence on our need to receive and offer forgiveness. Each of these activities demonstrated the nature of God's rule, but on their own they could easily be a series of unconnected events in the life of others without a fulfilling context. It is this final expression of the kingdom that provides the ultimate vision of the kingdom of God. The kingdom of God, the rule of God, is best understood as bringing together a new community, a new humanity in which the rule of the king is unhindered and unopposed, in which his rule is increasingly experienced and understood. This is a community in which there is only one ultimate rule and that is of love. As Paul taught, faith and hope will fade away and only the way of love will remain. (See 1 Corinthians 13.) Indeed, God's whole plan, as Paul himself understood it, was that through this community, which included both Jew and Gentile, "...the manifold wisdom of God should be made known to the rulers and authorities in the heavenly realms." (See Ephesians 3:6,10.) The formation of this new community brought together by the cross, and given the power and hope of the resurrection, was the aim of Jesus in his earthly ministry.

We must now trace the formation and empowering of this community through the ministry of Jesus. We shall look at three aspects of this community: firstly, that it was a diverse community but united by faith in Jesus and expressing itself through love; secondly, that it had at its heart the hope of resurrection; and, lastly, that it was a community which would never be at home in this world, so would be, temporarily, a community of exiles.

A diverse community

It is clear that from the beginning of the ministry of Jesus of Nazareth that it was his intention to bring together a new community which would, by degrees, demonstrate the reality of his reign. Later on in this book we must look more closely at the relationship of the church and the kingdom of God, but here we will look at some of the essential characteristics of this new community which Jesus brought into existence. It was marked by diversity and unity. In his teaching to the early church, Paul would highlight this fundamental characteristic of the church in his favourite metaphor for it, which is "the body of Christ". This phrase marvellously showed the combination of diversity and unity which should exist wherever Jesus' reign is truly found. Jesus made plain that his followers were not to be drawn from a single seam of society but from every section of it. This could not have been more clearly demonstrated than in his choice of the twelve disciples.

After an all night vigil of prayer, Jesus brought together a group of followers who were to be the leaders of this new community. Amongst their number were fishermen, a tax collector, a zealot, Simon, who was longing for the overthrow of the Romans, and a man who was later to betray him. They were undoubtedly a mixed bag, displaying great variety of occupation, background and temperament – from the "sons of thunder", James and John, to the more refined and cultured Philip; from the impetuosity of Peter to the caution and earthy scepticism of Thomas, who required argument or proof before believing. They were a diverse group who, it could be argued, had nothing in common except their loyalty to Jesus. Indeed, as Mark tells us in his account of the calling of the disciples, "He appointed twelve – designating them apostles – that they might be with him and that he might send them out to preach and to have authority to drive out demons" (Mark 3:14f). The dynamic of their relationship with Jesus was that they should "be with him" and be sent out by him to do those things (preach and drive out demons) which would show that the kingdom of God was here. This diverse group, in their relationships and activity, were to demonstrate the reality of the kingdom. The main way in which this was to be done would be through the reality of their love together in the context of diversity. This was and is the fundamental feature of the new community which Jesus was creating. In essence they were a new community revolving around a new commandment. The new community was one brought together by Jesus both by his call and by his death and resurrection. However the novel drumbeat of this community was love. As Jesus said, "A new commandment I give you: Love one another...." (See John 13:34f). Nowhere is this more cogently taught than when Jesus, having explained that he was dynamically related to this new community as a vine is to its branches, goes on to say repeatedly that, "My command is this: Love each other as I have loved you", and, "This is my command: Love each other" (John 15:12, 17). The very sap of this vine was love —the Father's love for those who acknowledge his Son, the Son's love in laying down his life for the members of the community, and the love that each had for the other as members of this community. All of this may be traced in the Christian community's horticultural handbook which is John 15:1-17.

Of course this sounds very comforting and plausible until we take seriously the quality of the love which Jesus is speaking about. It is not a love which simply endorses the all too human characteristic of "birds of a feather" who flock together. For Jesus calls us not simply to love those who are like us but those who are unlike us, for even sinners love those who are like them. (See Matthew 5:46-48.) If we are to love as God loves, as his kingdom requires, we are to love those who are unlike us; and in a community where there is real diversity there will be plenty of opportunity for that. This type of loving cuts across cultural barriers, ethnic diversity and intellectual outlook. One of the tragedies of the church in central Africa was to discover that despite such movements as the East African Revival, which affected Rwanda amongst other nations, Rwanda still remained fertile soil for ethnic hatred between Christians of different tribes. The resulting genocide of the 1980s, in which a million people were slaughtered in a hundred days, included Christian killing Christian. It showed that, despite the protestations of experiencing the kingdom of God in power, the bonds formed in the Christian community, which included different tribal groups, were less powerful and compelling than tribal

171

fears and loyalties. Nor is the history of Western Christianity any better. For hundreds of years Christians were divided by religious wars which destroyed countless lives. And today we are still far too ready to build church communities within our own cultural boundaries rather than ones which traverse these boundaries thoroughly.

So Jesus' command to love each other, which lies at the heart of the life of this community in which his reign is to be found, is no easy option. It challenges all those human barriers which we use to protect ourselves: barriers of culture, race, colour and background. The kingdom of God is the place and the dynamic where all these all too human ties are dissolved in the far greater allegiance to the King who, through his Son, makes us all brothers and sisters.

Love in a diverse community is the hallmark of God's just and gentle rule which is his kingdom. Not only that but the quality of this love was that it should encompass our enemies as well. In this way it was following the love of Christ who, when we were still his enemies, reconciled us to himself through his death. (Romans 5:10.) Jesus asked his followers nothing which he had not perfectly fulfilled himself. So he commands them in the Sermon on the Mount, "You have heard that it was said, 'Love your neighbour and hate your enemy.' But I tell you: Love your enemies and pray for those who persecute you, that you may be sons of your Father in heaven." It was precisely because the early Christians exhibited such love in the first centuries of their existence that they had such a profound effect on the Roman empire, eventually winning acceptance. Their love under pressure for those who oppressed them was unanswerable, and it precipitated the well-known exclamation of Tertullian, "See how these Christians love each other." This new community, which Jesus started to gather to himself with the twelve disciples, was indeed diverse, but was held together by the rule of love. It was also held together by the hope of resurrection, especially after Jesus' own resurrection from the dead.

The hope of resurrection
There is a difficult text, often puzzled over by commentators, at the beginning of Mark chapter nine, which is in fact part of a conversation between Jesus and the disciples about his death and resurrection and was followed by hard hitting teaching about the nature of discipleship. The conversation concludes with Jesus saying, "I tell you the truth,

some who are standing here will not taste death before they see the kingdom of God come with power" (Mark 9:1). Some may interpret the coming of the kingdom in relation to the second coming of Christ and the triumph of the kingdom, but Jesus must have known that such an event would be after his disciples' death. The coming of the kingdom in power may alternatively be referring to the sequence of events including the resurrection, ascension, Pentecost and the explosion of the early church. Since some of the disciples were to lose their lives during these times, notably James who was executed (Acts 12:2), it may be that Jesus was referring to this. If the coming in power of the kingdom of God refers to the resurrection and subsequent events leading up to the explosive beginning of the early church, then Jesus regarded the resurrection as the moment when the kingdom came in power. The old order was overthrown by the new order, of which the resurrection was both the harbinger and guarantee.

It was a community, as Paul so often tells us, that was defined by faith in Jesus as Lord, characterised by love in all its relationships, and founded on hope in the reality of the resurrection. Because of the reality of this hope of a kingdom which would one day be both perfected and fulfilled, the Christian community was empowered to love even its enemies because in Christ they knew that they were more than conquerors, and, as believers, could not lose. No one put this better than Paul who, in his peroration at the end of Romans eight, proclaimed, "Who shall separate us from the love of Christ? Shall trouble or hardship or persecution or famine or nakedness or danger or sword? …. No, in all these things we are more than conquerors through him who loved us..." (Romans 8:35-39). One consequence of the resurrection was that this community could never finally lose out.

Three years ago, while on a sabbatical in which I drove with a friend from Bath to Amman in Jordan, I stayed two days in Istanbul, or Constantinople as it has been for most of its life, on the way. Amongst other sites, including the great Constantinian church Hagia Sophia, we visited St Saviour's in Chora, well known for its remarkable cycle of mosaics which cover almost every wall, depicting biblical scenes from the Old and New Testaments. Amongst them, in a side chapel, is a striking fresco which I used as a front cover for the first book in this trilogy, entitled *Becoming Fully Human*. It shows a dynamic risen Christ hauling Adam and Eve from their tomb of death to new life.

It is a powerful and supremely energetic depiction of resurrection, conveying the great statement of St Paul, "For as in Adam all die, so in Christ all will be made alive" (1 Corinthians 15:22).What this early painter did in art, in illustrating Paul's great assertion, Handel likewise achieved in setting the same text to music in The Messiah. However, no Christian art can adequately depict the significance and meaning of the resurrection. It was, together with the cross, the theme of the early church's preaching. (See Acts 2:32-36; 17:31f.) It was the hope of their community life and, together with the gift of the Spirit, was the earnest of the kingdom to come. Tom Wright, in his formidable volume *The Resurrection of the Son of God*, asks this question: "Where did the resurrection show up in what the early Christians habitually did?" Answering his own question, he goes on to say, "Briefly and broadly, they behaved as if they were in some important senses already living in God's new creation. They lived as if the covenant had been renewed, as if the kingdom were in a sense already present, though, to be sure, future as well; often their present-kingdom behaviour (for instance readiness to forgive persecutors rather than call down curses on them) comes to the fore precisely in contexts where it is all too obvious that the kingdom has not yet been fully realized. The other elements of early Christian praxis, not least baptism, Eucharist and martyrdom point in the same direction. If challenged about their lifestyle as a community, the early Christians responded by telling stories of Jesus, particularly of his triumph over death."[1]

Hope based on the fact of the resurrection was a vital part of the make-up of the early Christians' mentality. Soon after the ascension of Jesus it was the firm expectation of the disciples that Jesus would return soon and the kingdom would be fulfilled. This was the thinking behind the question directed at Jesus by the disciples before his ascension. They asked, "Lord, are you are at this time going to restore the kingdom to Israel?" Although the thinking behind this question was of a political kingdom being established by the now risen Jesus – which in turn got a dusty answer from Jesus that it was not theirs to know the times and seasons of God's plan for his kingdom – the apostles persisted in their expectation of an early return of Jesus and the fulfilment of the kingdom.

Although, throughout their teaching, the apostles held to the imminent return of Jesus, the certainty that it would occur in their lifetime diminished. So Peter, answering the objections that Jesus had not returned yet, when he was writing his second letter, said, "But do not forget this one thing, dear friends: With the Lord a day is like a thousand years, and a thousand years are like a day. The Lord is not slow in keeping his promise, as some understand slowness. He is patient with you, not wanting anyone to perish, but everyone to come to repentance" (2 Peter 3:8f). We can see how the expectation was still there, but the confidence that it would happen during their lifetime had changed. But undergirding their perspective was the certainty that the kingdom would come, and of that there could be no doubt. As the writer to the Hebrews recognised, although the reign of God in Christ had begun, it was not yet perfected. So he wrote, "In putting everything under him, God left nothing that is not subject to him. Yet at present we do not see everything subject to him. But we see Jesus, who was made a little lower than the angels, now crowned with glory and honour because he suffered death, so that by the grace of God he might taste death for everyone" (Hebrews 2:8f).

Their hope was based on the resurrection, and all that meant for their future destiny. It looked forward to a completion of the kingdom at the return of Christ, and it recognised that, for the time being, not everything is subject to him. Later we shall study further the relationship between the now and the not yet, in relation to the kingdom of God; for now it is enough to see that hope together with faith and love constituted the marching orders of the early church. The same applies today.

The third feature of this community which Jesus came to found was that it was a community in exile, waiting for the fulfilment of the kingdom.

A community in exile

In almost every large metropolitan city around the world there are communities of exiles in particular parts of the town. If you were to go to the Edgware Road in London you would find strung along the street innumerable Middle Eastern cafés. There are people who are either voluntary or compulsorily exiles from their homeland. But in these characterful eating and drinking houses they re-create a little piece of Iraq or Egypt, or some other country; there are water pipes or hubble-bubbles, strong Arabic coffee; familiar fellow countrymen, as well as sought out conversations about the people, places and customs of home. All this reminds the exile of home, the nectar that the exile longs for. Likewise, the Christian community is one whose true home is elsewhere.

The community that Jesus formed was one that had a job to do in the present – making known the kingdom through similar means to those employed by him – whilst recognising that they were citizens of a community whose home is elsewhere. So they were exiles, too. "For here," as the writer of the Epistle to the Hebrews wrote, "we do not have an enduring city, but we are looking for the city that is to come" (Hebrews 13:14). And as Paul wrote to the Philippians, "But our citizenship is in heaven. And we eagerly await a Saviour from there, the Lord Jesus Christ, who by the power that enables him to bring everything under his control, will transform our lowly bodies so that they will be like his glorious body" (Philippians 3:20). Because Christians are citizens of a community whose abiding home is in heaven, they are consequently pilgrims here on earth, not at home in the world – in the sense that John used that word "world", as a place organised without reference to God – and waiting for better to come.

In Jesus' high priestly prayer at the end of John's Gospel, it is made clear that, although living in the world, the disciples were not of the world; instead they were to be sanctified by the truth. (See John 17:14-17.) They were a community passing through, on a journey or pilgrimage, with sights set on the abiding city and not on any settlement here on earth. It is true of many of us Christians in the West that we make ourselves so comfortable with all that we have in the here and now that we find it hard to say with Paul that, "to live is Christ and to die is gain" (Philippians 1:21).

The community which Jesus founded by calling together the disciples and appointing twelve of them apostles was to be the obvious expression of the kingdom of God here on earth: the place where the just and gentle rule of Jesus could be both seen and experienced. It was to be a community of faith expressing itself in love (Galatians 5:6); it was also a place of hope, looking to the consequences of the resurrection, but it would never be at ease in the world, from which it was fundamentally estranged. It was a group of exiles and pilgrims making their way to an abiding city. In this community the word would be preached and followed, the activity of healing and deliverance be found, justice would be proclaimed and followed, and forgiveness and acceptance would be the atmosphere of its life. What a community that would be! It also would turn on their head all the preconceived notions of power, religion and morality. More of that later! Before moving on to the final two sections of the book, and what I call this topsy-turvy world of the kingdom of God, it would be worth collecting together in our hand the threads of our journey so far.

Jesus spoke about so many things in terms of the kingdom of God. We might say that the kingdom was his world-view. This kingdom had been prefigured in the Old Testament in the great reigns (for the most part) of David and Solomon. It was a kingdom which had been dramatically glimpsed by Daniel in the exilic period, but which waited for its proper fulfilment in and through the Messiah. Jesus came both demonstrating and teaching the kingdom of God, and that is what we have looked at so far in this book. Firstly, he taught about what it was like, and he did this almost entirely through the parables. We have seen that in the parables he showed both what were the chief characteristics of the kingdom and what its demands were upon those who lived in it. Those characteristics were: that it was governed on the basis of grace and not of deserts; whatever problems it confronted, it would always grow; it operated on a new law of love; it demanded everything from its citizens; and it was moving inexorably towards a crisis in the future.

Then, in the second part of the book, we have seen the way in which Jesus demonstrated the reality of the kingdom in his own ministry. Jesus made known the ways of the kingdom through teaching and preaching, bringing healing and deliverance, standing for justice, offering forgiveness, and calling together an embryonic community in which these activities could be, quite literally, earthed. The truth is that where the kingdom of God is truly found, each and every one of these activities will be found.

Before we look at experiencing this kingdom for ourselves, we shall see how different this kingdom is to any other authority structure we may know of —hence the expression 'topsy-turvy kingdom', since it is upside down, inside out and round about.

PART IV

THE TOPSY-TURVY KINGDOM

Chapter Thirteen

THE UPSIDE DOWN KINGDOM

In October 2004 it was reported that a brawl broke out in the Church of the Holy Sepulchre in Jerusalem. It was the result of an ongoing rivalry between six Christian denominations which have a stake in this most holy of sacred sites, where it is thought by many that Jesus was both crucified and buried. The spark for the latest fist fight came when the Franciscans left their chapel door open as a Greek Orthodox procession approached. It is customary for the door of the Franciscan chapel to be closed when the procession passes and, since it was not, it was alleged that the one group was insulted and a fight ensued. One witness said that police were hit, monks were hit, and there was blood on people's faces. Two years previously, eleven monks from the Ethiopian Orthodox church had been taken to hospital. There is so much distrust between the six churches that locking the church has been left to successive generations of a Muslim family —an extraordinary outcome in a place dedicated to the reconciling death of Christ which it commemorates.

Why, you say, is it worth airing this particular piece of Christian dirty washing in public? It is a sad tale of interchurch rivalry and even hostility in a place remembering the greatest act of reconciling love in the world. Rivalry occasionally blazed amongst some of the early followers of Jesus during his earthly ministry, and even confronted him at the point of his own death, when the twelve were gathered in the upper room. We shall look more closely at that incident later in this chapter.

However, the revolutionary principle which Jesus introduced into the use of power, authority and privilege was that all these "trusts" were given not to aggrandize either an individual or community but for the service of others. Or, as Jesus put it in a nutshell, to be the greatest was to be the servant of all.

One of the most radical pieces of teaching that Jesus gave those who would both enter and be influential in his kingdom was that to to lead meant to serve. And it is this teaching that we are seeking to unpack in this chapter.

Becoming the greatest

There seems to be have been an ongoing debate amongst the disciples as to which of them was the greatest. In this sense, as in so many others, they were typical of most groups of men, vying between themselves as to who was the most talented or significant. On at least one occasion it was a topic of conversation whilst journeying together. Mark tells us that, 'They came to Capernaum. When he was in the house, he asked them, "What were you arguing about on the road?" But they kept quiet because on the way they had argued about who was the greatest' (Mark 9:33f). Naturally, they were embarrassed to be asked by Jesus their topic of conversation. It seemed so infantile, facile and self-centred to discuss such things, especially when some of them had just witnessed Jesus being transfigured, they had all been roundly rebuked for their lack of faith (see Mark 9:19) and, just before this conversation, Jesus had told them that he would be betrayed and suffer.

However, Jesus used their uncomfortable silence, and no doubt their mumbling into their cups, to teach them the true meaning of greatness. 'Sitting down, Jesus called the Twelve and said, "If anyone wants to be first, he must be the very last and the servant of all"' (Mark 9:35). He then took a child and placed him by him and said, "..whoever humbles himself like this child is the greatest in the kingdom of heaven" (Matthew 18:4). The natural meaning of these words and actions was that the true test of greatness was that a person should be prepared to be the last, to serve others before their own interests, and have the humility of a child. Nowhere was this more powerfully put in Mark's Gospel than in the following chapter (see Mark 10:35-45), a little after the incident about the disciples' furtive conversation on the road. This conversation in Mark chapter ten was precipitated by the question of two ambitious brothers. (In Matthew's Gospel the same incident is occasioned by an equally ambitious question from the mouth of their mother.) We shall look at both in turn.

In Mark, it is James and John the sons of Zebedee who ask, with no little brazenness, that Jesus do for them whatever they ask. They ask to sit at his right and left side in his kingdom. Jesus tells them it is not a privilege he can give, but goes on to link sitting in these exalted places with a willingness to suffer. This suffering Jesus describes as a baptism, a literal immersion in suffering which appears to be the gateway for privilege in the kingdom of heaven. But even if they were to suffer, such privileges are reserved for those for whom they have been prepared. When their ambition is reported to the other disciples, they are understandably indignant, so Jesus calls them together and tells them, "You know that those who are regarded as rulers of the Gentiles lord it over them, and their high officials exercise authority over them. Not so with you. Instead, whoever wants to become great among you must be your servant, and whoever wants to be first must be slave of all. For even the Son of Man did not come to be served, but to serve, and to give his life as a ransom for many" (Mark 10:41-45).

The parallel passage in Matthew (Matthew 20:20-28) is virtually identical except for the origin of the request. In this story it is the mother of the twins, James and John, who comes very deliberately before Jesus and petitions him for the places on either side of his throne, or seat, for them. She undoubtedly was an ambitious woman, but you wonder what kind of kingdom she envisaged. The response of Jesus is exactly the same, underlining that, although these two accounts are slightly different in their telling, they are probably relating the same incident.

Indeed, beneath both their requests, the brothers' and their mother's, there most probably lay a misunderstanding about the kingdom. Almost certainly the disciples, James and John, were once again envisaging the kingdom as an earthly one in which, by attaching themselves to Jesus, they would find power. At this stage of the ministry of Jesus, and in common with the rest of the disciples, they thought that the kingdom was most likely one in which the Romans would be overthrown and in which Jesus' closest followers would divide the spoils. Suffering would have been interpreted as sharing in the armed struggle, and naturally the most courageous would get the most privileges. This would be a typical way of understanding the outcome of a successful political or military movement whose aim was the overthrow of a corrupt and illegitimate regime. It had happened before in Jewish history, at the time of the Maccabees, and now they thought it might happen again, in the days of Jesus.

The final occasion in which this debate came up amongst the disciples was, amazingly, at the Last Supper. Just after the distribution of the bread and wine as solemn reminders of the new covenant made through Jesus' body and blood, we are told by Luke that a dispute arose amongst them. Once again they were discussing which of them was the greatest. (See Luke 22:24.) Again Jesus reminded them how they were to be different from the rulers of the Gentile nations, saying, "...you are not to be like that" [referring to the way of ruling amongst the Gentiles]. Once again Jesus teaches them that he is among them as one who serves. He will confer on them a kingdom but it will not be like the one they envisage, it will be entirely different. One of its hallmarks will be that, "...the greatest among you should be like the youngest, and the one who rules like the one who serves. For who is greater, the one who is at the table or the one who serves? Is it not the one who is at the table? But I am among you as one who serves" (Luke 22:26f). So, almost in the same breath, Jesus spoke of a kingdom which was coming, which he was inaugurating, but was one in which the greatest was the servant of all. The notion of the greatest being the servant of all is therefore fundamental to Jesus' understanding of the use of power and authority in the kingdom. He himself was the greatest example of this not coming to be served but to serve —giving his life as a ransom for all, and being among them as one who served. Before looking more specifically at the need for such servant leadership in the church today, we will look at the temptation of power, which is so prevalent in every aspect of human society.

The use of power
Power of itself is not evil. It is often grouped with sex and money. But rather as sex has great potential for good, and – when kept to its appropriate, rightful place – provides proper pleasure for husband

184

and wife; and just as money can be properly used in the service of the kingdom, so it is with power. It has its proper, godly use. The challenge is how we use whatever power or authority we have been given, whether by virtue of office, status, birth, gifting or circumstance. There are many types of power of which we commonly speak: we may speak of parent power, financial power, political or military power and so on. However, all power is based fundamentally on the power which God gives us. In the famous conversation between Pilate and Jesus, at the time of Jesus' trial, Jesus said to Pilate – in response to Pilate's assertion of his own power to execute or free Jesus – these important words, "You would have no power over me if it were not given to you from above" (John 19:11). Indeed at the end of Matthew's Gospel Jesus says, "All authority in heaven and on earth has been given to me. Therefore go and make disciples of all nations..." (Matthew 28:18f). What was unmistakable throughout the ministry of Jesus was his authority. And the authoritative nature of his teaching and actions (see Mark 1:27, Matthew 7:28f) resided in his intimate relationship with the Father, as Jesus repeatedly taught. (See John 7:16-18; John 5:19.) What Jesus taught in his ministry – that the power to rule came from God – Paul further explained in relation to the operation of power in the state when he taught the Romans that, "The authorities that exist have been established by God" (Romans 13:1b). So all power proceeds from God himself and power is entrusted to humans for all the various functions of life, whether raising a family, working for the state or for a commercial, voluntary or industrial organisation. Power is invested in us for a task, and it is then capable of being used creatively or abusively, effectively or damagingly.

We all have seen or heard of power being used destructively —notably by rogue rulers who intimidate and oppress their people. Equally, we will have heard of power being misused in commercial organisations. Extreme, high profile incidences of this become publicly known, as in the case of a newspaper proprietor now deceased, who raided the pension funds of his employees to resource his own business undertaking, or those found guilty of false accounting in certain large corporations, leading to financial ruin for investors or employees. These are examples of the abuse of power, used to aggrandize, or to intimidate or subjugate others. Such abuse of power originates from the temptation to pride or sheer greed.

It was abuse of power that Jesus observed in the Gentile rulers of his own day. He lived in an imperialist age, when Roman power was arguably at its height. The emperor Augustus ruled a territory which went from North Africa in the south to Britain in the north; from Spain in the west to Syria and Romania in the east. It was an extraordinary empire, held together by the might of Roman arms, the promulgation of its laws and the uniformity of its culture. Like all empires, it was passing. But its rulers, both great and petty, "lorded it" over their subjects. And to this often cruel method of rule Jesus drew attention. The kingdom which he had come to usher in was decidedly different in its use of power, and the great motif which described the exercise of this power was service.

The servant king

In reply to all the questions about power and ambition, there was always only one model of power with which Jesus answered his interlocutors. The model that Jesus held before them was that of a servant. In the Gospels, as we have seen, there are several occasions when people asked him for power in the kingdom he was inaugurating. We have seen that they invariably misunderstood the nature of the kingdom; nevertheless he answered their questions about power. To James and John, and their mother, who asked for the most powerful positions in this kingdom, to the disciples who argued amongst themselves as to which of them was the greatest, Jesus always replied in the same way. The greatest was the one who made himself least, and the one who would serve the others. Jesus summed it up: "Instead, the greatest among you should be like the youngest, and the one who rules like the one who serves" (Luke 22:26), because, "...even the Son of Man did not come to be served, but to serve, and to give his life as a ransom for many" (Mark 10:45). To lead, to rule, or to have authority, exercise power, in the kingdom of God is to serve. Nothing is more important to know than this in leadership.

At times the church, both past and present, has singularly failed to embody this, and has thereby failed to bear witness to the kingdom which is her chief function. Too often, its leaders in every age have shown that they are fascinated, beguiled and even intoxicated with power. This stems in part from the accident of history, the nature of Christendom and the misuse of authority. We shall look at each of these in turn.

With respect to the accident of history, if that is the right way of putting it, this goes back to the Constantinian settlement in the Roman empire. When Constantine was converted to Christianity, he made Christianity the state religion of the empire. He gave the church the trappings of power: bishops gained both civil and ecclesiastical jurisdiction, and buildings were constructed that communicated authority and grandeur as well as faith. Although they were built to the glory of God, they too easily could be used as symbols of earthly power. A process began by which the church community accrued wealth and legal jurisdiction. Its office holders, from the papacy downwards to bishops and clergy, were thereby able to hold considerable sway over the minds and lives of the people. This process of institutionalisation, which at root was based on a deal between the temporal and spiritual authority, in which both gained, led to and flowed from the establishment of Christendom. The construction of this arrangement between civic and ecclesiastical authority meant that the church conferred spiritual legitimacy on the state and the state conferred privileges and status on the church. In this arrangement it was all too easy for leaders in the church to move from being servants to being power-brokers; this was clearly discernible in the medieval and post medieval church; indeed, probably up to the time of the Second World War.

So what we might term the state of Christendom existed in Europe, (and outside Europe, in South America for example) from the time of Constantine until the twentieth century. Although Christendom took significant hits both at the time of the Reformation and the Enlightenment, it absorbed these body blows more or less in the West, until the complete secularisation of society which began in the 1960s. This secularisation ushered in the so called postmodern world. During the centuries of Christendom, which admittedly waxed and waned, the leaders of the church had great power. The nearest I have come to understanding the nature of that power presently is in countries like Nigeria, with which I am familiar, where the leaders of the church have almost unhindered authority. The temptation for leaders in such situations, past or present, was and is to use their power in just such a way that the apostle Peter warned against. He wrote to church leaders in the 1st century as follows, "Be shepherds of God's flock that is under your care, serving as overseers —not because you must, but because you are willing, as God wants you to be; not greedy for money, but eager to serve; not lording it over those entrusted to you but being examples to the flock" (1 Peter 5:2-4).

Peter puts his finger on those temptations that every leader in the church faces. There is the temptation to lead out of a spirit of compulsion or obligation, rather than a willing and free spirit. In such situations the leadership becomes heavy, overbearing and stultifying; there is little fun or enjoyment around, but instead a sense of guilt and "driven-ness" on the part of the flock. Or again, Peter tells leaders to shun temptations to financial or pecuniary advantage arising for leadership. In parts of the world such a possibility of making money from ministry may seem most unlikely, indeed almost laughable, considering the paltry wages of ministers, but in other regions ministry could be a way to real personal advancement. Such a motive in ministry must be resisted. Peter issues warnings to leaders which should have the effect of alerting us about the danger of getting on a power trip, in which egos are fed by dominating the flock and soaking them for either money or power.

Leaders in the church, as a result of this accident of history as well as the incipient temptations that leaders face, can become wolves in sheep's clothing —in name "servants", but in reality "devouring wolves". The apostles were well aware of such risks to the flock. (See Acts 20:29.) John Stott, in a book about Christian leadership entitled *Calling Christian Leaders*, which is a study of the first three chapters of 1 Corinthians, concludes with these words:

"During the last thirty five years or so I have had the privilege of travelling to many countries and observing the church and its leadership. As a result it is my firm conviction that there is too much autocracy in the leaders of the Christian community, in defiance of the teaching of Jesus and his apostles, and not enough love and gentleness. Too many behave as if they believed not in the priesthood of all believers but in the papacy of all pastors." He ends the book with the telling sentence, "My prayer as we come to the end of this study, is that Christian leaders who peruse these pages may be characterised above all else by what the apostles called "the meekness and gentleness of Christ" (2 Corinthians 10:1).[1]

Leadership in the kingdom, therefore, is characterised by the principle of servanthood but, perhaps worldwide, there are all too many examples of church leaders lording it over their flocks rather than leading them out gently to find pasture. On the other hand, Jesus' own ministry was fashioned by fulfilling in himself the Servant songs of Isaiah. These passages of Scripture describe not only the vicarious sufferings of the Messiah for his people but also the Servant's own attitude to his ministry. We are told of the Servant that a bruised reed he will not break and a smouldering wick he will not put out. Instead he will encourage and nourish all his people. Jesus embodied all the characteristics of the true servant. He was attentive to his Father to do his will (John 8:29), just as the servant in Psalm 130 was both attentive and patient to do his master's bidding. Karl Barth, commenting with great insight on that psalm, explains the concept of service as involving both will and action, where someone acts not according to his own purposes but for someone else. In his book *Money, Sex and Power*, Richard Foster describes various characteristics of creative power as he calls it, or true Christian service. He names a number of important attributes of service. The first is humility, which he describes as power under control, and which he points out is disciplined and able to be taught. In contrast, there is danger in power promoting arrogance. Secondly, it is self-limiting, choosing to use those resources which are for the benefit of the individual. Sometimes it may be unwise to give money or allow someone to become too dependent and not take up his own responsibility. Thirdly, a mark of true service is vulnerability. A well-known church leader and preacher told me that two qualities marked out his teaching: faithfulness to Scripture and openness about his own life —in other words, being vulnerable, as almost certainly others will share similar difficulties. Fourthly, there is weakness, which is closely related to vulnerability. In fact in God's hands our weaknesses can become our strengths as they make us dependent upon him, and conversely our strengths can become our stumbling blocks, as we can use them independently of his grace. Fifthly, submission is also a quality of true service —in that, if we ourselves know that we are accountable to another, our use of power and our service will be made all the more healthy. Finally, love is a mark of true Christian service since such service is done for the benefit of others. To be the greatest in the kingdom of God is to be such a servant to others. And nowhere was this more vividly demonstrated than in Jesus' washing of the disciples' feet.

In John's account of this, he prefaces the action of Jesus with these telling words, "Having loved his own who were in the world, he now showed them the full extent of his love.

"The evening meal was being served, and the devil had already prompted Judas Iscariot, son of Simon, to betray Jesus. Jesus knew that the Father had put all things under his power, and that he had come from God and was returning to God; so he got up from the meal, took off his outer clothing, and wrapped a towel round his waist. After that, he poured water into a basin and began to wash his disciples' feet, drying them with the towel that was wrapped round him" (John 13:1b-5). The actions of Jesus are rich in symbolism: the removal of the outer garment, the wrapping of a towel around him, the actual washing of the disciples' feet to enable membership of the new community (see John 13:8b). All these symbolic actions summarise the ministry of Jesus and our own needful response. At the end of the foot washing Jesus draws out the chief lesson for his disciples, which is that they are to follow his example. "Do you understand what I have done for you?" he asked them. "You call me 'Teacher' and 'Lord', and rightly so, for that is what I am. Now that I, your Lord and Teacher, have washed your feet, you also ought to wash one another's feet. I have set you an example that you should do as I have done to you" (John 13:12b-15). No event in the Gospels fulfils more clearly the servant ministry of Jesus than this, and no other teaching, accompanied as it was with this example, so demonstrates the call to service which is integral to true discipleship. Later Paul would teach the same in his famous Philippian hymn, in which he recalled that Jesus,

> ...being in very nature God,
> did not consider equality with God something to be grasped,
> but made himself nothing,
> taking the very nature of a servant,
> being made in human likeness.

Philippians 2:6-7

He prefaces this hymn with the teaching that we are to have the same attitude towards each other as Jesus had towards us. (See Philippians 2:5). The call to a servant form of leadership could not be clearer.

It is quite probable that we have become so acclimatised to such a style of leadership, in theory at least, that we are in danger of forgetting just how radical such teaching and such an example was, and still is. Although the vocabulary of service still permeates almost all titles given to leadership in our public life in Britain, it is easy for them to remain no more than names alone. In the UK, government ministers are called servants of the crown; we speak of public *service* as the work they do. Members of Parliament *serve* their constituencies, and leaders of churches are likewise servants of their flock, too. Such terms derive from what has become an archaic-sounding English usage: all employees, including managers, used to be termed, and perhaps this may still obtain in some legal documents, *servants* of their employers or companies. The secular world has various models of service, if not as many of servanthood. But the true spirit of service befitting disciples who are becoming citizens of the kingdom of God, derives from Jesus' own teaching and his supreme example as the servant king. He overturned all previous models of leadership, to bring in one which was – and is still today – both novel and revolutionary. The kingdom of God was to be a place where only this type of leadership was welcome, and in which it would eventually become uniform. In this respect, as in others, it was a topsy-turvy kingdom, inasmuch as normal human expectations were completely reversed.

Another central plank of Jesus' teaching about life in the kingdom is that he put far greater emphasis on the inside than on the outside —on the heart, as opposed to the *persona* or image.

Chapter Fourteen

THE INSIDE OUT KINGDOM

In this chapter we shall look at principles which underlie what might be called the ethics of the kingdom. In contradistinction to the ethics of the Pharisees and leaders of the Jewish people in the first century AD, Jesus placed his emphasis on the attitude of the heart rather than the outward observance of the law. Again and again we shall see that this was his primary concern. In a word, Jesus was more concerned with what was happening on the inside, rather than any outward display. The ethic of the kingdom of God could therefore be said to be "inside out". In fact this was no new ethic, it had always been part of the prophetic tradition of the Old Testament, but it was re-invigorated and restated by Jesus in his own distinctive teaching, and would be further elaborated by Paul in his teaching to the infant church, and especially in his summary of the gospel in his great Epistle to the Romans. But this teaching was nonetheless a radical departure from the way of life being taught by the Pharisees. In this chapter we will firstly look at the prophetic tradition which Jesus' teaching was both to fulfil and further apply, then look at the way this occurs in the teaching of Jesus particularly in the Sermon on the Mount, and lastly see how it continues in the teaching of Paul and John to the early church.

The prophetic tradition
There were certain issues which cropped up again and again between Jesus and the Pharisees. In the next chapter we will look more deeply at what underlay this ongoing controversy and so uncover the root of

the conflict. But superficially there were three areas which repeatedly caused controversy between Jesus and the Pharisees. These were ritual cleanliness, observance of the Sabbath, and righteousness under the law. (And we might add the issue of the temple, but this controversy was not specifically with the Pharisees). Jesus re-interpreted the true meaning of each of these three areas of contention with the Pharisees to show that outward observance without inner understanding of the purpose of each would only lead to sterile religion. In fact in every age, whether in Judaism or Christianity, there is an all too human tendency to replace a radical inner trust in God with outward observance of ritual, sacrament —or even with Scripture itself. (See John 5:31.) Jesus, in fulfilling the prophetic tradition, showed that the kingdom of God was about the attitude of the heart. For, as George Eldon Ladd pointed out in his book *The Presence of the Future*, the ethics of the kingdom puts fresh emphasis on the righteousness which is of the heart.[1] In the case of ritual purity (which together with possessing the Torah, circumcision and observing the Sabbath was a chief distinctive of Judaism) one of the most notable cases of Jesus' conflict with the Pharisees is recorded in Mark chapter seven.

Jesus and his disciples were being closely observed by the Pharisees as to their ritual washing, and were seen to come from the street or marketplace to eat without having ceremonially washed. As Mark says in his editorial aside, "The Pharisees and all the Jews do not eat unless they give their hands a ceremonial washing, holding to the traditions of the elders. When they come from the market-place they do not eat unless they wash. And they observe many other traditions, such as the washing of cups, pitchers and kettles" (Mark 7:3f). Given their customs which had become a litmus test of their religion, the Pharisees roundly condemned Jesus and his disciples for that lack of ritual washing. Jesus responded to the Pharisees' criticism with the telling riposte that, "Nothing outside a man can make him 'unclean'* by going into him. Rather it is what comes out of a man that makes him 'unclean'" (Mark 7:14f). [*'Unclean' in the strictly religious sense of that word.] Once again we can see that the Pharisaic tradition placed the emphasis on the outside whilst Jesus spelt out that it is what is on the inside that makes a person "unclean". (See especially the seven "woes" of Matthew 23.) Having to explain this further to the disciples, he gives a devastating critique of the heart of the human problem when he says, "For from within, out of men's hearts, come evil thoughts, sexual immorality, theft, murder, adultery, greed, malice, deceit, lewdness, envy, slander, arrogance and folly. All these evils come from inside and make a man 'unclean'." The problem is on the inside and not the outside. Cleansing the hands or the cup will not bring about the radical change that God is looking for from those who are entering the kingdom. Not surprisingly, Jesus shows that the Pharisees had missed the mark and had unwittingly fulfilled what the prophets had disparagingly said about them. So Jesus said, "Isaiah was right when he prophesied about you hypocrites; as it is written:

> These people honour me with their lips,
> but their hearts are far from me.
> They worship me in vain;
> their teachings are but rules taught by men.
>
> *Isaiah 29:13*

The Pharisees taught that it was enough to observe ceremonial washing regardless of what was in the heart, whilst Jesus, sitting lightly to the traditions of ceremonial washing, which was itself connected to ritual cleanliness and the food laws, pointed out that no amount of external washing was sufficient to cleanse the heart itself. Jesus pointed them to the inside rather than the outside, and in so doing challenged their understanding both of humankind and the salvation we need.

The second area of deep controversy with the Pharisees was over the Sabbath. Observance of the Sabbath, together with the practice of circumcision and ritual purity, was one of the great distinctives of Judaism. It still remains one of the chief distinguishing features of Judaism today. On many occasions Jesus was at odds with the Pharisees for doing good on the Sabbath, because they considered it work proscribed by Sabbath law. One such occasion, amongst many others, is recorded in Mark chapter 3, in a section devoted by Mark to the controversy between the Pharisees and Jesus about the Sabbath. Jesus is attending synagogue worship one Sabbath, as he normally did. His attendance at synagogue normally caused a stir —whether it was reading from Isaiah 61 at his home town of Nazareth and telling the congregation that what the prophet had written was fulfilled in him (Luke 4:14-21), or the reaction of a man possessed by an evil spirit, at Jesus' first recorded visit to the synagogue at Capernaum. (See Mark 1:23.) On this occasion in the synagogue there was a man with a "shrivelled hand". Perceiving the antipathy of the Pharisees and their hostility to helping this man on the Sabbath, he nevertheless asks him to stand, and challenges the watching Pharisees as to, "Which is lawful on the Sabbath: to do good or to do evil, to save life or to kill? But they remained silent." (See Mark 3:3f.) Jesus himself, we are told by Mark, is both angry and "...deeply distressed at their stubborn hearts". He goes ahead and heals the man's hand, and for their part the incensed Pharisees take stock with the Herodians as to how they might kill Jesus. (Mark 3:6.)

Once again it is an inside-outside issue. Jesus points the Pharisees to the deeper, if you like, internal reason for the institution of the Sabbath, which he does at the end of the previous chapter in which the Pharisees were objecting to the disciples' lack of Sabbath observance, just as they objected to their failure to wash and their failure to fast adequately. (Mark 2:18-22.) The disciples were picking ears of corn while walking through some cornfields; they were accused of doing what is unlawful on the Sabbath. The underlying question is whether man was made for the Sabbath or the Sabbath made for man. Of course the Sabbath was to be a day of rest, free from normal work, and was made for humankind's refreshment and enjoyment. As so often, the Pharisees had made it a day wrapped around with law and what today we might call "red tape". Instead of being a day of refreshment, it was one of anxiety. Why? Because they had forgotten its true purpose! Its inner significance was jettisoned in a welter of external rules. Once more the prophetic tradition of the Old Testament was endorsed and fulfilled by Jesus. Jesus pointed to the inner significance of the Sabbath which was to be observed —not mere external conformity to a scaffold of rules erected supposedly to support the law.

The third area where Jesus challenged the superficial conformity of the Pharisees to God's way was in relation to Scripture itself. Scripture must be added to ritual purity and the Sabbath as another place in which the Pharisees had the appearance of godliness but in fact turned something wonderful into something repressive and enslaving. Nowhere is this more powerfully put than in John's Gospel, where Jesus upbraids the Jews who had never heard his (the Father's) voice, "...nor seen his form, nor does his word dwell in you, for you do not believe the one he sent. You diligently study the Scriptures

196

because you think that by them you possess eternal life. These are the Scriptures that testify about me, yet you refuse to come to me to have life" (John 5:37b-40). Once again, the Pharisees and teachers of the law made reading of the Scriptures an exercise in obedience to the letter of the law, but they entirely missed the person of whom the Scriptures chiefly spoke. As we shall see again, they strained at gnats and swallowed camels! They were preoccupied with external conformity, but missed the true significance and meaning. As Ladd has shown, any reading of the Mishnah shows that rabbinic ethics generally focussed on *external* obedience to the letter of the law.

So in these three areas, as in fasting, Jesus makes it clear that the disposition of the heart is all important. Cleansing of the heart and not just of the body (or the drinking or cooking vessel) is needed. A heart turned to true worship of God, and time for re-creation and wholeness, is the true use of the Sabbath. Equally, leading a heart to the Messiah in repentance and faith is the true function of the Scriptures. Here is the true inner meaning of each of these pillars of Judaism. Without this true purpose there are simply burdens and an empty shell. Jesus showed that we must voyage from the outer to the inner. He also showed this was true in relation to the commandments. He made this abundantly clear during the Sermon on the Mount.

But I tell you; and rewards for secrecy

The Sermon on the Mount was the place *par excellence* where Jesus showed that he came to fulfil the prophetic tradition at a new and deeper level. As he himself said, "Do not think that I have come to abolish the Law or the Prophets; I have not come to abolish them but to fulfil them" (Matthew 5:17). Fulfilling the law and prophets meant applying them at a deeper level than hitherto. In this way, Jesus took several of the commandments and applied them not only to external actions but also to our thoughts and speech as well. So in relation to the commandment "You shall not kill", Jesus extended its application to being unjustifiably (as stated in some manuscripts) angry with your brother (fellow Jew), and swearing at him with the colourful Aramaic word, "Raca!" To express such anger would also, according to Jesus, be in breach of the commandments. Again, he famously reapplies the commandment against adultery —from action to thought. The Jewish male had construed the law of adultery in such a way as to let himself off lightly, both in this regard and in

197

the matter of divorce. Now, Jesus teaches, it is enough to look at a woman lustfully to commit adultery, and it is insufficient to simply write out a certificate of divorce unless the reason for it is marital unfaithfulness. (See Matthew 5:31f.) On both counts, Jesus extends the application of the commandments.

In all these instances the extension of application of the law is prefaced by Jesus' words, "But I tell you..." (See Matthew 5:22, 28, 32, 34, 39, 44.) What Jesus taught in relation to the sixth and seventh commandment he also applied to other practices current in Israel at the time. Thus our manner of speech should be simple and straightforward, unsupported by some escalating ladder of oaths related to creation or our bodies, Jerusalem or the temple, as was common at the time. About the customary law of retaliation, an eye for an eye, etc., which was based on the Old Testament judicial system (Exodus 21:24; Leviticus 24:20 and Deuteronomy 19:21), Jesus turned it on its head —calling for the turning of the cheek, generosity to the person who sues you, and going the second mile with someone who compels you. He even goes as far as to say, "But I tell you, do not resist an evil person" (Matthew 5:39). Finally, he calls on his disciples not only to love their neighbours but to love their enemies as well.

For Jesus, this extension – or in some cases redefinition – of Old Testament law was a fulfilment both of its original intention and of the prophetic tradition which accompanied it. In falling into legalism, the outward observance of the law without regard to intention or motive, the Jews failed to fulfil the law at its deepest level. The prophetic tradition in the Old Testament repeatedly attacked inadequate observance which showed itself in outward conformity but really camouflaged an inner rebellion. Nowhere was this more powerfully put than in the seventh century BC northern kingdom prophet Amos, who prophesied,

> "I hate, I despise your religious feasts;
> I cannot stand your assemblies.
> Even though you bring me burnt offerings and grain offerings,
> I will not accept them.
> Though you bring choice fellowship offerings,
> I will have no regard for them.
> Away with the noise of your songs!

I will not listen to the music of your harps.
But let justice roll on like a river,
righteousness like a never-failing stream!"

Amos 5:21-24

Jesus extended the scope of the law from the exterior to the interior; from the outward action to the attitude of the heart. The ethic of the kingdom was truly inside out. It also valued what was done in secret rather than for all to see. Once again, in this way the inner and the secret was cherished above the outer and the obvious. This applied in particular to the three great acts of piety: prayer, almsgiving and fasting. Jesus addressed all three, and emphasised the importance of secrecy.

Firstly, in regard to giving, he said, "So when you give to the needy, do not announce it with trumpets, as the hypocrites do in the synagogues and on the streets, to be honoured by men. I tell you the truth, they have received their reward in full. But when you give to the needy, do not let your left hand know what your right hand is doing, so that your giving may be in secret. Then your Father, who sees what is done in secret, will reward you." You cannot help noticing that in Jesus' teaching he exposes the deep desire for applause and praise in the hearts of some people for their philanthropy. It is a case of ostentatious giving being met with public applause. Jesus says such people have their full reward, now. But he then commends another way of giving, which is so secret that the left hand does not know what the right hand gives. There is to be what bankers call a "Chinese wall" between the hand and the brain; a kind of philanthropic amnesia which prevents recall of previous giving, seeks no plaudits from others and is content to be unrecognised; in which case such a person's reward, if there is to be one, is in heaven. The Father who sees the secret action will reward it. I have to say there are churches in the world that although they may be squeaky clean when it comes to sexual ethics have a curious weakness for money! The big givers are rewarded with publicity and status in church life and there appears to be little time for "secrecy" in this matter. Often only too happy to expose sexual misdemeanours, they are curiously blind to the use of money for influence, power and reputation. I wonder why that is? Jesus clearly, without prevarication or exceptions, requires "secrecy" in the area of all almsgiving.

199

Secondly, he calls for secrecy in our prayer life, too. Maybe for reasons of idleness or spiritual torpor we are happy to go along with this. If secret prayer is the order of the day, then no-one is going to know, this side of heaven, how much or little I pray. Whatever, Jesus makes it clear that we should, "...not be like the hypocrites, for they love to pray standing in the synagogues and on the street corners to be seen by men. I tell you the truth, they have their reward in full. But when you pray, go into your room, close the door and pray to your Father, who is unseen. Then your Father, who sees what is done in secret, will reward you" (Matthew 6:5-8). The same principle of secrecy applies with prayer as with giving. The movement again is from exterior show to interior integrity. And just as we are not to be showy where we pray, nor are we to be showy how we pray. God is not impressed by either length or liturgy; he is touched by earnest, believing prayer. And yet how often we are impressed by length ("so and so prayed for thee hours before he did anything"), or by a beautifully constructed prayer. Just as Jesus taught that the widow's mite was more valuable than all the giving of the wealthy that day (see Luke 21:1-4), so one brief, heartfelt prayer uttered in faith is more valuable than a host of prayers that are simply going through the motions.

The last area of piety in which Jesus looked for secrecy of practice was in the area of fasting. Once again Jesus teaches that, in this case, those fasting should eschew any form of exhibitionism. It was common practice amongst those whom Jesus called "hypocrites" to make it quite obvious that they were fasting. They did this by disfiguring their faces, perhaps by putting ash on their faces so fulfilling the maxim of putting on sackcloth and ashes. But once again such devotion in fasting was not to be accompanied by any kind of spiritual ostentation. Instead, those fasting were to make people think that far from fasting they were at ease and at rest, so washing their faces and putting oil on their heads. However, not only should fasting be unobvious, so surmounting the possibilities of temptation to pride, but it should also range further —not just giving up food but all forms of injustice. After all it was Isaiah who prophesied,

> "Is not this the kind of fasting I have chosen:
> to loose the chains of injustice
> and untie the cords of the yoke,

> to set the oppressed free
> and break every yoke.
> Is it not to share your food with the hungry
> and to provide the poor wanderer with shelter—
> when you see the naked, to clothe him,
> and not to turn away from your own flesh and blood?
>
> *Isaiah 58:6f*

The principle remains the same that the true faster's spiritual effort or exercise will be known to God, and that true fasting includes giving up and/or practising social justice.

So each of these three classic areas of spirituality – giving, praying and fasting – is to be performed in secret and not publicly. They are for the Father's eyes only, and not for the appreciation of onlookers or bystanders. The reward is in heaven and not on earth. He rewards what is done in secret, not what has been previously applauded by a human audience for whom the act of piety was done to impress. Throughout Jesus' teaching in the Sermon on the Mount, he shows that he is more concerned with the inside than the outside. The extension of the law's application to cover attitude, motive and thought, together with the practice of any piety secretly, shows the kingdom of God is very much "inside out". This is most clearly shown in Jesus' revolutionary teaching in the Beatitudes.

The Beatitudes are akin to a spiritual cardiogram, a way of both measuring and rewarding a commendable attitude of the heart. They give us a yardstick capable of detecting the inclinations of the human heart, as well as a standard to which to aspire. The Beatitudes are just what they say they are, blessed attitudes, or attitudes of the heart which bring deepest contentment or peace, not possible without the previous operation of God's grace. "Blessed" may not be the best translation of the Greek word *makarios* which R T France maintains stands for the Hebrew word *asre*, which means fortunate, rather than one whom God blesses.[2] So anyone with these attitudes of heart is indeed fortunate and will receive a reward in the kingdom of God, either now or when that kingdom finally and fully comes.

For our purposes, and sticking to the theme of this chapter, we can see that these commendable attitudes are generated internally, and then both shown and rewarded externally. So each beatitude begins with a description of that internal attitude, and then in the second part of the statement shows the reward which is carried with it. Poverty of spirit, or meekness, is the basic attitude which underlies all the others. It alludes to what the Old Testament prophetic tradition often taught as in Micah, for example:

> He has showed you, O Man, what is good.
> And what does the LORD require of you?
> To act justly and to love mercy
> and to walk humbly with your God
>
> *Micah 6:8*

And in Isaiah:

> For this is what the high and lofty One says—
> he who lives for ever, whose name is holy:
> "I live in a high and holy place,
> but also with him who is contrite and lowly in spirit,
> to revive the spirit of the lowly
> and to revive the heart of the contrite"
>
> *Isaiah 57:15*

A contrite, humble, trusting spirit is what the Lord looks for, and he rewards it. God also seeks an unworldly attitude, putting trust in him rather than the power and the expertise of the world, an attitude that longs for his righteousness or justice, and which may consequently mourn as a result of the world's indifference or cold shoulder. Beyond this, the blessed are those who are merciful, who seek purity in its widest sense, and who are "peacemakers". These are all commendable attitudes of heart, and although they may be neither commended nor recognised on earth they will be rewarded in the kingdom of heaven. More especially, any who suffers on account of espousing these attitudes, this kind of righteousness, will inherit the kingdom of heaven. The Beatitudes are the pattern for living in the kingdom of God, and they will far outlast their counterparts which exist in the world.

Continuing with St Paul

If what we have been looking at so far is essentially the spirituality for the kingdom of God as taught by Jesus, we shall briefly see how this same spirituality is continued in Paul's writings, as indeed in the apostle John's, whose Gospel and other writings use for the most part a different vocabulary to Paul or the synoptic Gospels. It is not that either John or Paul espoused a different spirituality, but their purposes in writing being slightly different, and their audiences being distinct as well – not to mention their own differing experiences and background – means that the terms in which they expressed this spirituality of the kingdom are different. All we are saying here is that in their writings too there is an emphasis on the priority of the heart over against the external, and both make this clear.

Of the two writers it is Paul who makes this more of an issue, not least because he is the apostle to the Gentiles, and therefore continually has to explain and defend what the essence of the gospel is, stating its irreducible minimum, which is in fact remarkably succinct. In his greatest teaching epistle, the letter to the Romans, Paul shows that the true Jew – that is, the true Israelite, or the one who is acceptable to God – is not the person with the right externals (i.e. race, birth or external actions), but the one who trusts from the heart. Thus he writes, "A man is not a Jew if he is only one outwardly, nor is circumcision merely outward and physical. No, a man is a Jew if he is one inwardly; and circumcision is circumcision of the heart, by the Spirit, not by the written code. Such a man's praise is not from men, but from God" (Romans 2:28). Nothing could be clearer than this teaching that God is interested in the heart, in the inner life and commitment, and not mere externals; even though originally those externals – whether they be circumcision, the law, the Sabbath or the temple – were given by God himself. Paul teaches the same elsewhere —for instance in Philippians when he says, "For it is we who are the circumcision, we who worship by the Spirit of God, who glory in Christ Jesus, and who put no confidence in the flesh" (Philippians 3:3). Or again, as Paul says to the Galatians with all the passion he can muster, "For in Christ Jesus neither circumcision nor uncircumcision has any value. The only thing that counts is faith expressing itself through love" (Galatians 5:6). Again and again, Paul argues that it is the heart exercising faith in God's promise fulfilled in Jesus that is the basis not only of our salvation but of all true spirituality, and in so doing he more than echoes the teaching of Jesus which we have already been looking at in this chapter.

The outcome of such faith, such trusting, is both an internal revolution and a way of life which is best shown in love, and at that point both John and Paul use the same vocabulary. Paul, like Augustine later, was the great psychologist of the effect of true faith —that is, he saw the internal revolution in the heart of the believer resulting from faith in God's promise of redemption, and charts it in his difficult but rewarding chapters of Romans 6-8. Although we shall look at the implications of that a little more in the next chapter, suffice it to say here that the Christian stands in a different relationship to both the old life of sin and the law, and this is the argument of those chapters.

In regard to sin Paul says, "For we know that our old self* was crucified with him so that the body of sin might be done away with, that we should no longer be slaves to sin —because anyone who has died has been freed from sin" (Romans 6:6). [*"old self" signifying our old way of life.] Paul argues that, in believing, something in us died when we came to faith in Christ. And the thing that has died is being under the control of sin, that is our own selfish ego, and we are freed to follow a new Christ-centred way of life in which we must continually, actively yield our bodies, or whole beings, in slavery to righteousness leading to holiness. (See 6:19.) It is not that we are insensible to the appeals of sin, nor that we do not face a continuing struggle, but that we now have a new power at work in us so that the Christian need not be led into sinful ways. In a sense we have simply been given the spiritual wherewithal to fight back, and not on our own but with the power of the Spirit, and a new mindset of wanting to please God. What Paul teaches is that an internal change takes place in us when we believe, the result of which is that through grace we can fulfil the law —both outwardly and, more importantly, inwardly; not perfectly, but it is now a real possibility.

The call then is, as always, to love both God and neighbour. On this, both Paul and John agree, for love is the fulfilment of the law (Romans 13:10) or, as John says, "Whoever lives in love lives in God, and God in him" (1 John 4:16b). Or, again, as Paul puts it in the context of the kingdom of God, his only mention of the phrase in the entire Epistle to the Romans, "For the kingdom of God is not a matter of eating and drinking," [referring to his previous discussion about what is permissible in the fellowship], "but of righteousness, peace and joy in the Holy Spirit, because anyone who serves Christ in this way is pleasing to God and approved by men" (Romans 14:17f). So faith in Christ leads to an internal change, and the internal change should have external evidence. The dominant feature of this new way of life is love in which there is integrity; and integrity is a true match between the inside and the outside —something which was absent through Judaism but is made possible by Christ. The spirituality of the kingdom of God is all about a new internal life being shown in a new external way. A new inside is shown outside. Another way of putting this, which we must look at now, is that grace made possible what the law could never do. So in the penultimate part of this section on the topsy-turvy kingdom, in which the leader is the servant and the inside is more fundamental than the outside, is the movement from law to grace which lies at the heart of kingdom life.

Chapter Fifteen

THE LAST IS FIRST KINGDOM

The third area which Jesus turned on its head was the very motivation for worship and discipleship itself. In other words, what is it that should truly motivate any person in their following of God? Is it conformity to rules and regulations? Is it a desire to win favour with the one we follow or worship, or with our peers who we are seeking to impress? Is it that we seek to tick off various check points of our own spiritual life? The answers to these questions or others like them may seem obvious, but they were not so in Jesus' day. What he seemed to be teaching was at complete variance with the teaching of the contemporary religious leaders. And I have a sneaking suspicion that, like the Galatians, having started out with a gospel of grace we too can revert, all too easily, to a religion of law, which as Paul said is no gospel at all. (See Galatians 1:7.)

In this chapter I hope to show that, in bringing back the central message of grace to the message of the kingdom, Jesus was indeed overthrowing a tradition that had grown up within Judaism. For in the previous four hundred years the observance of the Torah and its rules had become seen as the way of salvation. In overthrowing this law-centred spirituality, Jesus was reinforcing the message of the prophets and, more fundamentally, was restating the great Abrahamic covenant which had been obscured by the Pharisees' concentration on the keeping of the Mosaic law. In this chapter we shall look again at Jesus' dispute with the spirituality of the Pharisees and its fundamental concerns, observe his own teaching of the necessity of grace, and then look again at the way in which Paul in his two great epistles on this theme, namely Romans and Galatians, explains how the grace of God did what the law of God could never do.

We have already seen this theme well trailed in this book. In our survey of the parables we have seen that grace was a basic operating principle of the kingdom. God governed the kingdom through grace. Indeed the kingdom could not be entered without it. The parable of the prodigal son is the iconic story of being welcomed back by grace into the Father's presence. The parable of the Pharisee and the tax collector epitomises all that we shall be looking at in this chapter, namely that the one who is justified in the kingdom is the one who cannot even raise his eyes heavenwards, and who says, "God, have mercy on me, a sinner!" (Luke 18:13). But the theme we are treating here is best described by John in the prologue to his Gospel. He writes, "For the law was given through Moses; grace and truth came through Jesus Christ" (John 1:17). It was not a grace that was welcomed by the religious leaders of his day, who purported to follow Moses —yet, as Jesus told them, Moses rejoiced to see his day. (See John 5:46f.)   So Jesus had to face, full on, the false and hypocritical spirituality of the Pharisees in announcing this kingdom of grace. He does this powerfully in his blistering polemic against them in Matthew chapter 22.

Straining at gnats and swallowing camels
Jesus' most vehement condemnation of the scribes and Pharisees comes toward the end of his ministry. Throughout the Gospel accounts there have been run-ins with the Pharisees about healing on the Sabbath (see Mark 3:1-6; Luke 14:1-6; John 5:10; John 9:14), offering forgiveness (Mark 2:7-10), and supremely his claim to be equal with God (John 10:36: John 5:18: John 8:58f). Although there was always heat in the controversy between Jesus and the scribes and Pharisees, it reached boiling point by the end of his ministry. And the steam was certainly rising by the final chapters of Matthew and Mark. Although there is much common material which records this fierce controversy in both these Gospels, it is Matthew who gives us the fullest account.

In Matthew chapter 22 we see various groups coming with their venomous questions designed to discredit Jesus, and so make him vulnerable to a trial and punishment. These questions were not of only academic interest, like those on Mastermind or University Challenge (two well known British television quiz shows), for on Jesus' answers depended his reputation and life. The price of a mistaken answer was not simply the loss of a mark but, potentially, the loss of his life. In another translation Matthew graphically says of the Pharisees that they, "...went out and laid plans to trap him in his words" (Matthew 22:15b). The questions Jesus was asked concerned: paying taxes to Caesar— "Is it right to pay taxes to Caesar or not?" (v. 17); and the resurrection (posed by the Sadducees); and, lastly, what was the greatest commandment. The last question, before Jesus reversed the role and asked them a question of his own about whose son the Christ is, may seem fairly innocuous to us but it was a disputed part of the law as to which commandment was the most significant. As we know, he answered each question with consummate skill and authority, turning the tables on his questioners, who fled from his answers to lick their damaged pride. At the end we are told that, "... No-one could say a word in reply, and from that day on no-one dared to ask him any more questions" (Matthew 22:45).

The last question in this series, about which was the greatest commandment, was a chestnut, entering into an area of contemporary religious debate about the right interpretation of the law. It was nonetheless a test question. But, despite its intent to trip Jesus up and, if possible, destroy his reputation, it led to a conversation with the man who asked it which was in a way quite promising. In Mark's longer account of this question, Jesus, in his classic and defining answer about our true spiritual obligations, was speaking of the commandments. "The most important one," answered Jesus, "is this: 'Hear, O Israel: The Lord our God, the Lord is one. Love the Lord your God with all your heart and with all your soul and with all your mind and with all your strength.' The second is this: 'Love your neighbour as yourself.' There is no commandment greater than these" (Mark 12:29-32). It was in a rather patronising way that the questioner went on to say, "You are right...", confirming Jesus' reply. But the questioner also adds that such action, of loving God and neighbour, was "...more important than all burnt offerings and sacrifices" (Mark 12:33). Jesus lastly responds, seeing the wisdom of his reply, with the words, "You are not far from the kingdom of God" (v. 34).

How close was this questioner to the kingdom of God? He had understood the law in its essence. He knew the message of the prophets:

> "For I desire mercy, not sacrifice,
> and acknowledgment of God rather than burnt offerings"
>
> *Hosea 6:6*

and:

> With what shall I come before the LORD
> and bow down before the exalted God?
> Shall I come before him with burnt offerings,
> with calves a year old?
> Will the LORD be pleased with thousands of rams,
> with ten thousand rivers of oil?
> Shall I offer my firstborn for my transgression,
> the fruit of my body for the sin of my soul?
> He has showed you, O man, what is good.
> And what does the LORD require of you?
> To act justly and to love mercy,
> and to walk humbly with your God.
>
> *Micah 6:6-8*

So this questioner, unlike the other Pharisees and Sadducees who had questioned Jesus, understood the nature of the kingdom and that it was about grace and mercy as well as righteousness and truth, and that these were the foundations of the government of the kingdom. However, if he was not far from the kingdom and was commended for his wisdom by Jesus – a wisdom drawn from the prophets – he was an exception to the rule. The questioner did not yet know that the great commandment was a perfect measuring rod which could tell everyone that they had fallen short, that they were deficient and needed to enter by another route, marked grace. If this questioner at least recognised the standard, and maybe his own deficiency too, he was an exception, unlike most of the Pharisees whom Jesus would now go on to condemn.

In Matthew chapter 23 we have some aspects of the spirituality of the kingdom set out in contradistinction to the spirituality of the Pharisees. We see some of the marks of this topsy-turvy kingdom presented in a polemic of such sustained passion that the page almost seems to burn. When Jesus' questioners had slunk away at the end of Matthew chapter 22 (with its parallel of Mark 12:13-40), he turned to the crowds and to his disciples, and literally vilified the spirituality of the Pharisees, blowing it out of the water. In the first twelve verses of Mathew 23, Jesus on the one hand condemns the spirituality of the Pharisees and on the other hand upholds some of the principles of the kingdom which we have already seen. Before considering the seven charges (the seven woes) that Jesus lays at the door of the Pharisees, we will look at his challenge to them in these opening twelve verses of Matthew 23.

In these verses Jesus firstly exposes their spirituality. Although they tie themselves to Moses' teaching ("The teachers of the law and the Pharisees sit in Moses' seat") so that Jesus says, "So you must obey them and do everything they tell you", he also says, "But do not do what they do, for they do not practise what they preach" (v. 3). Here is the root of their failing! They are not in it because of a sincere love of Moses' teaching which they themselves are seeking to follow but because of the status it imparts by being associated with its moral authority, by making themselves heirs to Moses' central position in the nation and by deriving a sense of power from the burdens they can impose on others. Thus Jesus criticises them for the burdens they place on others (v. 4), for their love of publicity and show through their style as much as their clothes ("They make their phylacteries wide and the tassels on their garments long", v. 5), for their love of status and reputation (the best seats, see v. 6), for the recognition they get in the community (greetings in the market places, see v. 7), and the applause which they soaked up from each other (see John 5:44), and for being called teacher or rabbi. All this they loved; and it is easy to fall in love with it, not least in a denomination, as with my own, where there are special clothes to be worn, fine buildings to use, a connection with the state to be exploited and publicity to be found with the media. But Jesus' words taught that nothing like those things which so appealed to the Pharisees was to be sought. And in contradistinction to that, Jesus advocated a true spirituality of the kingdom in which leadership is not top down but bottom up: "The greatest among you will be your servant. For whoever exalts himself will be humbled, and whoever humbles himself will be exalted" (v. 11f).

Jesus once again showed the topsy-turvy nature of the kingdom with regard to leadership. In the seven woes or charges that followed he showed where, fundamentally, the Pharisees had missed the mark. The charges, briefly, were that firstly they prevented people from entering the kingdom because they made it out to be a place completely different from what it was (v. 13). A similar charge could be levelled at our churches, because all too few churches are windows into what the kingdom is truly like, and instead demonstrate a kingdom which is far removed from the kingdom of which Jesus spoke. (We shall return to this theme in the chapter on the church and the kingdom.)

Secondly, they erred because in bringing the people into a system of religion with no Messiah of mercy the Pharisees made their converts twice as much a child of hell as themselves. (See v. 15.)

Thirdly, their speech was peppered with oaths of little consequence, as we have already seen from Jesus' teaching on speech in the Sermon on the Mount.

Fourthly, they fulfilled their duty of tithing, but neglected what was supremely important (v. 24), to which matter we will return in a moment.

Fifthly and sixthly, they were concerned with the outside whilst concealing rottenness inside. What could be more graphic than the metaphor Jesus used to describe them here: "...You are like whitewashed tombs, which look beautiful on the outside but on the inside are full of dead men's bones and everything unclean. In the same way, on the outside you appear to people as righteous but on the inside you are full of hypocrisy and wickedness" (v. 27f). Here is irony indeed— the very people who set themselves up as the purveyors of the Mosaic law became "lawless" themselves!

The last charge was that they, like their fathers before, murdered those whom God sent. Happy to acclaim those past prophets who were dead and buried, by embellishing their tombs, they nevertheless persecuted any contemporary "prophet", like John the Baptist, who upset their sway over the people. They had learnt the art of turning history to their advantage while getting rid of any contemporary challenger who was in fact in a continuum with the very people who they deceitfully applauded but who were now safely dead!

So how was it that the promulgators of "law" had become "lawless", that those who spent their whole time in applying the law of Moses became a roadblock on the way to the kingdom, shutting the kingdom in people's faces? (See v. 13.) The most memorable statement of Jesus about this was that although they tithed the dill, mint and cummin from their herb gardens, they, "...neglected the more important matters of the law —justice, mercy and faithfulness.... You blind guides! You strain out a gnat but swallow a camel." (See v. 23.) Here, for me, is the central point. We must have a proper understanding of justice, mercy and faithfulness if we are ever to find the true role of the law. Or, to put it another way, we must firstly receive grace and mercy if we are to find the true value of law, for the law by itself will only ever condemn. The Pharisees, as Jesus said, were straining out gnats but swallowing camels. They needed to know the proper relationship of grace and law.

There is only one New Testament author who can properly guide us to a right understanding of grace and law, and he is Paul. Until the road to Damascus he strained out every gnat and swallowed many camels, but after his meeting with the Messiah he truly understood the difference between law and grace. To him we must now turn, and his writings, about the limits of the law and the limitless expanse of God's grace. For grace must abound for the law to be rightly understood.

The limits of law and limitless grace

We have seen that the Pharisees were those who strained at gnats but swallowed camels. This striking metaphor, so typical of Jesus' sharp use of language, and itself so much in the prophetic tradition, summed up much of the religion of the Pharisees. Their teaching, if not their example which Jesus had exposed (Mathew 23:3b), was based on a fundamental misunderstanding which Paul spent large chunks of his letters, especially to the Romans and the Galatians, trying to expose. Failing to appreciate the requirement of God's covenant with Abraham – in which faith in God's promise led to a right standing before God (justification) – the Pharisees made the outward observance of the law the litmus test of anyone's exclusion or inclusion in the covenant. However, Paul had to show the Jews that no one could ever be justified (put right with God) by works of the law. This was at the centre of his teaching. So to the Romans he wrote, "Therefore no-one will be declared righteous in his sight by observing the law; rather, through the law we become conscious of sin" (Romans 3:20). This is a key hermeneutical (interpretative) verse in understanding large parts of Romans. Or to put it another way, it is a key to the sardine tin of Romans. It undoes the lid and enables us to appreciate the innards of the epistle, especially when we come to chapters 7 and 8. The reason it is so important is that it categorically shows that the law is severely limited in what it can do; what it does it does well, but set it to do more than it was intended to do and it leads to a grievous distortion. The law, by which we mean the moral law here – although for the Jew it might well have been taken to mean the whole Torah – is like a stethoscope. If one sees the doctor, with symptoms of breathlessness and acute pains in the chest after exertion, he or she may well use a stethoscope, detect a heart condition and send one to hospital for further investigation. The stethoscope can detect trouble but cannot itself cure. It is perfectly good in its proper place in the diagnostic process, but you would never be sent home with a prescription to take one stethoscope a day! You cannot turn the instrument of diagnosis into the means of the cure; that is simply to confuse two different parts of the healing process. The Pharisees had done precisely this. They had taken the law and said that by keeping it one would become well, but since no-one could keep it perfectly (the only way by which it could prove helpful to us), least of all the Pharisees themselves, its work would only lead to condemnation —an important word in Romans. (See 8:1.) So the law can detect moral failure; it can condemn, but it cannot save us. That does not mean to say that it is bad; as Paul is at pains to point out, it is in fact very good and effective at its job, but it is limited. It cannot save, and it was never intended to do so.

So Paul argues that the law, the teaching of Moses (and, we might add, by extension, its distilled moral essence, the ten commandments) can never be properly and perfectly fulfilled. The Jew, as much as the Gentile, will fail its exacting standards. Indeed, he says to the Jew, "You who brag about the law, do you dishonour God by breaking the law?" (Romans 2:23). Indeed he does break it, like all people! So the law can never make us righteous because we all fail to keep it perfectly. We have to be released from this —and this is his argument in the much chewed over passage of Romans chapter 7. The purpose of this passage is to show further the limited power of the law; it has a power to convict and condemn, but it is on the other hand powerless to help. We have to understand this whole chapter (Romans 7) as one designed to show the limits of the law, especially for the person not yet a Christian. In this chapter Paul speaks of both his Christian and Jewish experience in relation to the law. The trick is to see when he is speaking about it from a Jewish standpoint and when he is speaking from a Christian standpoint. So at the beginning of the chapter Paul, speaking about the Christian's experience, says that when a Christian believes, he or she is freed from the law in the same way as death releases one married partner from any obligations to the other. It may not be a very affectionate illustration, but Paul's point is clear: death releases us from obligations; and in the same way, when a person becomes a Christian, he or she dies to an old way of life as well as trying to satisfy the law. (See Romans 6:6.)

However, before a person becomes a Christian, the demands of the law together with the old nature make for an explosive combination, dragging down to condemnation and spiritual death. Paul then deals with the question: since the law brings about this degradation, does that mean it is itself "sinful" (v. 7)? Not at all —that would be like saying that the stethoscope is diseased simply because it had rightly detected a heart murmur. It has done its job, but again its job is limited. In this section of Romans chapter 7, Paul is explaining how a Christian's relationship with the law has changed with his or her conversion, but since he is at pains to explain that the law is also good, he rows back after giving us a brief glimpse of a new and exciting way of life in the Spirit (see v. 6), in order to answer the question of whether the law is itself wrong or sinful, because this was an important question for the Jews. Again his answer is simply that it is good but its power is limited. (See v. 7.)

Paul embarks on a famous and complex personal argument as to how, in his own experience as a Jew, he found the law's action painfully effective in two respects. Firstly, it magnified his own sinfulness, detecting it where he had thought himself alright (see vv. 9-11). Secondly, he discovered a moral power crisis in himself, so that although he approved of the law's commands in his head he could not obey them in reality; worse than that, he did the very thing he did not want to do, and did not do things which both he and the law approved! (See v. 18.) Now, because this struggle closely resembles the ongoing struggle with the presence of sin in the Christian's life, it is often used as the classic expression of the struggle that a Christian experiences in fulfilling the commandments or leading a holy life. However, I believe Paul is using his personal experience here as a Jew to illustrate the inherent rightness of the law but its inability to help him, and his inability without the Spirit to fulfil the demands of the law (which, incidentally, he has heralded in verse 6). He will go on to describe the struggle we do have as Christians, but in the terms of a struggle between our flesh and the spirit in the next chapter (see Romans 8:5-17). Not only does Paul further explain in chapter eight what he had intimated (in 6:6), namely that the Christian has by dying to what once bound us, been released from the law so that we serve in the new way of the Spirit, but he further shows that Jesus did through grace what the law could never do. In one of the most important verses in the New Testament, explaining the limits of law and the limitless power of grace, Paul writes (in 8:3), "For what the law was powerless to do in that it was weakened by the sinful nature, God did by sending his own Son in the likeness of sinful man to be a sin offering."

If all this seems rather dense and difficult, the upshot of it can be simply put. It is this: the law is limited in what it can do. Mostly it can only do negative things, not because it is bad but because we are. It detects sin, it magnifies sin, it condemns sin, and it is powerless to help us because of our weakness. As Jesus taught, only if the law is perfectly fulfilled can it help us. "For I tell you that unless your righteousness surpasses that of the Pharisees and the teachers of the law, you will certainly not enter the kingdom of heaven." Or again, Jesus requires us to, "Be perfect, therefore, as your heavenly Father is perfect" (Matthew 5:48). However, since we can neither fulfil the law in its entirety nor be perfect, then there must be another way by which we can enter the kingdom.

Once again then, "...the law was given through Moses; grace and truth came through Jesus Christ" (John 1:17). It has rightly been said that the principal difference between Christianity and all other religions is grace. The Pharisees, in trying to enforce the Mosaic law, were always trying to navigate a canoe through dangerous rapids of finding salvation with only one paddle. The craft would always capsize and the occupants be left to the mercy of the foaming waters. "...know that a man is not justified* by observing the law, but by faith in Jesus Christ" (Galatians 2:16). [*Justified – put right with God.] But in making themselves the imperfect enforcers of the Mosaic law, the Pharisees were ignoring another vessel already made available, which would safely navigate the rapids, and that was the covenant with Abraham which was founded on grace and required the response of faith. The Old Testament text, "He [Abraham] believed God, and it was credited to him as righteousness" is probably Paul's most important and most often quoted verse from the Old Testament, for it shows that righteousness or justification may be obtained through faith in God's gracious promise. It was the foundation verse in both Romans and Galatians (see Galatians 3:6, Romans 4:3), and as Paul says in two seminal verses in Galatians: "The Scripture foresaw that God would justify the Gentiles by faith, and announced the gospel in advance to Abraham...." So what pertained to the gospel was present in God's promise to Abraham, and when Jesus came, "He redeemed us in order that the blessing given to Abraham might come to the Gentiles through Jesus Christ, so that by faith we might receive the promise of the Spirit." The law was given by Moses, which was powerless to help us, but grace and truth came through Jesus Christ.

So, curiously, it was not that the Pharisees were unbiblical; they knew the Scriptures well, but they were simply not biblical enough. They did not go back sufficiently far. They went back to Sinai, the giving of the law, when they should have gone back to Bethel, God's covenant with Abraham. They looked on the outside, when the prophets repeatedly looked to the heart and the inside. Grace, in the context of God's covenant with Abraham with the necessary response of faith, had always preceded the requirement of the law and its necessary response of obedience, but the Pharisees had strained out the gnats and swallowed the camels. They neglected the underlying principles of the Torah, "...justice, mercy and faithfulness" (Matthew 23:23b). They did not know that law was limited but grace was generous and regenerating. Paul could never find words sufficiently profuse to describe the extent of this grace. "For if the many died by the trespass of the one man [Adam], how much more did God's grace and the gift that came by the grace of the one man, Jesus Christ, overflow to the many!" (See Romans 5:15). So we have it: abundant, overflowing grace. What Jesus had come to bring was this overflowing grace; or again, as John put it in the opening of his Gospel, "From the fullness of his grace we have all received one blessing after another."

In stressing the importance of observing the law, without making known the availability of mercy, the Pharisees were putting the cart before the horse. Forgiveness would bring about change, as exhibited by Zacchaeus, which no amount of legal compulsion could ever produce. The kingdom could never be entered by a set of rules, but something more radical which we must now explore. Entrance could be gained by surrender and not by deserving or merit. It was uncomfortable, humbling, but it precluded boasting and made it open to all. Jesus had a way of encapsulating all this teaching in another of those sayings which I call kingdom reversals. He simply said that the first would be last and the last would be first. Those who thought themselves deserving of the kingdom by virtue or by their deeds, by their religious privileges or their birth, would find themselves sent either to the back of the entrance queue or excluded, whilst those who knew there was nothing in themselves to commend them found as they trusted in God's mercy that they were fast-tracked to the front of the entrance queue and welcomed with open arms. As I say, it is one of those three great reversals found in the kingdom which we have looked at here: upside down, inside out and last is first. Together they more than adequately describe the spirituality of the kingdom.

Chapter Sixteen

THE WAY IN IS
THE WAY DOWN KINGDOM

In this chapter we shall look at the basic question of how we enter the kingdom. We have looked at many of the kingdom's characteristics, seen the most important features of it, thought about the way in which the kingdom is expressed or manifested in the world; and we are currently engaged, in this section, at looking at the way in which it is quite unlike any other power structure you could think of, continually turning the generally accepted world order on its head.

For instance, its leaders should be the servants of all, its spirituality and life more concerned with the inside and not the outside (whilst most of the world spends huge sums of money and gives inordinate attention to the exterior), and it frequently surprises with its own revolutionary entrance system, so that those who the world thinks of as "last" (in Jesus' day the tax collectors, the prostitutes and the excluded) are admitted, through grace, into the kingdom "first". So, as Jesus often said, many who are first will be last, and many who are last will be first. What could be more, as the French might say, *boulverse* than that?

But here we see, in keeping with all of these other surprising paradoxes, that the way into this kingdom is also the way down, or to put it another way, entrance is by surrender!

Many have given their personal accounts (or testimonies) of surrendering to Jesus Christ. Entering the kingdom is by surrender —surrender of our pride as well as our weaknesses and sins; surrender of our own path of self-fulfilment for another path for which we were created; surrender of our own dreams in exchange for God's plan for our life, which surely must be better. Above all, surrender is of the whole self. We give him all that we are. And by grace he brings us into his kingdom. Scattered across the Gospels are insights as to what this entering means. Invariably it means the foregoing of certain things and embracing of others, leaving behind our own meritorious measurements and abandoning ourselves to someone who does for us what we could never do for ourselves.

In this chapter we will draw together sayings and stories of Jesus related to entering the kingdom in what I think is an unusual assembling of teaching not often brought together. This collection will take us to many scattered scenes and sayings drawn from Jesus' ministry. We will watch children being held up to the disciples as the best illustrations of what it means to trust and so to enter the kingdom. We will hear Jesus disown and condemn the ways of the scribes and Pharisees who by their teaching prevented others from entering. It will mean observing one of their number, Nicodemus, coming by night to Jesus, to have his world turned upside down by teaching about a second birth. It will mean seeing that humility can live alongside boldness when it comes to entering the kingdom, for boldness linked inextricably to faith was a quality always highly praised by Jesus. However, our basic point of departure must be that humility and surrender were the fundamental requirements for entering the kingdom, and this is the proper response to God's grace.

Humility and faith, our response to grace
Each of the authors of the synoptic Gospels records the incident of Jesus' rebuke of the disciples for the failure to welcome children. The disciples still had much to learn about who was fit for the kingdom of God and how it might be entered. People were bringing little children to Jesus that he might touch them. (Mark 10:13-16; Matthew 19:13-15; Luke 18:15-17.) The disciples thought that such action by the people was an intrusion into Jesus' privacy, or that such a great man should not be bothered by children who were comparatively unimportant; so the disciples rebuked the people for troubling Jesus with their children. But they in turn were rebuked for doing so. Indeed, we are told that Jesus was "indignant" with his disciples for their insensitivity and obduracy, failing to see that the kingdom of God was for exactly such as these. Not only did Jesus rebuke his disciples

but he pronounced: "Let the little children come to me, and do not hinder them, for the kingdom of God belongs to such as these." He went on to announce authoritatively, "'I tell you the truth, anyone who will not receive the kingdom of God like a little child will never enter it.'" At this, he took the children in his arms and blessed them. (See Mark 10:14-16.)

During a recent teaching series about the importance of welcome in church life (given the research which indicates that many people start attending church because of the welcome that they are given), I made the point that children are the model entrants to the kingdom of God because they easily trust, easily receive, and easily enter. For these reasons they are exemplars for us all. In other words they have no difficulty (or much less difficulty) in taking on trust and receiving themselves both the reality and blessings of the kingdom. Of course adults have any number of reasons for not receiving or entering the kingdom; such reasons might be intellectual questions about the existence of God, the origin of the universe or the problem of suffering. Sometimes these questions result from personal experience of neglect, suffering or exposure to scepticism. But Jesus is quite clear: entry to the kingdom is only possible through a childlike approach.

For a number of years we had as a member of our congregation in Bath a scientist who was and is at the forefront of his field of research. At an early age he was chosen for a chair at Cambridge University, probably one of the top posts in his field of scientific research and teaching anywhere in the world. What was always remarkable when he preached in our church was a combination of simplicity and faith. This demonstrated that knowledge need not deter or obscure faith, nor need it make belief any harder, but what is required is the willingness of all comers to lay their intelligence, privileges, position or importance, so to speak, in the dust and enter the kingdom by simple trust. It is not that faith is either a leap in the dark or the surrender of our intelligence, but that all knowledge is limited and a scientist or a poet must come to faith in God by a simple act of trust, just as the child. This surely is what the little children teach us, and it is the truth Jesus' words teach us. As we have seen in Mark 10:15, he could not have been more emphatic. Entrance to the kingdom requires faith and humility.

John Bunyan put it well in *Pilgrim's Progress* when he wrote of Christiana's entrance to the Holy City: "Then said the keeper of the gate, who is there?" So the dog left off to bark, and he opened to them. Then Christiana made low obeisance, and said, Let not our Lord be offended with his handmaidens, for that we have knocked at His princely gate. Then said the Keeper, Whence come ye? And what is it thou would have? Christiana answered, we are come from whence Christian did come, and upon the same errand as he; to wit, to be, if it shall please you, graciously admitted by this gate into the way that leads to the Celestial City. And I answer, my Lord, in the next place, that I am Christiana, once the wife of Christian, that now is gotten above. With that the Keeper of the gate did marvel, saying, what! Is she become now a pilgrim that but a while abhorred that life? She bowed her head and said, yes; and so are my sweet babes also. Then he took her by the hand and led her in, and said also, suffer the little children to come to me; and with that he shut up the gate. This done, He called to a trumpeter that was above, over the gate, to entertain Christiana with shouting, and sound of trumpet, for joy. So he obeyed and sounded, and filled the air with his melodious notes."[1]

A pivotal moment for Christiana, whilst standing at the gate waiting for admittance to the kingdom, was when she "bowed her head" and said "yes" in answer to the Gate Keeper's question, "Is she now become a pilgrim?" Her response perfectly illustrates the need for trust and humility which are the pre-conditions of entry. If Jesus used children to illustrate the kind of trust or faith necessary to enter the kingdom, it was a nocturnal visitor to Jesus that gave rise to the most illuminating conversation about entry to the kingdom.

Only on two occasions – in the Nicodemus passage, and later in conversation with Pilate at his trial – does John record a conversation or teaching about the kingdom. It has been widely suggested that the phrase "eternal life" in John is similar in meaning to the kingdom of God or heaven in the synoptic Gospels. The conversation between Jesus and Nicodemus is a further elaboration of that piece of teaching in his prologue where John summarises the gospel: "He came to that which was his own, but his own did not receive him. Yet to all who received him, to those who believed in his name, he gave the right to become children of God —children born not of natural descent, nor of human decision or a husband's will, but born of God" (John 1:11f). The theme of being born of God as a condition of entering the kingdom was further elaborated in the night time conversation with Nicodemus.

As on other occasions when Jesus was approached by a Pharisee, there is a little flattering circumlocution before the point of the interview was reached. So Nicodemus smoothly begins his conversation with the words, "Rabbi, we know you are a teacher who has come from God. For no-one could perform the miraculous signs you are doing if God were not with him" (John 3:2). Compare that with a later question asked by Pharisees about the payment of taxes, but with a powerful subtext of attempting to denigrate and defame Jesus' teaching, when a delegation spoke: "'Teacher," they said, "we know you are a man of integrity and that you teach the way of God in accordance with the truth. You aren't swayed by men, because you pay no attention to who they are"' (Matthew 22:16). There was a nefarious amalgam of truth and falsehood in that preamble; truth that Jesus was not persuaded by anyone's status but only by what they actually taught, and falsehood in that the Pharisees, whilst acknowledging his miracles, would not and could not acknowledge that he was really sent from God. To have done that would have undermined their whole case against him. Their problem was: what was the source or power behind these miracles? God or the devil? (See John 8:48.)

Nicodemus seems to have come to the conclusion that the miracles Jesus performed were definitely undertaken through God's power, but he had not yet understood the revolution in his own life that would be required for him to enter this kingdom. But before Nicodemus can even get his question out, Jesus seemingly cuts in on his preamble with the blistering statement, "...I tell you the truth, no-one can see the kingdom of God unless he is born again" (John 3:3). Jesus speaks of the need of this re-birth, both to "see", and later "enter", the kingdom (v. 5). So the phrase which is trailed in the prologue is a kind of overture to the symphony of John's Gospel. This is the Gospel in which we learn that Jesus enabled people to be born into God's family by receiving him (1:12f). This is spelt out with great clarity in the conversation with Nicodemus.

Now the way in which this birth would take place was through the operation of "water" and "Spirit". Water represents the waters of baptism, which were themselves administered on the basis of individual repentance; and the Spirit was the life-giving Spirit of God, whose action made possible such repentance and faith. For Nicodemus to see the kingdom, let alone enter it, he would need both to repent and to receive. The repentance would be symbolised by the water, and the Spirit must be received through faith. Jesus' words meant that only in this way would Nicodemus be born all over again and enter the kingdom. It is made clear that what was true for Nicodemus is indeed true for all: entering the kingdom requires a spiritual birth, which includes believing, washing and receiving. The rub for the Pharisee was that this method of entrance took no account of their so called "good behaviour", nor of their extensive study of the Scripture (see John 5:39), nor the position they held in the society of their day. However humbling this teaching was for someone as important as Nicodemus, it seems that Nicodemus may well have done the very things that Jesus requested of him, since he reappears at the end of the Gospel, with Joseph of Arimathea, to bury the body of Jesus after the crucifixion. This involved wrapping the body with linen cloths, interleaving its folds with copious amounts of myrrh and aloes (about 34 kilograms of spices). (See John 19:39f.) It was an act of both courage and care which surely must have sprung from faith! He had been born all over again; the entrance was by humility and faith —turning and receiving.

We are now building up a picture of what entering the kingdom involves. It entails trust and receptivity, like that of a child. It involves a willingness to make a dramatic turning in your life and go in a new direction; this is repentance symbolised by water used in baptism. It means having a spiritual rebirth, which necessitates believing that Jesus is the Christ or Son of God. Through these actions, entrance to the kingdom is possible. In reality, Jesus found that those who were outside the strict religious community of Judaism were more willing to accept and use this entrance than those who had long been accustomed to following its precepts, at least outwardly. Likewise, those who knew themselves to be in violation of the moral commandments were more likely to enter than those who spent their whole lives in a studied attempt to show that they fulfilled the moral commandments even if their obedience was superficial or only skin deep. As we have seen, such people, whether scribes, Pharisees or others, were concerned only with what was evident on the outside. Jesus knew all this only too well, so that in his short summary, following the parable of the two sons, he says, "I tell you the truth, the tax collectors and the prostitutes are entering the kingdom of God ahead of you. For John came to you to show you the way of righteousness, and you did not believe him, but the tax collectors and the prostitutes did. And even after you saw this, you did not repent and believe him." (See Matthew 21:31f.) Consequently, Jesus condemned them, saying, "Woe to you, teachers of the law and Pharisees, you hypocrites! You shut the kingdom of heaven in men's faces. You yourselves do not enter, nor will you let those enter who are trying to" (Matthew 23:13).

The supreme irony of this was that the very people who most desired the kingdom were prevented by the Pharisees from entering, and the Pharisees themselves, who felt themselves deserving of the kingdom, found they could never enter on the basis of their own deserts. Jesus made this abundantly clear in the parable of the Pharisee and publican. As we have seen previously, the publican, who had nothing to say for himself except "God, have mercy on me, a sinner" was the one who went home justified (see Luke 18:13), while the religious Pharisee, who could recount to God his good works of fasting, tithing and praying, found that he could not enter the kingdom. (See Luke 18:11.) One of the differences between the two men was that the publican earnestly and honestly prayed to God, while the Pharisee, we are told, prayed "to himself". (See v. 11, variant reading.)

How might this apply today? Recently I came across an account of a man who was totally unfaithful to his wife, having been with many other women, including prostitutes. His wife attended an Alpha course, became a Christian and, extraordinarily, forgave her husband. He, too, went on a course, became a Christian, and was healed from a chest complaint which he indicated had been brought on by his job. Concerning his former life, he expressed how appalled he now felt about the way in which he had treated his wife and children, and had put them at risk. He told of the wonderful relationship he now enjoys with his family, and how he is involved in a variety of forms of service in the church, including the church council. What a turn around!

As Jesus said, "The tax gatherers and the prostitutes are entering the kingdom of God...." Or, to recall once again one of Jesus' kingdom sayings, "...many who are first will be last, and many who are last will be first." Entering the kingdom was for the childlike, for the sinner who recognised their own true spiritual state, whatever sins they had committed, for the person who was willing to begin again, for the individual who would admit that they could never do for themselves what was necessary to gain admittance to this kingdom and who needed a spiritual rebirth. What Jesus often explained in story form in the parables, as we have seen, or in pithy sayings which are both memorable and radical, the apostle Paul was able to further elaborate. In his classic statement about entering the kingdom he says, "For it is by grace you have been saved, through faith — and this not from yourselves, it is the gift of God — not by works, so that no-one can boast" (Ephesians 2:8f). And this was made possible because, as Paul teaches in Romans, God has made known a way to be justified to which the law and Prophets testify: "This righteousness from God comes through faith in Jesus Christ to all who believe. There is no difference, for all have sinned and fall short of the glory of God, and are justified freely by his grace through the redemption that came by Christ Jesus. God presented him as a sacrifice of atonement, through faith in his blood." (See Romans 3:21-25b.)

So the key words in Paul's description of how entrance into this kingdom is possible are: "grace", "faith" "atonement" and "no boasting". Jesus himself says in one of his great "I am" sayings as recorded by John, "I am the gate for the sheep." He is the gate through whom we must enter the kingdom, and he is also the Shepherd who will guide us both to the gate – by his Spirit – and to the pasture we need. Simply put, the entrance to the kingdom is Jesus himself. Having entered by him, we may then forcefully lay hold of the kingdom he has qualified us to join.

Forcefully entering the kingdom

If I said that someone made a forceful entrance, I wonder what would spring to mind. Perhaps you would imagine a play in which one of the main characters made a powerful entrance, like Henry V addressing his troops before Agincourt. Or you might think of a meeting in which a politician or statesman came to the rostrum and made a forceful impact on the proceedings, changing the atmosphere and significance of the meeting. Or you might think that I was simply referring to a burglary! So what did Jesus mean when he said, "...the kingdom of heaven has been forcefully advancing, and forceful men lay hold of it"; or, in Luke's Gospel, "...everyone is forcing his way into it"? (See Matthew 11:12; Luke 16:16).

Before enquiring more precisely into the meaning of this saying, let us take a step backwards, to understand the context. It is quite probable that Matthew is the primary source for this saying; he certainly gives it the fullest context. But in both Gospels, Matthew and Luke, the saying is set in the context of John the Baptist's ministry and its place in the scheme of God's salvation history.

The saying in Matthew comes in the midst of an assessment by Jesus of John the Baptist's ministry. John, in jail, has had a moment of doubt about the identity of Jesus, so he sends messengers to him asking, "Are you the one who was to come, or should we expect someone else?" Jesus responds not the with Old Testament texts, or statements of doctrine, but with an account of what he has been doing: restoring sight to the blind, healing the lame, the leper, the deaf, and preaching good news to the poor. This is sufficient to reassure John; such activity is the true validation both of the coming of the Messiah and the kingdom he came to bring, the rule that he has come to exercise. However, for the sake of his hearers, Jesus not only extols John by saying that, "Among those born of women there has not risen anyone greater than John the Baptist" (Matthew 11:11), but then surprisingly also says that, "...he who is least in the kingdom of heaven is greater than he", before giving us the saying which is the focus of our study here. So how is it that John is the greatest born of woman, but that any in the kingdom of heaven is greater than he?

The answer to this conundrum lies in the greatness of this new era of the kingdom of heaven, compared to that which has gone before. As Luke puts in a nutshell, "The law and the Prophets were proclaimed until John. Since that time, the good news of the kingdom is being preached." In other words, John the Baptist's ministry marks the watershed between the age of the law and Prophets and the age of the kingdom, preached and made known by Jesus. The point Jesus surely is making is that because of the *nature* of the kingdom the least in it is greater than the greatest in the previous era, which was characterised by the law and the prophets.

Ladd has explained very clearly the way in which John's ministry concluded the old era, the new order being God's kingdom, which John announced. So there is no suggestion that John or his followers performed kingdom miracles. The preparation ended; what had been promised would now be fulfilled.[2] Having made this contrast between two eras of salvation history – the law and the Prophets and the coming of the kingdom through the Messiah – Jesus then says that the kingdom of heaven has been forcefully advancing, and forceful people enter or lay hold of it. So what did he mean? Who are these forceful people? Presumably they are not those who are worldly, rich or naturally impressive, but those whose are preparcd to stop at nothing to obtain what they glimpse in the kingdom of God as demonstrated by Jesus. The Gospels are sprinkled with such people: the Syro-Phoenician woman whose faith was noted by Jesus; Zacchaeus, who forwent his ill-gotten gains to enter the kingdom; even Nicodemus, frightened at first, so coming to Jesus by night, but who in the end identified himself powerfully with Jesus by burying his body, rather than with his party who had engineered Jesus' execution; and Mary Magdalene, whose total commitment to Jesus after her healing was obvious for all to see. These, and many others in the Gospels, "forcefully" laid hold of the kingdom. In other words, they were prepared to burn their boats, cut free from the past; and they were entirely committed to re-ordering their lives around the agenda of the kingdom, and to following the King.

The way into the kingdom is indeed the way down, involving a surrender of our human will to God's will, but it also involves a complete identification with the coming of this kingdom rather than an all too cosy settling down with the kingdoms and values of the world. Nor is it surprising that in a kingdom in which the leaders are servants, the inside is more important than the outside; the first shall be last, and vice versa; and that entrance into it will involve an about turn, in which surrender is the manner of acquisition.

So, lastly, we must consider the matter of how much fulfilment of the kingdom we can now expect, as well as thinking: what is the place of prayer and the church in the coming of this kingdom? To these final issues we must turn.

PART V

THE COMING KINGDOM

Chapter Seventeen

THE NOW BUT NOT YET KINGDOM

Anyone familiar with the British climate will know that at one and the same time in a given area the sun can be shining brightly yet nearby there can be dark clouds and actual rainfall. In Britain, where the hours of sunshine are limited, sunshine is what is appreciated most; in other parts of the world the rain would be considered the greatest blessing. Or again, in our climate we experience dark clouds gathering all around and filling the sky, but in another part of the landscape a remarkable pool of sunlight is to be seen, the more vivid because of the contrasting darkness.

This is an illustration of what we are thinking about in this chapter: the now and the not yet of the kingdom, or what the theologians like to call realised or unrealised eschatology (of which, more later). When there is general cloud, but broken by strong shafts of sunlight, we know that beyond the cloud it is a different story. Above the cloud, although we may not see its brightness, feel its warmth or experience its warming, we know that the sun shines brightly everywhere. If you were to ask an airline pilot what it was like up there above the cloud, he would tell you that when travelling across the face of the earth in daylight hours there is always sunshine, nothing impedes it, and that is the final reality. However, below him, clouds and weather patterns come and go. And night time only occurs when part of earth is turned away from the sun.

So here is an illustration of what is meant by the kingdom of God, now but not yet. The kingdom, like the sunshine in the illustration, bursts through the gloom of our normal cloudy existence —in the ministry of Jesus. And wherever his working or activity is to be found it continues to break through, hopefully especially in the church!

We might extend the metaphor and say that the reign of God, bringing light, warmth and nourishment, is evident wherever the working of Jesus is found, just as rays of sunshine break through cloud. Above the cloud there is perpetual sunshine, and that is the ultimate reality. However those under the clouds can often neither see nor feel the sunshine, and it is the duty of those who (by grace, through no merit of their own) live in the light of Jesus Christ, to "punch holes" in the cloud by faithful witness and ministry of the word in the power of the Spirit —so that the life and light of Jesus may shine through and be evident to others.

This picture may go a little way to help us understand that the kingdom has indeed come – it is present around the world – yet it certainly is not fulfilled or consummated. There is no uniform "spiritual weather map" across the world. Generally there are dark clouds, but there are also pinpricks of light continually moving across the landscape.

Jesus, having come from the Father and returning to the Father (John 13:3), knew perfectly well what the prevailing weather patterns above the clouds were. For only three years his ministry, like a beam of intense light, irradiated around Israel and her border regions. His words and actions, together with his life itself, were the living illustration of the kingdom which existed beyond the clouds of human existence. His words and actions were the perfect display of the kingdom or reign of God. But even with Jesus' presence on earth, it was a limited burst of sunshine. Not everyone enjoyed or experienced the evident wonders of the kingdom. Only some of the dead were raised, and there may have been many sick who were not brought to Jesus and his disciples and healed. Ladd[1] has suggested that such signs were tokens, not the kingdom being fully consummated. It is at the End (Gk. *eschaton*) that death and sickness will be no more. The "new order" brings salvation to those who receive it.

Jesus knew that he was the living embodiment of the new humanity. This humanity was promised to all who believed in him. He knew that through faith in him people could share in the blessings of this kingdom, but in the constraints of still living in the old order, and the tensions that this creates. As we saw at the outset, Jesus saw the kingdom of God to be the ultimate and only real world-view, because he knew that is what exists above "the clouds". In the end he knew that this world-view would both prevail and be seen for what it is. All other world-views, whether expressed politically, philosophically or religiously, would fall to the ground. His death on the cross enabled undeserving people to both taste and one day fully experience being in this kingdom ("today you will be with me in paradise", Jesus said to the penitent thief); and the resurrection blasted a way through death, confirming the effectiveness of all that he achieved on the cross, and promising the final outcome in time and space. However, as the apostles would say, "in this present age", we live with a foretaste of the future, with a glimpse of heaven and its perfected kingdom, but still very much in a world corrupted by evil and subject to its own mortality; in other words, a kingdom which is not yet but which breaks in – like occasional brilliant sunlight – into our world.

The not yet kingdom
There are a number of pictures of the kingdom in its final or fulfilled form given to us in the Bible. Naturally they are beloved by Christians, especially by those who are not living in ease, plenty or security —those living with daily hunger; those living in places of unremitting conflict; those who are persecuted for their faith in Christ. Such people have their longing for an end to hunger, disease, war and persecution chiselled ever sharper by the very circumstances of their daily life. Indeed their very lack of food, security and stability make them long for the kingdom of true pleasure, plenty, perfection and peace all the more. But above all they long for a place and community where the Lamb who was slain has begun his reign (see Revelation chapter five).

One of the greatest pictures of the reality of the kingdom of God comes in the last two chapters of the Bible, Revelation 21 and 22. We will look at some of the features of this vision of perfection described as, "the Holy City, the new Jerusalem, coming down out of heaven from God, prepared as a bride beautifully dressed for her husband." A city dressed as a bride is indeed a picture which is hard for us to get our heads round, but in a single sentence it merges the great themes of community and perfection in an amazing vision. Later in the same chapter, John is taken up by the Spirit to a high mountain where he is told: "Come, I will show you the bride, the wife of the Lamb. And he carried me away in the Spirit to a mountain great and high, and showed me the Holy City, Jerusalem, coming down out of heaven from God." Again the bride is a city prepared for marriage. At the heart of these pictures is a community purchased by the redemption of Christ, having passed through judgement because of his grace (see Revelation 20:11-15) and now prepared as a bride for perfect unity with the Lamb who has purchased it.

I have been privileged to take many weddings and nothing compares with the moment when a bride – radiant, beautiful and brimming with excitement – walks down the aisle of the church, to the amazement of the waiting onlookers, the admiration of her family and the astonishment of the groom! When one bride entered to the sound of a single oboe playing the opening piece from the film *The Mission*, it was as though every heart stopped! In the highly symbolic vision granted to John, a perfected bride proceeds from heaven, presumably to a renewed and remade earth, to be united with the Lamb of God. Once again our imagination, let alone our grasp of metaphors, can scarcely cope. But in these symbols we see a perfected community, a city of unparalleled magnificence ("It shone with the glory of God, and its brilliance was like that of a very precious jewel, like a jasper, clear as crystal" [v. 11]), and a wedding which is the destiny of all creation.

A voice from the throne said what had always been God's intention, "...the dwelling of God is with men" (v. 3). Once that is re-established and all other barriers, distractions and obstacles have been removed, then inevitably, "He will wipe every tear from their eyes. There will be no more death or mourning or crying or pain, for the old order of things has passed away" (v. 4). So when God is both perfectly present and his rule is undisputed and uncontested, then none of these things – death or mourning or crying or pain – can exist. The old order will have passed away. The marks of the new order are symbolised for us in a whirlwind of powerful pictures: there will be nothing impure in it (vv. 27f); there will be no more sea (the sea in ancient thought being a picture of untamed anarchy); every thirst will be satisfied (v. 6); the Lamb will replace the temple (v. 22); there will be no sun, "... for the glory of God gives it light, and the Lamb is its lamp (v. 23); it will be peopled by the nations; and its members will all be written in the Lamb's book of life; and, "On no day will its gates ever be shut, for there will be no night there" (v. 25). Here is perfection; here is the kingdom of God in its unhindered splendour. It is a symbolic vision which keeps hope alive while we travail under the clouds. And what it conveys is the final and only reality.

Alongside this final picture, with which the message of the Bible closes, is a more pastoral vision of the future conveyed to Israel by one of her greatest prophets, Isaiah. It was around eight hundred years before Jesus, but Isaiah prophesied of his coming like this:

> A shoot will come up from the stump of Jesse;
> from his roots a Branch will bear fruit.
> The Spirit of the LORD will rest on him—
> the Spirit of wisdom and of understanding,
> the Spirit of counsel and of power,
> the Spirit of knowledge and of the fear of the LORD—
> and he will delight in the fear of the LORD.
> He will not judge by what he sees with his eyes,
> or decide by what he hears with his ears;
> but with righteousness he will judge the needy,
> with justice he will give decisions
> for the poor of the earth.
> He will strike the earth with the rod of his mouth;
> with the breath of his lips he will slay the wicked.
> Righteousness will be his belt
> and faithfulness the sash round his waist.
>
> *Isaiah 11:1-5*

The one who will bring in the kingdom will be the Messiah from the line of David, the stump of Jesse; he will be endowed with the immeasurable power and the wisdom of the Spirit, and he will bring both righteousness and justice, especially for the needy and poor. The outcome of this ministry is then given an unusual twist— it is harmony and peace throughout creation, or the created environment. So Isaiah continues,

> The wolf will live with the lamb,
> the leopard will lie down with the goat,
> the calf and the lion and the yearling together;
> and a little child will lead them.
> The cow will feed with the bear,

235

> their young will lie down together,
> and the lion will eat straw like the ox.
> The infant will play near the hole of the cobra,
> and the young child put his hand into the viper's nest.
> They will neither harm nor destroy
> on all my holy mountain,
> for the earth will be full of the knowledge of the LORD
> as the waters cover the sea.
>
> *Isaiah 11:6-9*

Again it is a remarkable and almost inconceivable picture, in which animals and people, normally a threat to each other, live in harmony and peace —a further picture of a kingdom extending throughout creation, in which peace and security replace danger, death and destruction.

So through the Bible there are these glimpses of a coming kingdom, promised but not yet fully come —the not yet kingdom. But it is not simply a question of reading all about it and hoping for its fulfilment. There have been, in every age over the years of salvation history, as recorded in the Bible and since the years of the apostles, pools of sunlight breaking through the cloud to irradiate the landscape of human history, reminding all who would look that there is another reality above the cloud, about which these and other passages of Scripture speak. Sometimes they are as small as a pinprick, or even as large as a pinhead; like stars, they wax and wane, but they witness to the reality of the kingdom.

The kingdom now

We have been considering two biblical descriptions of the kingdom of God in its final form, both using highly symbolic language to convey eternal truths. But how much of this kingdom can we expect on earth? Theologians speak of the eschatological appearance of God's kingdom at the end of the age, but how much of that final manifestation may be realised here, in the present? Or, to use our running illustration, how much "sunlight" can we expect on the often bleak landscape of human relations? How much heaven can we expect on earth? In answer to this, what I hope has been made clear is that the kingdom of God has become powerfully active among people —in Jesus himself, and his mission on earth.[2] Looking back over history, we can see that the kingdom of God or the rule of Jesus has become evident in human affairs and history, sometimes strongly and at other times weakly. Whenever that truly happens, then the presence of the kingdom signifies that our infinite, eternal, transcendent God is at work here in this world.[3] Where do we look to find these pools of light? The answer is in countless places, down the years. Wherever women and men set themselves to yield their own will to God's revealed will, then there we have the beginnings of the kingdom come on earth. Wherever people submit their own wills to the revealed will of God, loving him and neighbour, then the kingdom of God is coming to the earth. So when a cup of hot soup is offered to a homeless person in a freezing city centre of one of our cities, then the kingdom is coming; when a person turns from leading their own self-centred life to yield their lives to Jesus Christ, then the kingdom is coming; when someone gives up hard-earned money to give hope to starving people in a faraway country, then the kingdom is coming; when a person blows a whistle on an unethical and unjust practice perpetrated by a government or company, then the kingdom is coming; when a family takes in a person displaced by earthquake or floods or conflict or AIDS, then the kingdom is coming; when release or healing comes to an individual who has been weighed down by disease, bitterness or hatred, then the kingdom of God is coming. It is coming wherever the government of God is brought to bear on the issues of our time —then the kingdom of God is coming now in the same way in which it will finally come at the end of the age, and in which it once came with full force in the life and ministry of Jesus. And I am quite sure that it is those people who have done these things in the name of Jesus who will be closest to the throne of God's government at the end. Each and every one of these things brings into focus the kingdom of God which is his rule.

But these are, at the most, pinpricks of light in a general outlook of gloom, signs of the kingdom to come, but all too frail and ephemeral. I well remember driving past biblical Antioch on a sabbatical journey from Bath, England to Amman, Jordan. It is now in the south eastern corner of Turkey, just a few miles from the border with Syria. There are no signs now, nor have there been for many hundreds of years, of the vital church that existed there for the first three hundred years after Christ, which sent out Paul and Barnabas on their missionary travels, and of which the apostle Peter was the first bishop. That witness has sunk without trace. Nor again is there very much evidence of the remarkable life of the church in Jerusalem in which, "They devoted themselves to the apostles' teaching and to the fellowship, to the breaking of bread and to prayer. Everyone was filled with awe, and many wonders and miraculous signs were done by the apostles. All the believers were together and had everything in common. Selling their possessions and goods, they gave to anyone as he had need" (Acts 2:42-45). For large tracts of time, that life almost entirely disappeared. The march of history, together with the dispersal of the church in Jerusalem for most of the period from 70AD to 1918, meant that, for the most part, the witness of the church was extinguished in the very place where it began. What is the purpose of drawing attention to these changes in the life of the church? The point is that if the kingdom of God is borne witness to chiefly by the church – and we shall look at this more closely in chapter 19 – then the glow of its testimony distinctly waxes and wanes. A vibrant revival of faith in God through Christ, together with a prophetic voice to the society in which it finds itself, and a missionary outreach to its own communities and beyond, can in a matter of two or three generations be extinguished. The sunlight is indeed patchy.

After the great Awakening in the mid 18th century in England under Wesley and Whitefield, which produced such movements as the abolition of slavery, the reformation of manners, and the origins of the worldwide missionary movements of the 19th century, the church lapsed into a more general form of religious formality by the mid nineteenth century. The chapels of Wales, brim full with people during the days of the Welsh revival, were decidedly empty sixty years later. The point is that continuous renewal or revival of the church, so that the kingdom of God can be seen in action, seems hard to maintain for more than a period.

In his book *The Dynamics of Spiritual Life*, Professor Richard Lovelace says the secret of maintaining revival, if that is not itself an oxymoron, lies in sustaining a "live orthodoxy". He writes, "We may conclude therefore that the key to live orthodoxy offered by the Puritan and Pietist traditions is the proper balance between the Spirit and the Word with appropriate attention given to the role of each. What this really means is that to proclaim Christ in living power it is necessary for us to depend on him in a double way. On the one hand, for accurate knowledge of the incarnate Word, we must look back in dependence on the written word which he inspired through the Spirit and which is the continuing instrument through which his mind is made present among believers. On the other hand, for illuminated understanding of the written word and power to transmit it to others, we must look with dependence on the risen Word, who alone is able to enliven the dead conceptual knowledge of the fallen human mind through the sanctifying operation of the Holy Spirit."[4]

Live orthodoxy was also what Jonathan Edwards longed for. Only when this was the outcome of revival would its fruits truly continue. In his work *Distinguishing Marks of a Work of the Spirit of God* (1741), he itemised the following five marks as proof of the genuineness of the revival in Northampton, Mass. Only when a revival exalted Jesus Christ, attacked the kingdom of darkness, honoured the Scriptures, promoted sound doctrine and involved an outpouring of love towards God and man was it really genuine. As Lovelace writes, "Edwards was especially concerned to make clear that fallen human nature is fertile ground for a fleshly religiosity which is impressively 'spiritual' but ultimately rooted in self-love. High emotional experiences, effusive religious talk. And even praising God and experiencing love for God and man can be self-centred and self-motivated. In contrast to this, the experiences of renewal which are genuinely from the Holy Spirit are God-centred in character, based on worship, and appreciation of God's worth and grandeur divorced from self interest. Such experiences create humility in the convert rather than pride and issue in the creation of a new spirit of meekness, gentleness, forgiveness and mercy. They leave the believer hungering and thirsting after righteousness instead of satiated with self-congratulation. Most important, their end result is the performance of works of justice and mercy."[5] Perhaps it was precisely because some revivals in the past did not adequately express themselves in actions of justice and mercy that they died out!

If there is some connection between the coming of the kingdom on earth and the incidence of revivals of faith at given times and places, then we would have to say that the glimpses of the kingdom we have seen on earth have, over history, been powerful, transforming, and at times society changing. But they have also been sporadic, relatively short-lived and often, as with all things human, mixed with a good deal of human frailty and sin. Glimpses of that kingdom – or rule of

God in human affairs – is exactly what we have been given, pinheads of bright light in an otherwise dark and bleak landscape. So with one eye on the future and the coming kingdom, as described by John and Isaiah, and with another eye on the past and its lessons about human response to the coming of the kingdom, we draw the conclusion that we live in what has been called the overlap period. That is the period in which aspects of this kingdom break out into human affairs, so that we are still in the "now" of human sin and evil, but also (with and through Christ) in the "not yet" of the kingdom of God coming in its fullness. The question we must look at is what kind of expectations we can have for this "time of the overlap". Quite simply, they can be either too great or too little —and there are pitfalls in both.

The overlap: living in between the now and the not yet
Expectations are important. They can liberate or they can burden and depress. If parents have no expectations of their child, then they can frustrate that child's potential, so that he or she is mired in either laziness or lack of aspiration or confidence. Conversely, to have expectations that are too great means that the child might be overburdened with something he feels is unattainable, and so could become depressed by those expectations which are neither realistic nor healthy. Finding the right balance of expectations means that the child reaches for their potential without being burdened by the risk of failure —and, in a real sense, grows to maturity. If we live in a time-span in which the kingdom of God has broken into our fallen world, what are the right expectations for ourselves and our churches, and indeed what could we hope to see in terms of our communities being transformed? Our expectations have to do with the extent of our own personal transformation, the measure of salvation we can expect to see now, and the degree to which the world can be impacted by the kingdom. Each of these expectations is important, each needs to be calibrated by Scripture, and when each is rightly calibrated the result should be a liberating expectation rather than an impossible burden. We shall look at each of these three areas of expectation in turn.

Firstly, what expectations can we have of salvation here and now? In a story told in another of the books in this trilogy, a bishop was once cross-examined by a member of the Salvation Army —he in his purple and gaiters, for the period in which this meeting took place was before the Second World War, she in her bonnet. "Are you saved?" she asked. The bishop, who was a Greek scholar, replied, "Which tense were you asking your question in? Are you asking have I *been* saved, or am I *being* saved, or *will* I be saved?" She was a little bemused by this. But he was perfectly correct, if a little pedantic, to further elucidate her question. For when it comes to our own personal salvation and what we can expect now, it is true that we have been saved from the penalty of sin (Colossians 2:13f), we are being saved from the power of sin now, though not yet perfectly (1John 1:8f), and one day we will be delivered from the very presence of sin (Revelation 21:4). So the bishop could rightly say that he had been saved from the penalty of sin and enjoyed assurance of forgiveness; he was being helped in his struggle with sin; and he would finally be delivered from the presence of sin. So in answer to her question he had been saved, he was being saved, and finally he would be completely rescued. Although the Salvationist may have got more than she was bargaining for, his reply is nonetheless both helpful and right. His reply also produces appropriate expectations calibrated by Scripture. There have been some holiness movements in the past which seem to indicate that there can come a time when a person in the here and now can enter into some state of moral or spiritual perfection. The doctrine of "perfection" as taught by John Wesley seemed to suppose this, and some of the holiness teaching of Keswick around a hundred years ago seemed to indicate that such a state was possible. But such teaching is quite erroneous and unhelpful; we will never be free entirely from attitudes, motives, thoughts or actions which are not in some way or other "sinful"; and if we think that we are free from all such impurities we will certainly be guilty of pride! To expect a complete holiness in the here and now is to confuse the "not yet" with the present, and if it is taught as a real possibility it generally leads to make-believe, hypocrisy or anxiety, which may well lead to forms of spiritual depression or neurosis. What we know is that we have been saved from the penalty of sin, we have a continual struggle on our hands with the presence of sin, but we are offered the safety net of ongoing forgiveness, and we have the assurance of one day being free from this present struggle. When it comes to personal salvation in relation to these matters, we must distinguish between the real now and the not yet.

The second area has to do with how much of heaven we can really expect on earth in relation to our own well-being. An interesting thing happened in our church staff meeting. Two members of our staff had been to two very different meetings over a weekend. One had been to a conference on the theme of accessing heaven on earth, while another had been to a nearby church to hear the paraplegic Joni Eareckson Tada speak. Confined to a wheelchair for the last twenty years, she has come to terms with a disability caused by an accident. This in itself was far from easy. She had learned through God's grace both to glorify him in her life and bear a powerful and unusual testimony in so doing. Contrastingly, the teaching at the conference was about bringing heaven's blessings to earth and encouraging people to reach out for God's miracles now. How much of those blessings which we see in Revelation 21 can we really expect now? And if we can expect them, what do we do when they simply do not happen? Some say the blessings of heaven can be realised in our time now, while others expect the outpouring of God's grace to help them with the pain, restrictions and suffering which they presently face. The framework with which I personally deal with these difficulties is as follows.

The kingdom of God is coming, but it has not yet come; its inauguration will only be complete after the second coming of Jesus. It is then that we can expect a new heaven and a new earth in which the vision of the kingdom given to us in passages like those in Isaiah and Revelation will be fulfilled. Until then we live in an overlap in which the blessings of the kingdom may break out in an uneven kind of way, partly in relation to faithful prayer but also in accordance to God's sovereignty. So in one instance there will be a remarkable healing, but in another, almost identical case, where much prayer is offered, nothing on the surface appears to happen. So the rays of kingdom sunshine will alight here and there, but they will not always be uniform in their result. (Who is to say which is more marvellous: a person keeping faith with God in severe difficulty and disability, or a person who is able to walk away from their burden? I am hard pushed to say, although of course we would all prefer the latter.) Nor will the sunlight bathe every human ill with obvious healing, just as in the ministry of Jesus he did not cure all those in Palestine or relieve all their needs. What does this mean? It means that we can earnestly pray for God's kingdom, his just, gentle and powerful rule, to come to all people in every situation, but there will not now be a uniform result. But in one way or another – in the way we want, or in the way we do not expect – his reign will come. It may teach the lesson that power is made perfect in weakness, or it may demonstrate the resurrection of Jesus in what seems to be a more victorious way.

However much of the kingdom we see on earth, we should always remember that any taste of it now is only a foretaste. We should pray for the sunshine to break through, but when in the clouds we should content ourselves that it is only a matter of time before the kingdom is finally and fully made known.

Thirdly, we cannot expect that this side of the parousia the kingdoms of this world will be subject to his rule. As the writer to the Hebrews said, "Yet at present we do not see everything subject to him" (Hebrews 2:8b); or again, later in the epistle, he says, "He waits for his enemies to be made his footstool" (see Hebrews 10:13). There is a lot of waiting going on as Paul tells the Romans, "The creation waits in eager expectation for the sons of God to be revealed" (Romans 8:19), another way of saying it waits for his kingdom to fully come. The whole world order, including creation itself, waits. But in the midst of conflict, war, brutality, corruption and the rest, there are pinpricks of light breaking through. Often actions by the "little people" (who are in fact the big people) who occasionally get reported amongst the machinations and posturing of international government, have the greatest effect. In 2003, as mentioned before, my wife's godson Tom Hurndall was shot in Rafa, Gaza while trying to help a Palestinian child. In his early twenties, he was the oldest of four children. He was one among so many who have lost their lives on both sides of that interminable conflict. I saw him with his mother in a London hospital after his unconscious and wounded body had eventually been returned to England. He died a few months later. Or again, a few weeks ago I heard of a Palestinian family, whose son was killed by Israeli soldiers, subsequently offering to Israeli children his organs for transplantation. Pinpricks of God's kingdom break through into the awful realities of our world. It is a world which, for the time being, is not yet subject to his just and gentle rule. But it will be, and that is our hope! And it is the creation, so spoilt by the human family, that waits for the redemption of that family to be complete for its own remaking and restoration. With creation we wait and groan, as Paul repeatedly says.

So we live in between the present pinpricks of kingdom life breaking out like sunshine on a cloudy day, and the full unhindered radiance of his kingdom. Like the sky above, his kingdom is already perfect. Given these two facts of our cloudy living and his already unhindered reign, we naturally pray, "Your kingdom come, your will be done on earth as it is in heaven." Perhaps our greatest task is praying the kingdom.

Chapter Eighteen

PRAYING THE KINGDOM

Understandably the now and the not yet of the kingdom of God gives rise to a prayer of longing. Now we see only a foretaste, a down payment of the kingdom that is to come fully. As Jesus taught, the kingdom is both among his people and within us, (see Luke 17:20f), but it is also still to come. The resurrection and the gift of the Spirit are guarantees of this future kingdom. Presently the power of God breaks through here and there, as trailers of what will eventually come, but for the moment it is all too passing and fragile. And, as we have seen, even these tokens of the future are mere pinpricks in a landscape of human misery and pain. You may say that is rather a bleak outlook, but it depends on where you stand. It might not look like this, on the surface at any rate, if you are a Christian in New Jersey, Guildford, Chantilly or Milan, but it most certainly does in Niger, Darfur, Fallujah, Gaza and the *favelas* of Rio de Janeiro, as well as many other places beside. The gap between present experience and the future reality of the kingdom necessarily gives rise to a longing for the consummation of the kingdom which is to come. Longing is the fundamental attitude and emotion of the prayer which prays "Your kingdom come" —a longing that the mercy and justice of this kingdom would come to all people and every situation.

In this chapter we will look briefly at this longing as it is demonstrated in the two thousand years of biblical salvation history. It is played out through the longings of the enslaved Israelites for freedom and a home; in the longing for the end of exile and return to

Jerusalem focussed especially in the lives of Nehemiah and Daniel; the longing in the preaching of John the Baptist for the arrival of the Messiah —the king who will inaugurate the kingdom; the lament of Jesus over Jerusalem; and then, lastly, in the great sweep of Paul's teaching in Romans chapter eight.

This survey offers us a panoramic view of the longings of God's servants in every age. Having felt some of the force and intensity of these longings for God's rule in the lives of prophets, leaders and many others, reflected in the Old and New Testaments, we will then look at the expression of this prayerful longing in the worship of the church, particularly in connection with the sacraments of baptism and the Eucharist, as well as in songs and hymns through the ages.

Longing in the Old Testament

In the Old Testament there were two great occasions when God's people longed for peace and security —longings which find their fulfilment only in the kingdom: firstly at the time of the exodus and then at the time of the exile. At both periods they hoped that they would find peace and security on earth. This "rest" on earth eluded them because of their disobedience. (See Hebrews 3:7-4:11.) And, as we have seen, their desire for rest was fundamentally a heavenly longing, a longing for God's kingdom which can only finally be satisfied there.

The writer to the Hebrews tells us that everything on earth is but a shadow of what is to come. Of all those who exercised such exemplary faith as to be mentioned in his great gallery of faith in Hebrews chapter eleven, he says, by way of conclusion, "These were all commended for their faith, yet none of them received what had been promised" (Hebrews 11:39). Indeed, as he further explains, "You have not come to a mountain that can be touched and that is burning with fire; to darkness, gloom and storm," referring to the Israelites' approach to Mount Sinai in Exodus chapter 20, "But you have come to Mount Zion, to the heavenly Jerusalem, the city of the living God. You have come to thousands upon thousands of angels in joyful assembly, to the church of the firstborn, whose names are written in heaven." Interestingly, he powerfully concludes, "Therefore, since we are receiving a *kingdom* that cannot be shaken, let us be thankful, and so worship God acceptably with reverence and awe, for our 'God is a consuming fire'" (Hebrews 12:28f, my italics). So the longings that a faithful Israelite as well as an expectant Christian have are basically longings that can only be fulfilled in the perfection of the kingdom. All else is but a pale imitation, a foreshadowing of the real thing.

The longing of the enslaved Israelites in Egypt for peace and rest was poignantly and powerfully expressed, and God heard their cry and longing: 'The LORD said, "I have indeed seen the misery of my people in Egypt. I have heard them crying out because of their slave drivers, and I am concerned about their suffering. So I have come down to rescue them from the hand of the Egyptians and to bring them up out of that land into a good and spacious land, a land flowing with milk and honey" (Exodus 3:7f). So the Israelites' longings for freedom and peace had come to God, and he, through Moses, promised to bring them out to a place "flowing with milk and honey". That was a longing which God fulfilled, but centuries later the Israelites found themselves once again in slavery in a foreign land, this time serving the Babylonians, followed by the Medes and Persians. The reason for their enslavement was their disobedience, as God had warned them. (See Deuteronomy 28, and especially verse 65). The period in exile heightened once again the longing of the faithful for his kingdom, and the two who best expressed this were Nehemiah and Daniel.

We cannot fully re-tell the faith journeys of Daniel and Nehemiah here, with the very considerable and unusual challenges that they faced. Both men found themselves in exile in the Babylonian/Persian empire, and both longed for the re-establishment of Israel in Jerusalem, although the visions granted to Daniel allowed him to look further beyond earthly kingdoms, which came and went, toward the establishment of a kingdom which would never wane.

Daniel's life spanned the governments of several emperors. On at least three occasions Daniel was vindicated by God in the face of fierce trial by Nebuchadnezzar, whom he was called to serve. Firstly he forewent the king's rich food for vegetables and was vindicated (Daniel chapter 1). Then he interpreted the king's dream of a vast multilayered metal statue (Daniel chapter 2). Lastly, he interpreted the dream which foretold Nebuchadnezzar's madness, at the end of which the king,

"...praised the Most High….

His dominion is an eternal dominion;

his kingdom endures from generation to generation"

Daniel 4:34

During his life in exile, Daniel witnessed the passing of the Babylonian empire, with the dramatic demise of Belshazzar and the arrival of a new king, Darius, a Mede, at the age of sixty-two. (Daniel 5:30f.) He was subsequently delivered from the punishment of the lions' den during Darius's reign (Daniel 6), not least because of his intense prayers, in which, "Three times a day he got down on his knees and prayed, giving thanks to his God, just as he had done before" (Daniel 6:10). He prayed at his window which was open and which faced toward Jerusalem. After the deliverance of Daniel from the lions, Darius concluded, as Nebuchadnezzar had done before, that, "...in every part of my kingdom people must fear and reverence the God of Daniel.

"For he is the living God
and he endures for ever;
his kingdom will not be destroyed,
his dominion will never end"

Daniel 6:26

There was awareness of some kind here, even amongst non-Jewish rulers, that the God of Daniel ruled a kingdom which could never be destroyed. And Daniel himself, after a vision of a succession of kingdoms rising and falling (namely Persian, Greek and Roman), saw another kingdom coming, which would outlast all others. He saw that, "...the sovereignty, power and greatness of the kingdoms under the whole heaven will be handed over to the saints, the people of the Most High. His kingdom will be an everlasting kingdom, and all rulers will worship and obey him" (Daniel 7:27). And at the centre of this kingdom there were two great figures: "the Ancient of Days" of course (Daniel 7:9); also, he meets a man whose, "..body was like chrysolite, his face like lightning, his eyes like flaming torches, his arms and legs like the gleam of burnished bronze, and his voice like the sound of multitude" (10:6). As Ronald Wallace observes,[1] the identity of the latter figure is left rather vague, but the passage may be a Christophany. In any case, from both his visions and dreams, Daniel was aware that after a succession of human empires, which would wax and wane, there would come a godly kingdom with two great figures at the centre. This eternal kingdom was the one to which the whole of history was moving. In the meantime there would be glimpses of this kingdom on earth.

Nehemiah, who was another well-placed Jewish exile, who longed for the rebuilding of Jerusalem and was cupbearer to the king, Artaxerxes, yearned that God's name be exalted once more in the city bearing his name. He longed for the end of disgrace typified in the broken down walls of Jerusalem, and a temple no longer functioning. Longing was the essence of his prayer. (See Nehemiah 1:5-11.) He mourned, fasted and prayed. What Isaiah and Ezekiel, those two great prophets of the pre-exilic and exilic periods, had promised, Nehemiah longed to see come about —namely the restoration of Jerusalem. Although in their own day this had an historical fulfilment with the return of the exiles to initiate the rebuilding of Jerusalem, there is also a further level of prophecy here, in which the kingdom of God is equated with the heavenly Jerusalem. (See Revelation 21:2.) No one puts this prayerful longing in relation to the restoration of Jerusalem more wonderfully than Isaiah, who writes,

> I have posted watchmen on your walls, O Jerusalem;
> they will never be silent day or night.
> You who call on the LORD,
> give yourselves no rest,
> and give him no rest till he establishes Jerusalem
> and makes her the praise of the earth.
>
> *Isaiah 62:6-7*

So throughout the Old Testament there are periods of powerful longing, not least during those times of enslavement in Egypt and exile in Babylon. Equally, when we come to the New Testament we see further longing for the coming of God's kingdom. It is time to consider this now.

Longing in the New Testament

Isaiah had prayed prophetically, "Oh, that you would rend the heavens and come down, that the mountains would tremble before you!" (64:1). And a little later he had prophesied of new heavens and a new earth when he cried out, "Behold I will create a new heaven and a new earth. The former things will not be remembered, nor will they come to mind." In the final chapters of his book of prophecy he clearly envisaged a time of fulfilment transcending the restoration of Israel after the exile when,

> The wolf and the lamb will feed together,
> and the lion will eat straw like the ox,
> but dust will be the serpent's food....
>
> *Isaiah 65:25*

But this vision of a new earth, depicted in vivid metaphors, would find its fulfilment only at the end of time, and before this could take place Messiah must come. The Messiah combined in himself, as we now know, the two contrasting figures of the Suffering Servant of Isaiah (see especially chapter 53) and the glorious figure of the Son of Man as described by Daniel. Jesus, we also know, was to fulfil both these roles in himself. So the Jews longed for their Messiah, and looked for him intently in the years around Jesus' birth. Communities like that at Qumran on the Dead Sea waited rigorously for his coming, but when Jesus came the leaders of the Jewish nation would not recognise him. However, one person specially sent to prepare the way for the Messiah did —and he, of course, was John the Baptist.

John's whole life was tensed like a bowstring for the recognition of the Messiah, who himself would inaugurate the kingdom. Even as an unborn child, John leapt in the womb of his mother, Elizabeth, at the greeting of Mary. (See Luke 1:41.) His entire being was tuned to both recognise and proclaim the Messiah, which he did. (See Luke 3:1-20; Matthew 3:1-12; Mark 1:1-8; John 1:19-34.) Indeed, John ends his account of John the Baptist's testimony with the words, "I have seen and I testify that this is the Son of God" (John 1:34). In the Gospel accounts John recognises Jesus as the Messiah by the dove descending bodily on him at the time of his baptism. (See John 1:32; Matthew 3:16; Mark 1:10; Luke 3:21f.) John tells us that Jesus will baptise with the Holy Spirit, and will bring judgement to Israel. (See Luke 3:16.) After John's arrest, as we have seen, he had a moment of doubt about the identity of Jesus, and sends messages to Jesus to be reassured that Jesus really is the Messiah. Jesus' reply points to the evidence of his ministry, or in other words to the signs that the kingdom is present with him: "The blind receive sight, the lame walk, those who have leprosy are cured, the deaf hear, the dead are raised, and the good news is preached to the poor" (Matthew 11:5; see also Isaiah 61:1-3). In other words, John longed both for the coming of the Messiah before whom he would gladly retire (John 3:30), and for the kingdom he would inaugurate. How much of his time was spent praying in the Judean desert for the revelation of these two events to Israel and the world?

Jesus not only heralded the kingdom by his preaching, healing and deliverance ministry, giving glimpses of its reality in his time – a foretaste of the future – but he himself longed that all would respond to the presence of the kingdom that he brought. In two ways he demonstrated this fundamental desire: his weeping over Jerusalem and his instructions to his disciples about prayer.

Anyone who has visited Jerusalem and the Mount of Olives will surely have seen the small chapel on the Mount of Olives opposite the temple mount, called the church of Dominus Flavit. Although it is twenty-six years since I visited, I can recall it clearly. The church, formed in the shape of a tear, faces the city. Through its main window, you can gain a perfect view of where the temple would have been. Somewhere near here, on his triumphant entry into Jerusalem, on what we know as Palm Sunday, the Lord stopped and in a dramatic change of mood wept for the city he was about to enter, and where in less than a week he would be crucified. His lament for Jerusalem, which may have been uttered on different occasions, is recorded by both Matthew and Luke. Matthew's record of it is at the end of Jesus' series of woes for the empty ways of the Pharisees, at which we have already looked. Here Jesus cries out, "O Jerusalem, Jerusalem, you who kill the prophets and stone those sent to you, how often I have longed to gather your children together, as a hen gathers her chicks under her wings, but you were not willing. Look, your house is left to you desolate" (Matthew 23:37f). And Luke records Jesus saying, "...If you, even you, had only known on this day what would bring you peace —but now it is hidden from your eyes. The days will come upon you when your enemies will build an embankment against you and encircle you and hem you in on every side. They will dash you to the ground, you and the children within your walls. They will not leave one stone on another, because you did not recognise the time of God's coming to you" (Luke 19:42-44). In other words, the king came to his capital, and the kingdom came to another seat of government, but they refused both king and rule. Nevertheless, Jesus urged his disciples to keep on praying, "Your kingdom come, your will be done". This petition lies at the heart of the prayer Jesus gave his disciples to pray. (See Matthew 6:10; Luke

11:2.) Discipleship means going on praying this kingdom prayer in a spirit of longing and hope that one day it will be brought about. Praying, "Your kingdom come, your will be done on earth as it is heaven" is our basic response when faced with the injustice, disease, poverty, sin, rebellion and cruelty of humans as well as all the many other destructive urges of our world. It is a perpetual prayer, applied to the specific situations where God's heavenly will must reverse all too earthly activity. But just as even the presence of Jesus working his miracles and giving his teaching did not transform the hardened wills of his opponents, so our prayers and action, so compromised by comparison with his, may not bring about his kingdom on earth, but may at the least, like sea defences, hold back a creeping tide of evil. This prayer is at the centre of our discipleship. The fervent prayers of his disciples for his kingdom to come must be at the very heart of that corporate discipleship of which Archbishop Sentamu spoke in his enthronement address in York Minster in 2005. Without it our preaching and activity will be in vain.

Finally, Paul longed for the kingdom to come, and nowhere does he put this more clearly than in his great teaching in Romans chapter eight. Although the chapter is primarily about living the Christian life by the power of the Spirit, it also exudes the longing for God's kingdom to come fully. This longing is described as the final phase of our salvation which is both the redemption of our bodies along with manifestation of a new heaven and a new earth. (See Romans 8:21ff.) Once more, this longing is placed in the context of the present abused created order yearning, indeed groaning, for the "not yet".

Romans chapter eight has been variously entitled the chapter about Christian assurance or the chapter about victory over death or the chapter which outlines the Spirit-filled Christian life. Of these three the first is possibly the best, since it encompasses the other two. Throughout the chapter, Paul is at pains to show the way of life to which the Christian is called. It involves living now by the Spirit; it involves the inner knowledge that God is our Father, Abba, as God's Spirit bears witness with our human spirit that this is so, and it involves the deep assurance that nothing can separate us from God's love. It is this final sense of assurance that inspired Spafforth to write the hymn "It is well with my soul", having lost his children in the Atlantic en route to Jerusalem to join him in his missionary work there.

So Paul turns to how the Christian can live with the sufferings of this present age. Paul's response is not to deny the reality of this suffering but to place it in an eternal context. His simple answer is that it is, "...not worth comparing with the glory that will be revealed in us" (Romans 8:18). Such is the expectation of something far better, in which our bodies are redeemed and the whole of creation is liberated, that these present sufferings are drawn of their despair-making power. Because of this hope of glory to come, creation groans, we ourselves groan, and lastly the Spirit interprets our prayers with groans that words cannot express. If there was no hope there would be no groaning or yearning, but because there is the hope of a liberated creation as well as redemption of our bodies and all that that implies, there is copious groaning. So what should shape our praying for the kingdom are: expectation, hope and groaning —because, although presently surrounded by suffering and mortality, God's people yearn for the off-putting of these things and the consummation of the kingdom. Praying for the kingdom, in the New Testament as in the Old, involves longing for it all the more because the life, death and resurrection of Jesus has made it such an assured eventual certainty.

So as we turn to look at the praying of the people of God, whether in the context of the sacraments (liturgy) or in its prayers or sung worship, we see that this longing also comes through powerfully.

Longing in the worship of the church

Firstly, we will look at this in relation to the sacraments of baptism and the Eucharist or Lord's Supper. Baptism is not only a sign of an individual's incorporation into the body of Christ and of a dying to an old way of life and a rising to a new one (see 1 Corinthians 12:13 and Romans 6:4), it is also the sign of belonging to the new humanity, the new community of which Jesus is the firstborn. (See Hebrews 2:11-13; Colossians 1:18.) As such, baptism has an eschatological perspective: the individual is not only born anew to a new way of life of which baptism is the sign, but also he joins a community which is already spread through earth and heaven. He or she is part of that great concourse of witnesses to whom the writer to the Hebrews draws attention when he says, "...since we are surrounded by such a great cloud of witnesses ... let us run with perseverance the race marked out for us." (Hebrews 12:1.) We diminish baptism if we so individualise it so exclusively that both its corporate and eschatological sides are neglected. In baptism we join the Body of Christ —and that community which is nothing less than God's new humanity.

This emphasis is reflected in the prayers and responses in the Anglican baptismal service in *Common Worship*. The sense of pilgrimage and heavenly longing is reflected in the prayer immediately following baptism, when the minister prays, "May God who has received you by baptism into his church, pour upon you the riches of his grace, that within the company of Christ's pilgrim people you may be daily renewed by his anointing Spirit, and come to the inheritance of the saints in glory."[2] Again a balance is struck between the equipping through baptism of the individual for a life of service and their mission now and the sense of journey initiated in baptism which only concludes in heaven.

So in another prayer following baptism these words are prayed, "Today God has touched you with his love and given you a place among his people. God promises to be with you in joy and in sorrow, to be your guide in life, and to bring you safely to heaven. In baptism God invites you on a life-long journey. Together with all God's people you must explore the way of Jesus and grow in friendship with God, in love for his people, in serving others. With us you will listen to the word of God and receive the gifts of God." The elements of baptism are here: a break with the old, past way of life; the beginning of a new life lived in submission to Christ; the reception of his gifts through the Spirit; being equipped for mission now; the sense of a lifelong journey and the culmination of it in heaven. Baptism is both a way of life now, in which God's kingdom comes through the orientation of our lives with Jesus as Lord, and the assurance that we will be safely brought to the place where his kingdom is consummated. It has both a now and a not yet side to it, reflected in this liturgy of baptism.

Secondly, the Eucharist is also a sign of the kingdom. Jesus himself saw it as an act of remembrance which both recalled his death for us and looked forward to the consummation of his kingdom in heaven. Just as the Passover was to be eaten by the Jews with an urgent sense of anticipation, indeed in haste (see Exodus 12:11), so the Lord's Supper or Eucharist was to be eaten with more than a glance to the future. In giving his disciples the cup of wine at the Last Supper, Jesus said, "Drink from it, all of you. This is my blood of the covenant, which is poured out for many for the forgiveness of sins." He went on to say, "I tell you, I will not drink of this fruit of the vine from now on until that day when I drink it anew with you in my Father's kingdom" (Matthew 26:27-29). The Eucharist was therefore a celebration and thanksgiving for the Lord's death, a means of grace through which we are spiritually strengthened, an assurance of our forgiveness, a proclamation of Christ's return — and a looking forward to his kingdom coming fully. The supper on earth looks forward to the banquet in heaven, when the kingdom of God would be perfected. This is well put in one of the Eucharistic prayers which I particularly like, when the minister leading prays, "Lord of all life, help us to work together for that day when your kingdom comes and justice and mercy will be seen in all the earth." Or again, the Eucharist looks forward to a time when all God's people will be gathered together, so we pray, "Gather your people from the ends of the earth to feast with all your saints at the table in your kingdom, where the new creation is brought to perfection in Jesus Christ our Lord."[3] The service of Holy Communion looks forward to the perfection of the kingdom, the full manifestation of his just and gentle rule. Both sacraments anticipate this fulfilment.

Next, the church in its worship both prays and sings for the coming of the kingdom. We shall look first at the songs. From earliest times the church has set its convictions to music, and sung together. The psalms of David and others set prayerful longings to music, and made them corporate expressions of worship. So the psalmist wrote,

> Come, let us sing for joy to the LORD;
> let us shout aloud to the Rock of our salvation.
> Let us come before him with thanksgiving
> and extol him with music and song.
> For the LORD is the great God,
> the great King above all gods.
>
> *Psalm 95:1-3*

> It is good to praise the LORD
> and make music to your name, O Most High,
> to proclaim your love in the morning
> and your faithfulness at night,
> to the music of the ten-stringed lyre
> and the melody of the harp.
>
> *Psalm 92:1-3*

Ever since then, and before, praise has never been far from God's people, and this praise was often about the kingship of God and his coming kingdom. (See Exodus 13.) In the New Testament writings Paul made use of hymns (e.g. the hymn to Christ in Philippians 2:6-11), and doxologies (e.g. Romans 11:33-36) in his teaching, and it is possible that such doctrinal statements or ascriptions to God were sung. More recently in the church, from the 18th century onwards, yearning for God's kingdom has often been set to music, which itself only heightens the emotion of longing in the prayer. Favourite traditional hymns at Advent proclaim the coming kingdom —for instance, "The Advent of our king, our prayers must now employ," which continues in the third stanza:

> As Judge, on clouds of light,
> He soon will come again,
> And his true members all unite
> With him in heaven to reign.[4]

Or again, the hymn,

> O come, O Come, Emmanuel,
> And ransom captive Israel
> That mourns in lonely exile here,
> Until the Son of God appear[5]

This expresses a yearning for God's kingdom to come.

Another hymn of kingdom longing is from John Milton, of *Paradise Lost* fame, who wrote,

> The Lord will come and not be slow,
> His footsteps cannot err;
> Before him righteousness shall go,
> His royal harbinger.

And finally, a hymn which carries an intense longing for God's kingdom is,

> Thy Kingdom come, O God,
> Thy rule, O Christ, begin;
> Break with thine iron rod
> The tyrannies of sin.

It continues,

> Where is thy reign of peace
> And purity and love?
> When shall all hatred cease,
> As in the realms above.

And it mingles prayer and worship together with these words,

> We pray thee, Lord, arise,
> And come in thy great might;
> Revive our longing eyes,
> Which languish for thy sight.[6]

Whether in modern spiritual songs or in older hymns, there can be no doubting the church's desire to sing about the coming of the kingdom.

And finally – in line with the petition in the Lord's Prayer for God's kingdom to come and his will to be done on earth as it is in heaven, – there is a whole body of prayer offered by the church for God's kingdom to come, whether in extempore or set prayers.

Some of the prayers most redolent of the kingdom are those set for the Sundays preceding Advent. Such a prayer is this one:

Almighty Father, whose will is to restore all things in your beloved Son, the king of all: govern the hearts and minds of those in authority, and bring the families of the nations, divided and torn apart by the ravages of sin, to be subject to his just and gentle rule.[7]

And a modern postcommunion prayer reads:

God of peace, whose Son Jesus Christ proclaimed the kingdom and restored the broken to wholeness of life: look with compassion on the anguish of the world, and by your healing power make whole both people and nations; through our Lord and Saviour Jesus Christ.[8]

One of the church's great tasks in its corporate worship and prayer is recollection of Jesus' death and resurrection. This helps to equip people both for the journey to the kingdom and in their service in the kingdom now. The prayer of God's people is for the coming of the kingdom in increasing measure in our broken world. Both in its prayer and witness, the prayer of the church points to the kingdom of God. In the next chapter, before concluding, we must consider the relationship between church and kingdom.

Chapter Nineteen

THE CHURCH AND
THE KINGDOM

So what is the relationship between the church and the kingdom? They are definitely not the same. As I wrote in another book in this trilogy, adapting the words of a well-known nursery rhyme, when the church is good it can be very, very good, but when it is bad it is horrid! If you have heard it said once, then you have heard it said a thousand times: "Jesus I love, but it is the church I can't stand." Many have been bruised by the church, whether it is through its having seemed exclusive rather than welcoming, condemning in tone rather than engaging and attractive, or being insensitive to those crying out for care and not just texts.

The catalogue of misery inflicted by the church down the ages on people both inside and outside is too lengthy to recount. And as the quip goes, "If you find the perfect church, don't join it as it will no longer be perfect!" The divisions, suspicions and hostility in the church towards others who name the same Name require repentance. The church is still an all too human collection of people, but where there is true faith it is the place where God promises to dwell, despite its many imperfections. Peter makes this abundantly clear in his words to the small Christian communities of Bithynia, Cappadocia, Asia, Galatia and Pontus, when he writes, "But you are a chosen people, a royal priesthood, a holy nation, a people belonging to God, that you may declare the praises of him who called you out of darkness into his wonderful light. Once you were not a people, but now you are the people of God; once you had not received mercy, but now you have received mercy" (1 Peter 2:9f). In other words, once they were nobodies but now they are the body of Christ on earth. But however great this transformation of being and status is, they are still not yet the kingdom of God. The church is not the kingdom, but it is a sign of the kingdom. The kingdom is God's perfect rule, which makes its way painfully into human affairs. As Tomlin points out in *The Provocative Church*, "Christians are not meant just to try and do good, be nice and help the world work a little better. They are instead to act as signposts to another order, another way of life and another kingdom, which can be glimpsed in this world, but has not yet completely arrived. Those who believe in God's kingdom and kingship will want to act as signs of that kingdom, offering reminders, aromas, tastes of what it might mean to live under God's rule, not the iron rule of sin and death."[1] In short, the church is not the kingdom, nor can it bring in the kingdom, for that is God's prerogative alone; but the church at its best can be a sign of the kingdom to a world which has lost sight of anything different from what it knows. The church can provide a number of signposts.[2]

The church, a signpost to the kingdom

It has been said, especially eloquently by the French theologian Jacques Ellul, that the most urgent need of the Western church is to develop a lifestyle that is recognisably different from that of the world around it. Indeed Tomlin, summarising Ellul's insights, goes as far as saying that, "He suggests that the rediscovery of a genuinely Christian way of life (rather than just getting doctrine right) is the key to the rebirth of Christianity in the West." This means, he goes on to say, living by a practical wisdom that impinges on our total perspective of life and informs our attitude towards all aspects of living. "Such wisdom will mean living as if it really is true that this planet is made and loved by a creator God; that each person we meet is a precious being crafted in God's image, to be treated with dignity and reverence; that God's judgement on a sinful world is real and imminent; that sin and death are empty, broken forces since the death and resurrection of Jesus; and that one day God will bring in his new kingdom of justice, peace and joy."[3] The Christian needs both to believe this to be true and to live in such a way as to demonstrate it in a new and attractive way of life. This is the challenge that faces the Western church today. There are a number of ways in which such a demonstration can be made.

It has become a truism that the church should be the community which makes the gospel credible. Once it was possible to announce the gospel in large impersonal meetings and expect a response, but that kind of invitation or that kind of evangelism is far harder in today's word-resistant world. The last time I took part in such a venture was ten years ago, when we took busloads of people to a half-empty football stadium in Bristol to hear an articulate evangelist speak for an hour and then ask for a response then and there. It did not work. And even a well constructed evening of drama, film clips, music and a clear explanation of the Christian faith is difficult to make palatable to the average person who is ready to open their mind to Christianity. No, more than anything else, I have seen that it is a credible Christian community which authenticates the reality of the gospel which in turn both touches and changes people. When Christians demonstrate in their life together the just and gentle rule of the King, then the gospel has real transforming power. It is not that the gospel has changed, far from it, but more than ever the gospel needs to be incarnate, fleshed out in the body of Christ, the church, in its multi-form, rainbow coloured community. Lesslie Newbigin famously asked how the gospel should be believable; he suggested that the way the gospel can be apprehended is through a body of believers whose lives are governed by its message.[4] Nor do they have to live by it perfectly, but they do need to be genuine, and then they can demonstrate the hope of change. In this context of belonging to such a believing community, there is the hope. In our own church we have a Wednesday night event at which a meal is served in a refurbished centre for many groups who come together: some are preparing for marriage, some are doing an Alpha course, some are groups which have done Alpha courses one or two years previously, others are involved in a leadership training course. As the pastor I commit myself to being there, and get to know as many of the participants as possible. It is, in fact, midweek church, community around a meal, people at different stages. Some have found faith in God, others are still exploring a year or so later. All are welcome, but people evaluate what we say by how we are, and they have had time to do that. People today want to see whether a Christian faith is credible, and for that they need to be part of a community where it is expressed. And, as I often say, the most important thing about church is, as Paul himself said, "...The only thing that counts is faith expressing itself through love" (Galatians 5:6b). Doctrinal exactitude is not of itself sufficient!

So the church is to be a community which makes the gospel credible. It is not that the church validates the gospel, for no-one and nothing can do that; God himself has done that through the events at its heart. It is that, in our world today, people need to see the gospel in action and to see what difference it really makes.

A second way in which the church is a signpost to the kingdom is that it is a place of healing and wholeness. As we have seen, there is no final end to suffering or sickness this side of heaven, when the kingdom will come in perfection. Until then, the church is a community in which the offer of wholeness is made, but in the knowledge that, for the Christian, paradoxically, death is the gateway to abundant life. However, in the here and now, we may experience many healings of physical, spiritual, emotional or mental kinds; they are part of a process which we call a movement into wholeness. Healing is not a one off single event, however dramatic it may be; it is simply part of the process whereby we are becoming as whole as we can be in this life. Nor is healing an end in itself, as it is often wrongly thought to be; to be healed is as much being healed *for* something as it is being healed *from* something. It is much more common in our therapy-centred culture to think of something we are being healed from than of the purpose for which we are being healed. So the church as a community is offering, in the power of Jesus Christ, healing along the axis of cure to care. If we cannot cure we can at the very least care, and if we care then we can also pray for cure. The church needs to offer both, not withdrawing care when a dramatic cure does not take place – as tragically happens in some so called healing ministry – and not being so cautious that it dare not pray for cure. The church is a community where there are glimpses of the healing which will one day be perfectly complete, when there is no more pain, disease or suffering or death. Until that perfection comes, the church must continue to be a place where healing, at whatever level, is both offered and received.

Next, the church as a sign of the kingdom must be a place of transformation, where all its members are on a path to "becoming fully human". God, whose characteristics include love, faithfulness, mercy, forgiveness, generosity and justice, became man, one of us, and his will is that those qualities should begin to characterise our lives. Becoming fully human, realising our full humanity, is for our lives to become marked by those qualities of which God is the source. If you described the qualities you most admire in people, you would probably include those characteristics. This process will not be completed this side of heaven, but in the meantime the church as a community can be a signpost to those values and qualities which will finally prevail in the kingdom of God. Ideally, the church in its relationships should be a microcosm of the kingdom, the rule of God. And the more human we become, in the best sense of that word, the more attractive we will be.

Fourth, the church should be a signpost through its compassionate action. Compassion is in danger of becoming an overused word; every political party in Britain wants to annexe it for their own political purposes. We have compassionate conservatism, compassionate socialism, and so on. It is now the necessary, indeed politically correct, prefix to every modern political creed. Earlier in the book we saw that the call to become a disciple involved the disciple in compassionate action toward his neighbour, and this was clearly expressed in the parable of the Good Samaritan. There is little doubt that churches which run programmes of care for the homeless, the outcast, the refugees, the ex-convicts, are displaying something of the compassionate love which lies at the heart of the kingdom. They also, by these compassionate actions, gain a hearing for the gospel that inspires them. In the 11th century, the Benedictines, the Order which had dominated the monastic scene for six centuries, subdivided into two further orders, the Augustinian canons and the Cistercians. Both were to become highly influential in their own ways, but the more easy engagement of the Augustinian canons (monks) gained far more influence amongst the population than the way of the more austere Cistercians. The Augustinians practised compassionate action amongst the town folk, whilst the Cistercians fled the towns for the edges of human settlement, becoming highly organised communities dedicated to agricultural and spiritual development.[5] The point is that compassionate action not only demonstrates the gospel in practice but also it opens others to receive its teaching and helps them glimpse the kingdom of God.

Lastly, the church at its best is subversive of the world in the interests of the kingdom, and the example that Tomlin effectively uses is that of Robin Hood! The point about Robin Hood was that he bore allegiance to a king who was outside the country, Richard Coeur de Lion, who had been captured whilst returning from the second Crusade. Whilst kidnapped abroad, his brother John, of Magna Carta fame, took over the reins of government, subjugated the people with onerous taxes to sustain his illegitimate court, and it was one of his sheriffs, the Sheriff of Nottingham, that Robin Hood took to opposing so that by robbing the rich he could give to the poor. Tomlin goes on to offer the surprising analogy of the church today to Robin Hood's band of resistance fighters. "They live under an oppressive regime, but they can laugh merrily because they know that the present system is not the last word. They know that the true king is coming, and that things will one day be different. From time to time, they still remind the false powers that their rule is temporary and bogus, by acts of rebellion that recall the true king. They also whisper around the good news that things don't need to be like this. The king is coming, in fact he has already landed, and others can begin to live joyfully in the light of this coming kingdom."[6]

In these ways the church at her best can be a signpost of the kingdom. It is not in itself the kingdom – which is God's just and gentle rule – but where that rule is given as full a sway as possible it exhibits what kind of rule and what kind of a kingdom it is, hopefully attracting more adherents to it.

Pilgrims and exiles

Pilgrims and *exiles* are two metaphorical expressions often used in the Bible which signify that God's people have literally not yet arrived, or still await the perfect fulfilment of God's kingdom. And it is probably true that these images have now a greater resonance in the church in the West than in previous generations. The church can more easily perceive itself today as a pilgrim or an exiled people than it could in previous generations, when it was more in step with the secular rulers of the time; indeed, for long periods the rulers were not "secular" but saw themselves both appointed by and accountable to God. For large tracts of time from the conversion of Constantine until the 1960s, the moral consensus was basically underpinned by wide acceptance of the church. However, from the 1960s that broad consensus began to break, so heightening in the mind of the church its sense of pilgrimage and exile. It is not that pilgrimage was not an important concept to the medieval church, as it spent huge energy encouraging or enabling pilgrimages to take place, but the meaning of pilgrimage has significantly changed. We shall look at each metaphor in turn. But it is worth saying at the outset that what is common to both terms is the sense of the church either being away from (exile) or journeying to (pilgrimage) its final destination. We will begin with pilgrimage.

Anyone acquainted with the psalms will know that the idea of pilgrimage often surfaces in them. Indeed, some were written for pilgrimage itself. Every male Jew was expected to go to Jerusalem three times a year, for the major festivals of Passover, Weeks or Firstfruits and Tabernacles. The last feast, Tabernacles, was itself a reminder of the pilgrimage of the people of Israel in the desert, and they were required to live outside in tabernacles to remind them of the journeying with Moses. (See Leviticus 23; Numbers 28:29.) If each male Jew went to Jerusalem for the observance of these feasts, then a large proportion of time was spent in pilgrimage each year, and it was a significant part of their worship. The psalms of pilgrimage were used by the pilgrims on their ascent to Jerusalem, and these can be found in Psalms 120-134. But other psalms, too, record the pilgrim life of the people of Israel, for instance Psalm 84:

> Blessed are those whose strength is in you,
> who have set their hearts on pilgrimage.
> As they pass through the Valley of Baca,
> they make it a place of springs;
> the autumn rains also cover it with pools.
> They go from strength to strength,
> till each appears before God in Zion.
>
> *Psalm 84:5-7*

If we now transpose the earthly destination of the Jew's pilgrimage, which was the city of Jerusalem, to the heavenly city of Jerusalem which is the final destiny of the Christian (see Hebrews 12:22; Revelation 21:2 and Isaiah 65:17-19), we can see that Christian discipleship can also be viewed as a pilgrimage to the heavenly city. On our way there, we will experience both tears and joy (Psalm 126:5); we too will search for peace (Psalm 122:6-8); we will find deliverance (Psalm 124:1-8); and we will pin our hopes on the coming of God (Psalm 130). The psalms of ascents are rich with the attitudes which will sustain and nurture any serious pilgrim. Attitudes which were necessary to sustain the Jew on the way to earthly Jerusalem are equally important to sustaining a Christian on the way to the eternal city. The whole notion of pilgrimage, so prevalent in the Old Testament, reminds us that church at its best is not only a signpost of the kingdom it is actively journeying to the kingdom. The culmination of the journey is also the moment of fulfilment.

Alongside the metaphor of pilgrimage we must place the complementary idea of exile. The theme of exile is one of the chief themes of the Old Testament. It is present in the exodus narrative; it was the experience of the northern kingdom after the destruction of Samaria by the Assyrians; and then was the seminal experience of the southern kingdom after the fall of Jerusalem to the Babylonians. A large proportion of the Israelites from Jerusalem and the southern kingdom were taken to Babylon, to begin a period of exile which lasted in its entirety for nearly 150 years. The rebuilding of Jerusalem under Nehemiah did not take place until around 450BC, followed by the restoration of the temple. But that narrative of exile and restoration is a story which must be pursued at another time. Suffice it to say that, for the Jews, the experience of exile was etched on their hearts and minds. After all, their greatest feast, the Passover, involved remembering a first deliverance from a kind of exile in Egypt, and their more recent history from 589BC until the coming of Jesus was a continuous history of exile in the successive empires of the Babylonians, Medes and the Persians. After they returned home it must have felt as though they were exiles in their own land, under the successive governments of the Greeks and the Romans. It is not surprising then that the apostle Peter, in particular, takes this familiar theme in Jewish history and experience, and uses it to describe the way of life of Christian communities. They too were exiles! Writing from Rome towards the end of his life and ministry, Peter says at the outset of his epistle, in a moving introduction, that they are strangers and exiles in the world. (See 1 Peter 1:1 and v. 17.) They are awaiting a salvation to be fully and finally revealed from heaven, and they are to live like pilgrims and exiles on earth.

Christians in this world are to recreate on earth a taste of heaven; since none have ever been there, their blueprint is the way of life demonstrated by Jesus, taught by the apostles and made possible by the work of the Holy Spirit. People entering Christian communities should be struck by the description that Peter himself gives: "Finally, all of you, live in harmony with one another; be sympathetic, love as brothers, be compassionate and humble. Do not repay evil with evil or insult with insult, but with blessing, because to this you were called so that you may inherit a blessing" (1 Peter 3:8f). Christian communities are to be expressions of what is to come; they are not yet the real thing, but they are to be credible witnesses of it.

As we have pointed out here, the church is not the kingdom but at its best it is both a witness and signpost to it. In our society, where 90% of the population does not attend any church but where 70% of our population say that they believe in God, the task is to make known the kingdom in such a way that people have the opportunity to change their nominal belief in God into a real experience of living under his just and gentle rule. It is when they see others living themselves under that rule and being transformed by it that they may be drawn there too. Many of us, if asked, would not begin our witness in the place where we find ourselves; we might want to start from somewhere else. But we have no choice. Two thousand years of Christian history in Europe and the Near East and India cannot be erased; we must take the bad with the good. But it is now imperative, whether in fresh expressions of church or in making old church new, to build communities where the rule of God can be seen. It is that which makes the gospel credible in today's world. People like Thomas need to see to believe. (See John 20:29.) And there are many Thomases around. The church, because of its many failings, is not the kingdom, but only if it witnesses credibly and authentically to the kingdom will others be able to see it and be born into it themselves.

Chapter Twenty

CONCLUSION

It would be foolish indeed to think that any book, least of all this one, can encapsulate the concept of the kingdom of God. But over past pages we have tried to consider the greatness of it. To grasp its significance requires something of a mind shift, a change of perspective in which we become as convinced of its reality as Jesus himself was. That may not be possible to the same degree as in the case of Jesus because our grip on the idea is all too transient. The point is simply that the kingdom of God will be the final form of government in this universe and it will fill all and be in all; and for this finally and fully to happen is only a matter of time. But as I said in the introduction to this book there may be Christians who are or were like me who, for the first fourteen years of my new Christian life, barely paid much attention to the notion of the kingdom, even though it was what Jesus talked most about and continually demonstrated in both his teaching and actions. A combination of the writings of Eldon Ladd and the ministry of John Wimber, the founder of the Vineyard Movement, helped me to see and grasp more of its significance, and placed it centrally in my thinking and understanding of the way the world really is.

Perhaps the most important thing to know about the kingdom is that it is coming! And nothing will halt its final arrival. The kingdom of God is the corresponding entity to the gospel statement that Jesus is Lord. And "Jesus is Lord" is as good a summary of the gospel as any. It means that Jesus is King and nothing or nobody else is. It may not always seem that either Jesus is Lord or that there is a kingdom of God which is coming, but that is because the rule of God is either obscured by the sufferings of the world or by the inept witness of the church. But the resurrection of Jesus from the dead has inaugurated a new age, a new humanity, a new cosmos, and it is the guarantee of the inexorable rise of the kingdom in the world, which is the invisible rule of God in the hearts of people.

We have traced in this book some of the main features of the kingdom. We have noticed that Jesus' own world-view, indeed we could say his universe-view, is based on the idea of the kingdom of God. He announced the kingdom breaking into the world of humans with a new vividness, concentration and power in his own presence, ministry, death and resurrection. Jesus inaugurated this ministry with his Nazareth synagogue address, in which he said that the prophecy of Isaiah 61 had been fulfilled. He reassured a doubting John the Baptist, who asked, "Are you the one who was to come, or should we expect someone else?" (Mathew 11:3) with the words, "The blind receive sight, the lame walk, those who have leprosy are cured, the deaf hear, the dead are raised, and the good news is preached to the poor. Blessed is the man who does not fall away on account of me" (Matthew 11:4f). And he opened the kingdom to all people of faith in him, in fulfilment of God's covenant with Abraham.

The kingdom of God is governed by a policy of grace —undeserved love to all who welcome Jesus the King. Complete allegiance to him is required of all who enter it. Whatever the difficulties, it will assuredly grow and it is moving to a time of crisis. When Jesus was on earth the kingdom was vividly and memorably made known in his very life, a kind of continual acted parable. It was made known in his teaching which was a continuum of revelation that moved from parable to saying, to sustained discourse, to polemic, to exposition of the Old Testament Scriptures, to a word of insight or wisdom. The kingdom was supremely made known in his actions of healing, deliverance and forgiveness which both revolutionised and transformed the lives of so many individuals whom he met. He argued for justice and compassion of the deepest kind with those who used power to crush or condemn. It was not that Jesus healed everyone or reversed all injustice but in the limits of his own physical life (being in one place at one time) he demonstrated unequivocally the nature of the rule of God, the nature of the kingdom for which Israel had been waiting. The fact that Israel did not recognise the kingdom when it came was because it was looking for something different, something in the end which was ungodly. The kingdom was also both subversive and "reversive": it reversed all commonly accepted principles of government; the master would be the servant; the inside was more important than the outside; the last would be first, and the way in was not by merit but by surrender. It was different from all other power structures hitherto and heretofore. It was a kingdom to which a new community of faith must bear witness, for which it was yearning in its soul expressed through prayer and which was coming, silently, invisibly, inexorably and indestructibly. This was what Jesus knew and is also what we should know and live in the light of. For many of us it requires a change of perspective, or more deeply a change of heart.

On the front cover of this book is a painting by the Spanish artist Murillo, who came from Seville. The picture is The Return of the Prodigal Son, and it hangs in Dublin in the National Gallery of Ireland. Murillo himself had a change of heart or perspective which was a pivotal moment of his life. "As a young boy he already showed considerable promise in the visual arts, but was yet to find a patron or any real source of encouragement. In his childhood home there hung a picture of Jesus as a deadly serious shepherd boy. It portrayed him, in the style of the time, standing bolt upright, his shepherd's crook like a sentinel's bayonet. About his head shone an obligatory halo. Young Murillo detested the picture. So one day when his family was out of the house, he impetuously took the painting down from the wall and went to work on it with his paint box. In his youthful brilliance he was able to create a richer image of Jesus. Upon their return the Murillos were aghast to see their Lord had been defaced. The stern, unflinching face now had a lively grin, his eyes alive with mischief. The halo had become a battered straw hat and the plastered-down hair had been tousled into an unruly mess. His crook had been transformed into a gnarled walking stick, and the limp and sad looking lamb at Jesus' feet was now a troublesome puppy. The shepherd boy had become a lively, excited hiker in search of adventure."[1] Murillo was severely beaten for his pains, but a local merchant, seeing his skill, became his patron! A change of perspective had given a fresh vision of Christ and a new future. My hope is that this book will change our perspective of the kingdom, giving us new hope and life in Jesus.

What then should our response be to this coming kingdom, this coming rule of God? To those who consider themselves outside the kingdom, Jesus had two words for them: repent and believe. "The time has come," he said. "The kingdom of God is near. Repent and believe the good news!" (Mark 1:15). Repentance is not a forbidding, bleak word or action but one of immense hope and promise. It means turning from the kingdoms of this world, and whatever ephemeral fruits that they offer, to the kingdom of God and his Christ. "It involves a turning from and a turning to —from a life characterised by sin, separation from God, submission to evil and unfulfilled potential of God's image, to a new life characterised by the forgiveness of sins, obedience and renewed fellowship with God the Holy Trinity."[2] To those who have surrendered and entered this kingdom then, the task is to be an ever better witness to it so that in our own lives, and life together with other citizens, we may commend this kingdom which has at its beginning and end the just and gentle rule of the King. And finally it is to join with other Christians, across the world and down the ages, in their invocation, "Maranatha!" (Our Lord, come!) in the longing for an end to injustice, oppression, poverty, hunger, persecution, and to struggle for the coming kingdom of which Jesus is both the exemplar and the King.

NOTES

Chapter 1

[1] See *David Lloyd George* by Professor Grigg.

[2] In his introduction to the *UK Christian Handbook*: Religious trends 2004, Marc Europe. Used by permission.

[3] See *Churchless Faith* by Jamieson.

[4] Philip Jenkins in *The Next Christendom*. By permission of Oxford University Press, Inc.
See also Professor Alister McGrath's address to SOMA 2004.

[5] Dr William Abraham *The Logic of Evangelism* (Hodder) p. 83.

[6] Dr Alison Morgan *The Wild Gospel* (Monarch Books) p. 167. Used by permission.

[7] Lesslie Newbigin *Truth to Tell* (SPCK and Wm B. Eerdmans).

[8] Jean Paul Sartre *Nausea* (Penguin) p. 61.

Chapter 2

[1] Eldon Ladd *The Presence of the Future*, p. 46.

[2] John Bright Nashville *The Kingdom of God* (Abingdon, 1953).

[3] See Joachim Jeremias *The Parables of Jesus* (SCM Press, 1972) p. 58.

Chapter 3

[1] See Jeremias *op.cit.* p. 132.

[2] *Ibid.* p. 133.

[3] *Ibid.* p. 134.

[4] *Ibid.* p. 135.

[5] See Jeremias *Parables of the Kingdom,* and Deuteronomy 21:17.

[6] See H J M Nouwen *The Return of the Prodigal*, p. 129.

[7] See P Yancey *What's so Amazing about Grace?*

[8] *Ibid.*

[9] M Volf *Exclusion and Embrace*.

[10] *Op.cit. The Parables of Jesus*, p. 142 in revised (2003) edition.

[11] N T Wright *The New Testament and the People of God* (SPCK) p. 187.

Chapter 4

[1] Jeremias *op. cit.* p. 199.
[2] *Ibid.* p. 201.
[3] John Stott *Basic Christianity* (IVP) p. 110.
[4] Alison Morgan *The Wild Gospel* (Monarch Books) p. 78. Used by permission.
[5] *Rough Guide to a Better World* (DFID) p. 7.
[6] Jeremias *op. cit.* p. 195.

Chapter 5

[1] Jeremias *op. cit.* p. 149.
[2] *The Next Christendom* p. 183. By permission of Oxford University Press, Inc.
[3] South American Missionary Society (SAMS).
[4] Jeremias *op. cit.* p. 150.

Chapter 6

[1] See *Parables of Jesus. Op.cit.* p. 177.
[2] *Ibid.* p. 173.

Chapter 8

[1] G Tomlin *The Provocative Church* (SPCK, 2002) p. 56.
[2] *Ibid.* p. 57.
[3] Ian Stackhouse *The Gospel Driven Church* (Paternoster, 2004) p. 99.
[4] See, for example, the "Fresh Expressions of Church" website.
[5] See John 3:4; John 4:11f; John 14:5; John 14:8; John 13:36f; John 16:17 —just a few questions that give us some of the most fundamental teaching of Jesus.
[6] See William Abraham *The Logic of Evangelism* (Hodder, 1989) p. 171.

Chapter 9

[1] George Eldon Ladd *The Presence of the Future* (SPCK, 1974) p. 139.
[2] John Woolmer *Healing and Deliverance* (Monarch, 1999).
[3] Tom Wright *Jesus and the Victory of God* (SPCK, 1996) p. 195, and Augsburg Fortress. Used by permission.
[4] Irenaeus *Adv. Haer* 2:32.

[5] See John Woolmer *Healing and Deliverance* pp. 159-164, and Michael Green *Evangelism and the Early Church* (Hodder and Stoughton, 1970).

Chapter 10

[1] As documented by Hastings in *History of English Christianity*.

[2] Walter Brueggemann *Prophetic Imagination* 2nd edition (Augsburg Fortress, 2001) p. 82.

[3] *Ibid*. p. 88.

[4] *Ibid*. p. 101.

[5] See J Wallis *God's Politics*, pp. 290-292.

Chapter 11

[1] See *Exclusion and Embrace* (Abingdon Press, 1996) p. 123.

[2] *Ibid*. p. 111.

[3] L Smedes *Forgive and Forget* (Harper Collins, 1984) p. 133.

[4] P Whitworth (Ed.) *Qualities of Enduring Love* (Terra Nova Publications, 2005).

[5] P Whitworth *Becoming a Spiritual Leader* (Terra Nova Publications, 2005).

Chapter 12

[1] Tom Wright *The Resurrection of the Son of God* (SPCK, 2003) p. 578f.

Chapter 13

[1] J R W Stott *Calling Christian Leaders* (IVP, 2002).

[2] R Foster *Money, Sex and Power* (Hodder, 1985) p. 202.

Chapter 14

[1] George Eldon Ladd *The Presence of the Future*, p. 292.

[2] R T France *Matthew*, Tyndale NT Commentaries (IVP, 1985) p. 108.

Chapter 16

[1] John Bunyan *Pilgrim's Progress* (Religious Tract Society, 1915) p. 196.

[2] *Op.cit.* Ladd *The Presence of the Future*, pp. 201f.

Chapter 17
[1] *Ibid.* p. 204.
[2] *Ibid.* p. 139.
[3] *Ibid.* p. 17.
[4] Richard Lovelace *Dynamics of Spiritual Life* (InterVarsity Press, USA) p. 279.
[5] *Ibid.* p. 45.

Chapter 18
[1] Ronald Wallace in *The Bible Speaks Today*, Ed. Alec Motyer (IVP).
[2] *Common Worship: Services and Prayers for the Church of England* (Church House Publishing 2000) copyright ©The Archbishops' Council 2000, Baptism Service.
[3] *Common Worship: Services and Prayers for the Church of England* (Church House Publishing 2000) copyright ©The Archbishops' Council 2000, Order One Eucharistic Prayers E & F.
[4] C. Coffin (1676-1749). (Trans. from French original by John Chandler 1806-76). See *Hymns A&M New Standard edition* (1983). SCM-Canterbury Press Ltd, Norwich.
[5] This hymn has its origins in a Latin Advent antiphon later translated by John Mason Neale (1818-66). See *Hymns A&M New Standard edition* (1983). SCM-Canterbury Press Ltd, Norwich.
[6] Lewis Hensley (1824-1905). See *Hymns A&M New Standard edition* (1983). SCM-Canterbury Press Ltd, Norwich.
[7] *Common Worship: Services and Prayers for the Church of England* (Church House Publishing 2000) copyright ©The Archbishops' Council 2000, Collects.
[8] *Common Worship: Services and Prayers for the Church of England* (Church House Publishing 2000) copyright ©The Archbishops' Council 2000.

Chapter 19
[1] Graham Tomlin *The Provocative Church* (SPCK) p. 22.
[2] *Ibid.*
[3] *Ibid.*
[4] *The Gospel in a Pluralist Society* (London, SPCK, 1989) p. 227.
[5] See R W Southern *Western Society and The Church in the Middle*

Ages, Pelican History of the Church Vol 11 (Penguin Books, 1970) p. 250.

[6] *Op. cit. The Provocative Church*, p. 29.

Chapter 20

[1] See Michael Frost and Alan Hirsch *The Shaping of Things to Come* (Hendrickson, 2003) p. 106. Used by permission of Hendrickson Publishers, Peabody, Massachusetts.

[2] David J Bosch *Transforming Mission* (Orbis Books, 2005) p. 413.

BIBLIOGRAPHY

W Abraham *The Logic of Evangelism* (Hodder & Stoughton,1989)

P Ackroyd, Sinclair Stevenson *Dickens*, 1990

W Brueggemann *Prophetic Imagination* 2nd edition (Augsburg Fortress, 2001)

H Chadwick *The Early Church* (Penguin, 1993)

Mission Shaped Church (Church House Publishing, 2004)

A Better World (Department for International Development, Rough Guides, 2003)

J Ellul *The New Demons* (Seabury Press, 1975)

J Ellul *The Presence of the Kingdom* (Helmers and Howard, 1989)

R Foster *Money, Sex and Power* (Arrow Books, 1990)

M Glenny *The Balkans* (Granta Publications, 1999)

R M Grant *Irenaeus of Lyons* (Routledge, 1997)

J Grigg *Lloyd George: The People's Champion 1902-1911* (Penguin, 2002)

A Hastings *A History of English Christianity 1920-85* (William Collins & Co, 1986)

A Jamieson *A Churchless Faith* (SPCK, 2002)

P Jenkins *The Next Christendom* (OUP, 2002)

R Jenkins *Gladstone* (Macmillan, 1995)

J Jeremias *Jesus and the Message of the New Testament* (Fortress Press, 2002)

J Jeremias, *The Parables of Jesus* 9th impression 3rd revised edition (SCM Press, 2003)

F Keane *Season of Blood* (Viking, 1995)

G E Ladd *The Presence of the Future* (SPCK, 1974)

G E Ladd *The Gospel and the Kingdom* (Paternoster, 1981)

C S Lewis *Surprised by Joy* (C S Lewis Signature Classics Edition, HarperCollins, 2002)

R L Lovelace *Dynamics of Spiritual Life* (Paternoster, 1979)

M Marshall *The Gospel Connection* (Darton, Longman and Todd, 1991)

A Morgan *The Wild Gospel* (Monarch, 2004)

L Newbigin *The Gospel in a Pluralist Society* (SPCK, 1989)

L Newbigin *The Open Secret* (SPCK, 1995)

H J M Nouwen *The Return of the Prodigal Son* (A Story of Homecoming)

R Parker *Forgiveness is Healing* (Darton, Longman & Todd, 1993)

J P Sartre *Nausea* (Penguin, 1965)

S Smalley *John —Evangelist and Interpreter* (Paternoster, 1998)

L B Smedes *Forgive and Forget* (HarperCollins, 1996)

R W Southern *Western Society and the Church in the Middle Ages* (Penguin, 1970)

I Stackhouse *The Gospel Driven Church* (Paternoster, 2004)

BIBLIOGRAPHY

J R W Stott *Basic Christianity* (IVP, 1958)

J R W Stott *Issues Facing Christians Today* (Marshall Morgan and Scott, 1984)

J R W Stott *The Contemporary Christian* (IVP, 1992)

J R W Stott *Calling Christian Leaders* (IVP, 2002)

R V G Tasker *Gospel According to St Matthew* (Tyndale, 1961)

H Thielicke *The Waiting Father* (James Clarke & Co, 1960)

G Tomlin *The Provocative Church* (SPCK, 2002)

M Volf *Exclusion and Embrace* (Abingdon Press, 1996)

J Wallis *Agenda for a Biblical People* (Harper Row, 1976)

J Wallis *God's Politics* (Harper, San Francisco, 2005)

D Watson *Discipleship* (Hodder & Stoughton, 1981)

P J Whitworth *Becoming Fully Human* (Terra Nova Publications, 2003)

P J Whitworth *Becoming a Spiritual Leader* (Terra Nova Publications, 2005)

J Woolmer *Thinking Clearly about Prayer* (Monarch, 1997)

J Woolmer *Healing and Deliverance* (Monarch, 1999)

N T Wright *Jesus and the Victory of God* (SPCK, 1996)

N T Wright *The New Testament and the People of God* (SPCK, 1992)

N T Wright *The Resurrection of the Son of God* (SPCK, 2003)

P Yancey *What's so Amazing about Grace?* (Zondervan, 1997)

P Yancey *Where is God When it Hurts?* (Marshall Pickering, 1998)

T Zeldin *An Intimate History of Humanity* (Minerva, 1994)